The Cerne Giant
Landscape, Gods and the Stargate

Peter Knight

Best wishes
Peter K

Stone Seeker Publishing
Wiltshire UK
Honouring ancient wisdom and the Earth

Published Spring 2013
by Stone Seeker Publishing,
Wiltshire, England, UK
www.stoneseeker.net
email: stoneseeker@waitrose.com

ISBN: 978-0-9560342-2-9

Also by Peter Knight

Ancient Stones of Dorset - 1996
Sacred Dorset: On the Path of the Dragon - 1998
Dorset Pilgrimages: A Millennium Handbook (with Mike Power) - 2000
Earth Mysteries: An Illustrated Encyclopaedia of Britain (CD-ROM) - 2004
Thirteen Moons: Conversations with the Goddess - 2007 (& 2012 ed.)
The Wessex Astrum: Sacred Geometry in a Mystical Landscape (with Toni Perrott) –
    2008
West Kennet Long Barrow: Landscape, Shamans and the Cosmos - 2011

website: www.stoneseeker.net
Follow Peter Knight on FaceBook

Cover images:
Front cover: Left: Peter Harlow
            Right: Adrian Gilbert ©
Back cover: Top images: Peter Knight
            Bottom left: Klaus Peter-Simon

Cover design: Peter Knight

Printed and bound by CPI Antony Rowe, Chippenham, on FSC paper.

MIX
Paper from
responsible sources
FSC
www.fsc.org   FSC® C013604

This book is dedicated to
Sir Patrick Moore (1923 – 2012)
who first ignited my love for
the night sky.

Acknowledgements

I would like to thank the following for granting permission to use their images, or for placing them in the public domain on Wikipedia or other websites: Gary Biltcliffe and Caroline Hoare, Sue Wallace, Adrian Gilbert, Mark North of Dark Dorset, Yuri Leitch, Peter Harlow, Klaus Peter-Simon, J Chartrand, Cambridge University, Nigel Mykura, USGS, RCHM, Cup Cake Kid, 'Mouser', Rory Bowman, Steve Jurvetson, and Luc Viatour.

I would also like to thank wholeheartedly the following people who imparted their wisdom and their time, some of whom walked with me across the landscape of the Giant: Sue Wallace, Gary Biltcliffe, Caroline Hoare, Bob Trubshaw, Marie Moon, and Phil Carter.

I would also like to thank Rodney Castleden and Paul Newman, who have both furthered our knowledge of hill figures through their outstanding books.

I thank the printers, CPI Antony Rowe, who once again did a fantastic job in producing this volume.

Finally, I thank Sue Wallace, for proof-reading the manuscript, offering wisdom and insight, accompanying me on site visits, and encouraging me from start to finish.

Contents

Chapter 1.
Introduction - will the real Cerne Giant please stand up?

'All things begin and end in Albion's ancient, Druid rocky shore.'
(William Blake)

O**ver** many years I have read various accounts and theories concerning the Cerne Giant, and my response to these was to quest through his ancient landscape, seeking out his mysteries for myself. He has long fascinated me, mainly because we seem to know so very little about him. Etched out in white lines on the hillside, he looks like the victim at a crime scene, still clutching the club that he used in a vain attempt to repel his murderer. I have visited the ancient fellow countless times, sometimes whilst leading tours around the area, on other occasions to simply ponder his mysteries, to try and get inside his head, so to speak. And the more I delved, the more questions and contradictions were thrown up. But this has always been fine by me, as mysteries of any kind compel me to venture into realms anew, enticing me to think *'outside the box'*. Referring to the Giant, Mary Jones concurs: *'One thing is sure. Profound mystery is here… the unheard voice of the primeval things of the hills'* (Jones, 1952).

Academics and archaeologists have been split down the middle concerning the Giant's age, as to whether he is prehistoric, Roman or post-medieval. Debate still rages as to why he was 'erected' (a term that seems so appropriate!), and why in the Cerne Valley. Was he an Iron Age god, a fertility prop, or a figure of mischievous fun at Cromwell's expense? And if he is ancient, why has he endured for so long, when so many other sacred sites have been destroyed or at the very least modified? So many questions and so many viewpoints; he is perhaps the original *'bone of contention'*. Sue Clifford, of Common Ground, sums up this state of affairs, as well as emotions I can relate to: *'The Cerne Giant attracts and emanates a cluster of meanings, only some of which I can articulate, all of which lead me to question upon question'* (in Darvill et al 1999, p. 152). How did he survive more pious times, when such a work would normally have been regarded as, at the very least, a risqué and subversive piece of art, verging on the pornographic? As Rodney Castleden comments: *'It is the survival of the Giant that is remarkable, not its creation'* (Castleden 1996, p. 15). And why, other than his obvious 'big boy' attributes, does he continue to hold our attention today?

Nowadays, the Giant graces t-shirts, fridge magnets, key chain fobs, biscuit tins and tea towels; there is even a clock, the second hand of which is his phallus; as it approaches 12 O'clock, it renders him a very excited fellow, only to be followed, inevitably, by a more limp state of affairs some thirty seconds later! He has also been used and abused for advertising campaigns and demonstrations. However, it was not so long ago that this powerful symbol was regarded less flippantly; the Giant was held in reverence, perhaps imbued with totemic and god-like powers.

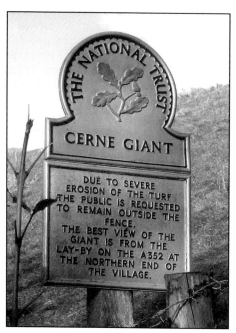

The Cerne Giant gazes out to us from a Dorset hillside, and yet speaks to us in a language we cannot comprehend, projecting symbolism we can interpret any number of ways. His left hand seems to beckon us to follow him into his mystery, into the bosom of the hill itself, back to times long gone; to an age, perhaps, when gods and giants walked the land, and fertility rites and phallic worship were not regarded as deviant cult practices, but fundamental to cultures throughout Europe and beyond.

History is constantly being rewritten, based on new debate and discoveries, and fresh interpretations; for history is not finite or set in stone, and the 'truth' is also dependant on whose history one is reading. We can employ history to create a whole host of new, alternative histories, depending on one's point of view. It is this process of constant reinvention and controversy that has taken history beyond stuffy academic circles to engage a wider public audience. The Giant of Cerne Abbas is part of this ongoing process, bringing together people from a broad range of disciplines and interests: *'For many generations… the Cerne Giant has been an archaeological mystery waiting to be solved. It is one of the best known but least-understood monuments in Britain'* (Darvill et al 1999, v).

I would suggest, as have others, that to solve the mysteries of the Giant we need to look beyond archaeology (whilst at the same time utilising that invaluable science) and venture beyond 'history' as it is defined, to turn to the rich heritage of indigenous myths. This is a precious and deep repository that affects our lives even today, as Anthony Thorley eloquently observed: *'… myth is the living undercurrent of our culture, the journey of our folk-soul richly enacted through legend and powerfully supported by unfolding history'* (Thorley 2012, p. 9). The London Olympic Games of 2012 created many new heroes who, like their mythic counterparts, overcame trials and tribulations to obtain their goals, their personal Golden Fleece or Grail, through heroic deeds that inspired us. The Olympics and the Olympians have become etched on our national mythos, helping us to remember who we are and what we stand for. The Giant reverberates of times long gone when tales of heroic deeds were commonplace, when cultural and racial identity was defined by one's myths.

6

I have briefly delved into the Giant's mysteries within the pages of some of my previous works (Knight 1996, 1998, 2000). These were written primarily to help **me** answer questions **I** had concerning ancient sites and the landscape; I offer this work as my personal pilgrimage into the Cerne Giant's personal space. I lean upon and acknowledge those who have gone before me, and heap particular praise on Rodney Castleden's *The Cerne Giant* (Castleden 1996), Bournemouth University's *The Cerne Giant – An Antiquity on Trial* (Darvill et al, 1999), and Paul Newman's seminal *Lost Gods of Albion* (Newman 2009). These works helped my research immensely, and I thoroughly recommend them.

But 13 years have passed since the publication of a book purely devoted to the Giant, and I feel it is timely to reassess the hill figure in the light of new insights and discoveries. I have set out the latest academic theories, as well as many lay people's thoughts concerning the Giant's identity, age, mythology, as well as what he might represent to us today. I also present my own original research into the astronomical alignments concerning the Giant, and his place *within* his landscape, subjects that have never been substantially dealt with before. I would suggest that my findings answer some of the questions posed in earlier debates; yet I seek not to deprecate previous findings, rather to add to the pot of understanding about this landscape wonder.

If we rely purely on science and archaeology, we may never know the full meaning of the mysteries of the Giant. We need to perceive him and interact with him as our distant ancestors did many centuries ago. He was always more than a piece of art or

The Cerne Giant from the air, with the Trendle above.
(Image: Peter Harlow. Wikipedia Common Licence.)

graffiti – he was a living element of a living landscape.

During research for my previous work (Knight 2011) I realised I had to walk the landscape of West Kennet Long Barrow and Avebury in order to truly connect with it, to hear what it had to say to me; I had to enter the mindset of the Neolithic shaman, to quite literally walk in his or her footsteps, and this is how I approached this current study. For our destination is never a place, but rather a new way of looking at things. The real Cerne Giant is already standing up, and maybe at last he is ready to tell us why.

'Many things that have been hidden will arise
and expose themselves to view'.
(Thomas Sprat, Bishop of Rochester, 1667)

Chapter 2.
The hills are alive -
hill figures of Britain

'Archaeology began with folklore.'
(Jeremy Harte)

Britain has more hill figures than any other country. One reason for this maybe the availability of a medium that facilitates the production of such art forms, i.e. white chalk downlands with escarpments providing abrupt slopes. One of the striking aesthetic effects of chalk figures is the contrast between the green grassland and the lines of white chalk, which can render them visible for miles. Hill figures are usually created by the removal of turf, exposing the white/grey bedrock beneath. Some are also rock-cut on occasion, because the soil and turf is thicker; the chalk at these places was scoured away in a series of trenches, and refilled up to grass level with chalk rubble. This is the practice carried out during the maintenance work on the Giant in recent years.

That said, not all hill figures are fashioned on chalk, the Red Horse at Tysoe and Gog and Magog at Plymouth being two notable exceptions. The Plymouth figures were in fact carved into limestone; where there is no local chalk, it would seem that any surface would suffice. Perhaps locations were purposefully chosen to obtain specific aesthetic effects depending on the colour of the exposed bedrock. (Two excellent guides to Britain's hill figures are Castleden, 2000, and Newman, 1997.)

Hill figures are amongst our most enigmatic ancient monuments, and ones that do not give up their secrets easily. Rodney Castleden concurs: *'Of all British antiquities, the older hill figures must rank as the most difficult to date and interpret'* (Castleden 1998, p. 27). Some hill figures are truly ancient, such as the Uffington White Horse, which has recently yielded a date range of 1200-800BC, whilst others are 'modern', such as the Cherhill Horse (1780), the Fovant military badges (1916-18), and the Whipsnade Lion (1933). The Osmington Horse is a Dorset cousin of the Cerne Giant, which depicts King George III riding on horseback, and was created in 1790. But we shall concern ourselves here with examples that are truly ancient and/or relate in some way to the Cerne Giant; these figures offer clues to aid our study.

The Cerne Giant is a good example of the problems encountered when studying hill figures, in so much that subsequent scourings and, in some instances, deliberate modification, have left little doubt that what we see today is not the original form. Sometimes we find that changes to a hill figure were intentional, for various reasons such as dogma and cultural intolerance. A good example of such modification is the

Westbury Horse, in Wiltshire. Although the present figure was cut in 1778, it replaced an older, more primitive design that was recorded on a map of 1773, and faced the opposite direction! The present horse was cleaned up in 2012 for the Queen's Diamond Jubilee.

There were once several more hill figures, for we have records of ones that have completely vanished, and may never be found. Some of these might have been created to commemorate some special event but not maintained thereafter, destined to disappear from the collective memory of the community. Plumpton Cross, west of Lewes, has now completely grassed over, even though it was 30m (98ft) across and shown on a plan as recently as 1923, when it was barely discernable; it may not have been maintained in the previous 250-300 yrs (Castleden 2000, p. 35). Tradition says it was cut by the Priory of St Pancras, which would date it 1537-8.

A chalk giant is suspected to have graced a hill near Wallington, Hertfordshire, not far from where Gog and Magog, two mythical giants, were buried with a golden chariot. At the Gogmagog Hills, a giant once adorned Wandlebury Camp, gifting the hills their name. It is no longer visible, yet was recorded in 1605 as, 'A Giant called All Paunch'. In 1954, Tom Lethbridge carried out a controversial survey of the site, producing an elaborate diagram that included multiple figures *outside* Wandlebury Camp. Later researchers have cast doubt on his methods, advocating that any hill figures were probably *inside* the enclosure.

More hill figures described as giants *(Gog and Magog)* were once seen at Plymouth, and at Shotover, east of Oxford. The latter was reported in the 17th century, but not drawn, and little else is known. The Red Horse of Tysoe (at Edgehill in the Cotswolds) appears to have been at least two figures (possibly up to five), the oldest record dating from 1606 (a reference to *Red Horse Vale*). The name Tysoe derives from *Tiw, the* Germanic equivalent of the god Mars. Resistivity surveys in the late 1960's suggest that the largest horse may have been of a comparable size to that at Uffington. In the 12th century local land was given over to the Knights Templar, who had a foundation in the area; a nearby village is called Temple Tysoe.

Fortunately, some figures *have* survived; the Watlington White Mark is a long thin triangle 59m (193ft) high, and is undated, as is the Whiteleaf Cross, which looks across the Vale of Aylesbury. The Bledlow Cross, on Wain Hill in the Chilterns, may be pre-1350, when there was reference to *'Henry at Bledlow Cross'*.

Long Man of Wilmington

This giant figure, at Wilmington in Sussex, measures 70m (230ft) from head to toe, and is the most colossal of the UK hill figure giants; globally, he is second in size only to the Giant Of Attacama in Chile, who stands at 119m (390ft). He has been known variously as the Wilmington Giant, the Lanky Man, the Lone Man, and the Green Man. He stands motionless, both feet pointing east, holding two staves 72m (236ft) long. His arms are bent, like the Cerne Giant, but he lacks facial features, genitalia, ribs or nipples; *'He is naked, featureless and enigmatic'* (Castleden 2000, p. 74). He appears in sketches dated 1681, 1710 and 1776, and in some of these he has facial features, and his feet both face outwards.

He stands on Windover Hill, on the South Downs, and graces a canvas that rises at an angle of around 28°, increasing to 40° above him. Recently, he was redefined by 770 white concrete blocks, replacing the original chalk, and later brick, versions.

One local story says the Long Man of Wilmington was a giant, slain in combat by another, and that originally both giants were depicted on Windover Hill, the lost one having survived until the mid-19th century. Legend says that locals drew the outline around the fallen giant before burying him in an adjacent long barrow. There are

The Long Man of Wilmington, Sussex, as seen from the north, near the church.

many different stories about how he died. Some say he was killed by a shepherd who threw his dinner at him, whilst a further tale says he tripped and broke his neck; yet another recounts how he was killed by pilgrims on their way to Wilmington Priory. However, the most popular folklore is that he was killed by a giant who lived on Firle Beacon. Also, it is said that a golden coffin is buried under the figure.

The best place from which to view the Long Man was formally the magnificent old yew in the churchyard to the north. It was planted in 400AD, before the arrival of Christianity to the area. This ancient viewpoint was rendered obsolete when the church was built, spoiling the view, a premeditated act to Christianise a Pagan gathering place. Cerne Abbey was built directly betwixt the sacred spring and the Giant, no doubt to engender a similar result.

The profuse number of Neolithic sites near the Long Man has been advanced as evidence that he might date back to that time, whilst some believe the figure represents a Bronze Age priest or warrior (Newman 2009, p. 138-9).

In 1925, the Duke of Devonshire gave the Long Man into the care of the Sussex Archaeological Trust (now Sussex Archaeological Society). During the Second World War it was painted green to prevent it being a landmark for German aircraft. At dawn on May Day, the Long Man Morris meet at the foot of the figure, and he also hosts Pagan rituals on the Sunday closest to the eight annual 'fire festivals'. At times the Long Man has suffered vandalism, just like the Cerne Giant, such as on the night of 17/18th June 2010, when a giant phallus was painted on the figure, resulting in him temporarily rivalling his Dorset cousin.

As with the Cerne Giant, there have been plenty of proposed candidates for the Long Man. These include Beowulf (who holds a spear in each hand), Mercury, Woden, Apollo, Bel, Herne the Hunter, and Samson (who supposedly stands betwixt the two pillars he will pull down); Hunter's Burgh barrow nearby certainly invites comparison with Herne the Hunter. Some have advocated that the lack of internal features means that

The Finglesham Buckle, showing a naked Odin holding two spears. (Image Rory Bowman.)

'he' could equally be a 'she' (Carr-Gomm 1993, p.100-1).

Perhaps the Long Man is Balder (or Baldur) the Beautiful, of Norse/Teutonic mythology, who opens the doorway to the heavens, letting through the light of the sun in the spring. This *'god of light'* was widely revered in Northern Europe as the son of Odin, and in one tale objects are thrown at him, one of which kills him, reminding us of the folklore of the Long Man. Interestingly, a 7th century Anglo-Saxon belt buckle found in Kent, known as the Finglesham Buckle, depicts a nude man (but for helmet) holding a spear in each hand (image above). Archaeologist Christopher Hawkes suggested that the character on the buckle and the Long Man both represent Odin, confirming the Scandinavian influx at that time (Hawkes 1965). Beowulf, the great hero of Norse mythology, can likewise be depicted holding a spear in each hand. Hawkes also advocates that the hill figure was later Christianised by the placing of crosses on the top of each spear. Rodney Castleden speculates as to whether the staves are ceremonial tools or weapons, like Thor's hammer or the double-axe of a Minoan goddess.

Some alternative researchers have regarded the two vertical lines as surveying or ranging rods held by a *'dodman'*, an ancient surveyor, whilst others have proposed that the figure is not carrying rods at all, but rather holds open a door, an entrance into the hillside, into the Underworld. Castleden seems to concur, seeing the two lines as portals, as the Long Man holds out his hands as a hieratic gesture, *'... perhaps directing summer crop ripening'*, and that he is, *'... the divine herald of the harvest'* (Castleden 2000, p. 80).

I would also like to add that it does not take a great leap of the imagination to see the giant as not looking *out* from the hill, but rather facing *into* it. Is he beckoning us to follow him into other realms?

The Long Man of Wilmington.
(Image: CupCakeKid. Wikipedia Common Licence.)

Academic John North has advocated an alignment with the constellation Orion (North 1996, p. 203); the adjacent *Hunter's Burgh* barrow also implies a link with Orion, *'the Hunter'*. The Egyptians had a celestial *'Stargate'* situated in Orion, which I shall later correlate to the Cerne Giant. Several internet writers have also regarded the Wilmington Long Man as Orion. North found further alignments with Orion at the Whiteleaf Cross and Bledlow Cross hill figures. These were vital pieces in the jigsaw for me, as I was to unravel the celestial elements of the Cerne figure. Perhaps the Long Man inspired the Giant at Cerne, as the latter is almost certainly younger.

Rodney Castleden and others favour a Neolithic origin for the Long Man, as he stands midst a landscape packed full of Neolithic (and Bronze Age) sites, such as long barrows, ancient trade routes, a causewayed enclosure, as well as flint mines. Roman pottery was found *halfway* down one of the trenches during the 1969 restoration and this is significant for it means anything *below* this level must be older. A resistivity survey in 1969 proved inconclusive regarding the Long Man's age, but did confirm that there had been prior alterations. Although more investigations need to be done, some have dated the Long Man to be as recent as 1545AD, based on brickwork found and dated in 2003. Rodney Castleden, however, thought that the methods used to obtain this date were flawed, in as much that deeper layers were not sufficiently studied; it was from these lower levels that a Neolithic scraper and a flint flake had previously been obtained.

As at Cerne, the problem with identifying the Long Man is that the figure has been modified. Drawings from 1710 and 1766 show him fully clothed, with facial features, and with his feet pointing in different directions. A record of 1873 describes a local tradition that boys once knew him as *'The Green Man'*, suggesting that the figure was either overgrown, or that they were describing literally what they saw - most of the Long man, as at Cerne Abbas, is green!

The Long Man is positioned within a depression between two spurs, creating a natural amphitheatre, which apparently produces special acoustic properties. A person speaking loudly on the Long Man can be heard a lot further away than normal, suggesting it may have been used for public speaking; the Long Man's powerful image behind a speaker would certainly have added weight to his authority. Recent studies at other prehistoric sites have proven that acoustics were often an important component of prehistoric ritual and monument design (Knight 2011).

Windover Barrow, a Neolithic burial mound at the top of the hill, is aligned with the Long Man, and the phallicism of such elongated mounds has been discussed elsewhere (Knight 2011).

All in all, the Long Man and the Cerne Giant might well be close cousins, and nearer to each other in terms of age than to any other figures. That the Long Man has an Iron Age origin is the conclusion of Paul Newman: *'... the Long Man's origins are essentially Celtic, like those of the Cerne Giant, and relate to the cult of Lugh or Lugus, in which the principles of light and fertility are yoked with meditation and balanced judgement'* (Newman 2009, p. 150). Whilst the Cerne Giant displays antagonistic action and movement, the Long Man stands guard over hidden mysteries.

Uffington White Horse

This hill figure, Britain's largest, gallops across the Berkshire Downs at White Horse Hill, south of Uffington village. It is 110m (361ft) from head to tail and 40m (131ft) high, its scale ensuring that it commands the vale below, which bears its name. Its sheer size makes it somewhat difficult to comprehend close-up, but from a distance, or indeed from the air, its beauty and dimensions become apparent. Rodney Castleden has queried why the White Horse was installed on a section of the hill that offered a relatively gentle 20° incline, making it difficult to perceive from below. If it were further down the slope it would be more impressive from the vale. The Cerne Giant is scoured into a steeper slope, enabling the figure to be viewed somewhat better from the valley below.

The slender, artistic lines of the White Horse project an eerie presence, with brush-like strokes that look as if they were painted onto the hill by the giants of old. The axis of the figure is almost north-south, and it gallops (although it has no hooves) towards the south, as if about to leap over the embankments of Uffington Castle. Below the horse plunges the Manger, a coomb whose steep slopes invite red kites to ride the thermals. To the south of the figure an ancient ridgeway runs to and beyond Wayland's Smithy, the Neolithic chambered mound.

The Uffington Horse has the earliest documented record of our hill figures. It is recorded in 9-10th century Saxon charters; known as *'Ecclesbeorg'*, it was a clear and well-known boundary marker. Local legend accredits the horse to King Alfred, who was born at nearby Wantage in 848AD, and that it is a construct commemorating his defeat of the Danes at Ashdown in 871AD. By 1072 and 1084, accounts tell us the locality was known as *'White Horse Hill'*.

During excavations in 1994, dates were obtained through a technique known as optically stimulated luminescence (OSL), which measures the time that soil has been cut off from sunlight. This gave a range of c.1200-800BC, making the figure a Bronze Age creation and by far the oldest dated figure, older than England itself, as G K Chesterton recounted in 1911:

'For the White Horse knew England,
When there was none to know.'

This is an incredible age and, considering it is such a slight, fragile work of art, demonstrates a feat of survival that verges on the miraculous; we can only wonder what inspired the countless 'grooming' repairs by all those generations. It is almost inconceivable that scourings have taken place for around 3000 years!

The style of the horse is unlike any other. It may possibly have started out looking more like a real horse, but is now very stylised and somewhat conceptual, even expressionistic. Its design, however, is like certain art on Iron Age coinage. There is a 'beak' of sorts, a huge ghostly eye, and one of the back legs might be seen as a phallus! This figure, perhaps more than all others, leaves much to the imagination, and interpretation really *is* in the eye of the beholder. The horse has a melancholy, timeless quality, and although the vulnerability of its thin white lines is only too obvious, it seems to hold mysteries as yet untold. Those who gaze upon its form

The Uffington White Horse. This view looks north, showing the head in the foreground and Dragon Hill in the middle distance.

know that it will outlive them, and that this is how it should be.

Horses feature heavily in classical and Iron Age myths. Recent thinking by archaeologists now suggests that the 'Celts' were inhabitants of Britain before the Iron Age, and that 'Celtic' beliefs were indigenous long before later migrations from the European mainland. Like at the Cerne Giant, above the Uffington figure is an Iron

Age enclosure and prehistoric tumuli. The Celts revered the horse as a precious prestigious animal associated with nobility and it was only fitting that the horse found its way into religious beliefs and myths. Rhiannon and Epona are goddesses who both have equine associations, and Epona is often depicted astride a horse; such was her importance that she was worshipped in Rome. She was the protector of Roman cavalry and may have held a similar status to free Celtic horsemen (Green 1989, p. 16-24). Sun gods such as Apollo and Helios are often depicted driving a horse-driven chariot across the heavens, and horses are often portrayed on Romano-British coinage. The close link between sun gods and horses in Celtic religion is born out by Celtic coins that bear both: *'The most common form in which the Celtic sky-gods are depicted is as a warrior on horseback'* (Green 1989, p. 124-7). Some warriors were buried with their horses, to be ridden by them in the Afterlife, but this practice may have also been due to their sheer reverence for the horse. The White Horse may have been a political marker on one level, staking claim to the land, and on another level a semi-religious badge or insignia of their deity, who watched over them from on high.

During excavations in 1857, forty-six Roman burials were found in the mound between the White Horse and Uffington Castle; there was evidence that this was a Neolithic mound put to later use by the Romans. This complements the pottery found in the trenches of the Long Man of Wilmington, and it could well be that datable Roman-British artefacts await discovery at the Cerne Giant.

To the north rises Dragon Hill, a good locality from which to view the horse and a place clearly connected with it. A natural outcrop, it was modified by human effort, and its circular flat summit suggests it was used for ceremonies involving the hill figure; in fact a narrow ridge connects the hill to the horse. A bald spot on the top of Dragon Hill, where no grass will grow, is said to be where St George killed a dragon and its blood was spilt onto the earth. Another legend tells of how King Arthur died here and was buried under the hill, and that the figure was cut to celebrate his victory

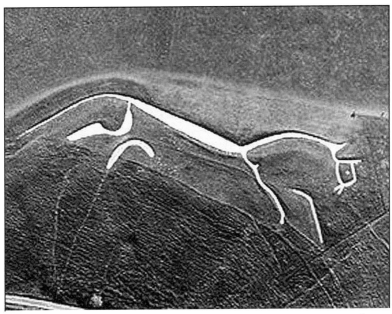

The Uffington White Horse. Was it previously a bull or a dragon?
(Image: USGS, Wikipedia Common Licence.)

over the Saxons at Badon Hill. These tales were meant to usurp the myths of the old Pagan horse deities, for it was now Christian heroes, such as St George, St Michael, Sir Gawain, and King Arthur, who rode noble white steeds, not the gods of old. Local folklore tells us:

'If it is true as I heard zay,
King George did here the dragon slay,
And down below on yonder hill
They buried him as I heard tell.'

In more recent times, the White Horse has been the focus for fairs, games and seasonal festivities, especially around the September equinox and at midsummer. Sometimes these were held when scouring was undertaken, which was on average every seven years. These celebrations probably evolved from Pagan religious festivals, in much the same way that Christmas Day, Easter, and Halloween are modern veneers of ancient Pagan observances.

Enter the dragon

For years, alternative researchers, and many Druids, have regarded the Uffington White Horse not as a horse, but a dragon - hence the naming of the hill from where best to view it; I too have held this view for some time. As long ago as 1926 Harold Massingham suggested that it was a dragon (and that Wayland's Smithy was the grave of a warrior-lord, such as a Arthur Pendragon) and pointed out numerous British dragon folklore (Massingham 1926). Earth mysteries pioneer Paul Screeton also regarded the figure as, *'...unlike any horse, and is, I believe, representative of a dragon and all that the fabulous beast symbolises'* (Screeton 1977, p. 91).

Dowser Guy Underwood concurred: *'...it is clearly a dragon, i.e. a serpent with legs. This is supported by the naming of the hill below'* (Underwood 1969, p. 141). The 'horse' does indeed have a slim, sinuous form, lacking the hanging equine under belly. The plot thickened when Underwood dowsed not one but *two* outlines, one being a horse, the other that of a dragon, laid down at different times. A curios 'beak' adorns the head of the existing figure, but Underwood dowsed the remnants of a much longer, snout-like feature extending from the present head, as well as dowsing a more substantial body. He also dowsed that Dragon Hill was very active energetically, with coils of spiralling energy (op. cit. p. 148).

The Spine of Albion, by Gary Biltcliffe and Caroline Hoare, is the new authoritative guide on the long distance alignment known as the Belinus Line. They dowsed the Belinus and Elen energy currents of the line through the White Horse, Uffington Castle and Dragon Hill; the two serpentine currents actually crossed at a node point on Dragon Hill. They call the hill figure the *'White Dragon'* and regard it to be the centrepiece of a *'Prehistoric Ritual Centre'* (Biltcliffe and Hoare 2012, p. 124). I too have dowsed the horse and found powerful nodes of spiralling energy at the eye; there is folklore that says it is lucky to stand on the eye and make a wish. I can also confirm a flow that goes down the spine of the horse and continues to Dragon Hill where, as Underwood found, nodes of energy converge on the bald patch attributed to St George's heroic dragon slaying. I shall come back to dowsing and earth energies in Chapter 6, when we will look at the Giant's energetic imprint.

Paul Devereux and Ian Thomson have advocated an alignment involving local sites. It runs almost north-south for nearly 10 miles, involving St Mary's at Uffington, Dragon Hill, a long barrow close to the horse, Uffington Castle and further earthworks and tumuli (Devereux and Thomson 1979, p. 100). It has also been noticed that the white horses of Uffington, Cherhill and Pewsey can be joined up to form an isosceles triangle, and that one line extends to Glastonbury Tor, whilst another goes to the Preseli Mountains. I have elsewhere demonstrated how the white horses at Cherhill, Westbury, and Alton Barnes all stand on alignments converging on Avebury (Knight and Perrott 2008).

John North found that the constellation of Taurus was involved with the White Horse (North 1996, p. 190-6), and I shall comment on this later. North suggests that the figure may have originally been a bull, which may explain the curious horn-like extensions on its head, and that later it 'evolved' into a dragon, and finally into the horse we perceive today. Working on the Belinus Line, Biltcliffe and Hoare (2012) found further astronomical alignments at the White Horse, notably involving Dragon Hill, the star Vega, and the North Celestial Pole; I have found similar alignments involving the Cerne Giant, which will be detailed later.

In the image below, one can see how the belly of the 'horse' was formerly plumper, how the front leg is attached to the torso, and how the head is more dragon-like. Grace Cooke, well known writer and clairvoyant (and channeller of *White Eagle*), was under no illusion that the figure was a dragon. She saw Dragon Hill as a great gathering place, '*... a concentration of the light'*, and she took the dragon to represent, '*... the battles between good against darkness and evil'.* She saw this as symbolic of humans slaying the *'evil within themselves'*. In conclusion, she asks a question: *'Could it be that this place where we are now sitting, this Dragon Hill, is one of the ancient sites where the god-men once dwelt and left their light and blessing for future races of men?'* (Cooke and Cooke, 1971). Cooke was also 'told' that an observatory had been built here, '*... from which people of the light watched the heavens'.* I think this is interesting, as this was 25 years prior to John North's astronomical research. Cooke had shamanically tuned-in to 'otherworlds', a practice that can be initiated at sites of great sanctity. Perhaps being within sight of potent images, such as the White Horse or the Giant, can trigger such trance states.

The form of the White Horse has changed over the last three millennia, a situation it shares with the Giant, as we shall soon discuss. It could be said that both figures changed along with the landscape into which they were implanted, evolving with the people who adopted and adapted them. At the end of the day, the horse has transcended the original intentions of its designers, whatever they were, becoming something much greater, as this excellent homily tells us:

A 19th century scouring of the Uffington White Horse.

'*The Anglo-Saxon ancestry projected on to the hill horse, complete with Alfred the Great, liberty, law, defence, constitution, and chivalry born of heroic Christianity, was firmly rooted at the heart of the national identity'* (Edwards

2005). Perhaps to the ancient settlers in the vale below, the horse was akin to the 'prancing horse' of Ferrari, an icon that encapsulated their very ethos.

Unlike the present situation at Cerne Abbas, the fences that once corralled the White Horse have now been removed, a situation that would be most welcome at the Giant. People can now interact with the figure - the horse is unshackled and unbridled, set free to roam the hills once more.

> 'Before the gods that made the gods
> had seen their sunrise pass
> The White Horse of the White Horse Vale
> Was cut out of the grass.
>
> Age beyond age on British Land,
> Aeons on aeons gone,
> Was peace and war in western hills
> And the White Horse looked on.'

(From *The Ballad of the White Horse,* G K Chesterton, 1911.)

Chapter 3.
Tall stories –
Giant folklore

*'… their minds were wrapped up with
notions of primeval giants and dragons,
which kept a jealous watch over their hidden treasures'.*
(T Wright, *The History of Ludlow*, 1841)

Myths are part of our cultural heritage; they are priceless legacies from an age when wisdom was mainly passed down by word of mouth, dispensed around campfire and hearth. Many were developed over the thousands of years of prehistory, a long period of time when literacy was either minimal or non-existent. Geoffrey Ashe observed that, *'Mythology is a long-term creation'* (Ashe 1990, p. 11), acknowledging it as a trans-global phenomena that transcends time, culture, race and dogma. Nor are myths the work of a few people with overactive imaginations, for something more universal, more archetypal, is at work:

'Myths and folklore are not created by the individual mind, yet neither are they the work of a group or a committee. Myths are the collective expressions of a society… over a long period of time… every single detail carries a meaning' (Bailey 1998, p. 9).

Myths are often difficult to decipher, comprising layers of hidden meaning, codes and riddles. Yet this, in fact, is what gives them potency and value. Although they may be modified over long periods of time, they retain their power and mysticism, providing a cohesive authority that can bind a culture, giving it identity.
I have advocated elsewhere (Knight 2011) that the very landscape itself is the originator of myths, which can be perceived by developing an intimate relationship with the land; it is the landscape that 'gifts' the stories to the people. In ancient times the land was as alive as people's imaginations:
'… Drawing upon both archaeological evidence and ethnographic analogy, we can begin to create a picture of a landscape not only invested with myths, meanings and histories, but one perceived as a potent and animate realm inhabited by spirits and diverse non-human agents' (Pollard & Reynolds, 2002, p. 29). To put it another way,

prehistoric people inhabited a *living landscape* of constant cycles, a dynamic manuscript, so to speak, on which tribal myths were, '... *captured by the very outlines of the landscape*' (Lévy-Bruhl 1983). And giants were very much part of these *'mythologized landscapes'*, and as such have been an imperative element of Man's psychological and sociological evolution. Giants represent a deep part of ourselves that is feared, the dark side of our psyche we are reluctant to confront.

Giants once walked every corner of the earth, and straddled the starry skies, a result of Man's yearning to explain his world. Myth was part of archaic science: '*One should pay attention to the cosmological information contained in ancient myth, information of chaos, struggle and violence. They are not mere projections of a troubled consciousness: They are attempts to portray the forces which seem to have taken part in the shaping of the cosmos*' (Santillana and von Dechend 1977, p. 150).

Global tall stories

Before we deal with our indigenous British myths, let us look at giants as global phenomena. Tales of giants come to us from the Vikings, the Indian *Vedas,* ancient China, South and Central America; in recent times, they perpetuate through the alleged sightings the Himalayan Yeti and Big Foot of North America. Tales of giants may not all be the result of gross exaggerations, for human 'giants' walk among us today; many people have reached 2.4m (8ft) and taller in modern times. A tale from Lancashire speaks of Childe of Hale, who stood 2.82m (9ft 3ins) tall and who died in 1623. Gigantism also occurs in Nature, with huge trees, dinosaurs, whales, etc, all demonstrating how life experiments with *'super-sizing'*.

In various Indo-European mythologies, gigantic peoples are featured as primeval creatures associated with the wild side of Nature, and they are frequently in conflict not only with humans, but with the gods themselves. The mythology of many cultures includes giants who are of human appearance, and yet are attributed with extraordinary strength and physical proportions. *Giant* is derived from the Greek word *gigantes,* and according to the Greek poet Hesiod, they were the children of Uranus and Gaia (making them beings of both the sky *and* the Earth). Giants were involved in a battle, called the *Gigantomachy,* with the Olympian gods, a conflict that was eventually settled when Hercules sided with the Olympians. Greeks also believed that earthquakes and volcanic eruptions were the

Many prehistoric sites were thought to have been the work of giants.

result of the *'tormented wrythings'* of giants. Homer, in *The Odyssey,* tells of one giant who devoured some of Ulysses' comrades. He also described the Cyclops, one-eyed giants who forged thunderbolts for Zeus: '*The Cyclops are accredited with being the master masons who built the formidable walls of ancient cities like Tyrins*' (Norvill 1979, p. 94). Cyclops were usually the offspring of the Olympians gods and nature spirits (the nereids, naiads and dryads), Polyphemus being a noted example. Hesiod also mentions Bronze Age men being, '*... of a monstrous size',* whilst according to Plato, Atlantis was inhabited by *'men of double normal size'.*

In his book, *The Comparison of Romulus with Theseus,* Plutarch describes when Athenians found the body of Theseus, who was *'more than ordinary size'.* Pausanias wrote that the kneecaps of Ajax were exactly the size of a pentathlon discus, suggesting he may have been around 4.3m (14ft) tall. And there is also the Greek hunter-giant Orion, whom we shall return to at length later.

In Finnish myths, Antero Vipunen is a giant shaman who possesses mighty spells dating back to the creation. In Slavic folklore, there was a giant called Rübezahl, who lived in the Giant Mountains, on the Czech-Polish border. Native American myths speak of child-eating giants, and Inca creation myths tell of how the deity Viracocha: *'... created a world of darkness, populated by a race of giants... who he had fashioned out of stone'* (Willis et al 1993, p. 255). William Cody's autobiography tells of a Pawnee Indian legend: *'While we were in the sandhills, scouting the Niobrara country, the Pawnee Indians brought into camp some very large bones, one of which the surgeon of the expedition pronounced to be the thigh bone of a human being. The Indians said the bones were those of a race of people who long ago had lived in that country. They said these people were three times the size of a man of the present day'.*

Many dolmens across Europe bear the title of Giant's Grave, so huge were they that only giants could be buried in them or, indeed, were capable of building them. Giants were believed to have built many of the huge, ancient city walls that are now crumbling away; Saxo Grammaticus argued that giants simply had to exist because nothing else could explain the existence of such massive walls, and other stone monuments, that we now know were built by pre-Roman cultures.

David and Goliath. An 1888 lithograph by Osmar Schindler.

Giants are frequently mentioned in the Bible, especially the first five books of the Old Testament, attributed to Moses; *'There were giants in the earth in those days'* (Gen. 6:4), and, *'That was also accounted a land of giants: giants dwelt therein in old time... called Zamzumummins'* (Deut. 2:20-21). And again (Deut. 3:11-13): *'For only Og, King of Basham, remained of the remnants of giants... Basham that was called the land of the giants'.* A giant named Gog is also mentioned (in Ezekiel 38), and we shall meet his namesake soon. In Numbers (13:33), we are told, *'And there we saw the giants, the sons of Anak'.* The Egyptians described the *Ph'anakes,* providing a link with these *'sons of Anak'.* The Bible also tells of how Joshua entered the Land of Canaan to destroy the *Ammorite Giants,* whose leader was called Og. This character also appears in English mythology as a Celtic giant associated with the sun. The legacy of this is found in many fables of man-eating giants called *Ogres* (Shrek excluded, of course!).

The most famous Biblical giant is of course Goliath, who met his demise at the hands of the hero David. Do we believe that all these tales are true testimonies, or mere flights of fancy? For this opens up deeper issues, as Roy Norvill concludes, *'If we decline to cast doubts on the biblical texts, then we can no longer disbelieve in the existence of giants'* (Norvill 1979, p. 152). Hebrew texts speak of a race of giants, the Nephilim, regarded by specialist scholars to be from the root Aramaic word *nephila*, which is one name for the constellation Orion. This heroic hunter will be a key player as the story of the Cerne Giant unfolds.

Regarding Norse creation mythology, an ancient poem tells of Ymer, the primary giant of the earth, from whose scattered body the world was created (Santillana and von Dechend 1977, p. 92). Norse/Viking settlers brought with them tales of the god Thor, who had an axe hammer, symbol of thunder and lightning. He was himself a giant, and in some tales he also defeats fellow giants, such as Geirrod and Hrungnir, in mortal combat. His deadliest enemy was apparently the World Serpent, the sea-giant Hymir, whom he had to slay, inviting comparison to one of Hercules' tasks. The Norse fertility god Freyr was fated to fight the fire-giant Surtr but was defeated because he had lost his sword. Loki is another northern European giant, who was a constant thorn in the side of the gods. However, Nordic

The giant Merlin building Stonehenge, according to myth.

colossi are not always menacing: *'The land-spirits included benevolent mountain giants, who protected men and women from hostile beings and helped in severe weather'* (Willis et al. 1993, p. 201).

Giants feature in a great many fairy tales, such as *Jack the Giant Killer* and the closely related *Jack and the Bean Stalk*. These have fostered the modern perception that giants are violent, if somewhat stupid, man-eating monsters, linking them with ogres, who are distinctly cannibalistic. However, in some recent portrayals, giants are both intelligent and friendly, as in Roald Dahl's *The Big Friendly Giant,* and the benevolent Hagrid of the *Harry Potter* series.

British giant folklore

If the numerous and widespread folklore concerning giants is anything to go by, the hills and valleys of Britain must have once constantly resounded to cries of, *'Fe Fi Fo Fum'*. Some tales are humerous and quite modern, and yet others go back to more distant times, where we may glimpse ancient wisdom; it is here that hidden histories and universal archetypes lurk in the wings.

Many geographical features and prehistoric monuments are linked to giants. Giant's Rock, at Zennor in Cornwall, could be rocked by the mere prod of a giant's gnarled finger. In the same area legend has it that huge boulders of granite magically sprang out of the ground at the behest of giants (Miller and Broadhurst 2000, p. 74 & 76). Cornish legend speaks of Bellerus (a variant of Bel or Beli), who was a one-eyed giant. Other Cornish giants include Holiburn, Wrath, Bolster (who is celebrated at *Giants Well*, St Agnes) and Cormoran; the local neighbourhood was terrorized by Cormoran until he was eventually killed by a local lad called Jack, giving rise to the *Jack and the Beanstalk* tale. Cormoran and his wife, Cormelian, are associated with

St Michael's Mount, where they dwelt in a cave; Giant's Well can be found on the mount today. Its French counterpart, Mont St Michel, was created by giants; it was once called Mount Gargan and the father of the giant Gargantua was buried there.

Another Cornish colossus resided at Bosporthennis, and was known as the *Giant of Morvah*. He was said to perform a magical rite on Lughnasad (August 1st) that

18th century engraving of the giant Ascapart, formerly on the Bargate at Southampton.

rendered him harmless, and that thousands of people came to drink to his health. Other reminders of Cornwall's giant population survive in place-names, such as Giant's Wheel, Giant's Coffin, Giant's Cradle, Giant's Quoit, and Giant's Castle.

Even natural geological features were attributed to giants, such as the massive basalt columns of the Giant's Causeway on the coast of Northern Ireland; giants provided the least complicated explanation for such features. The Strathclyde Isle of Staffa and the legendary land of Lyonnesse were both said to be inhabited by giants.

Tales of conflicts with giants are a common theme in Welsh, Scottish and Irish folklore. In the small Scottish village of Kinloch Rannoch, a local myth concerns a nearby hill that resembles the head, shoulders, and torso of a man, and is called the Sleeping Giant. Apparently the giant will awaken only if a specific musical instrument is played near the hill. Also in Scotland, there is a circle known as Tomnaverie, meaning, *'hill of the giant's grave'*, and the Great Grey Man, said to be over 3m (10ft) tall, is a spectral apparition said to appear on the summit of Ben MacDhui in the Cairngorms. Orkney and Shetland were strongholds for giants, including Saxi, Herman, Sigger and Atla, as well as two female giants, Fenia and Menia. They were all nocturnal creatures, for the rays of the sun would turn them into stone.

In Irish folklore the Fomorians were the *'giants of the night... who came from the sea'*, whose chieftain was the one-eyed Balor. His name sounds similar to the Mesopotamian god Baal, *'... which is synonymous with Bel or Beli... Bel is represented as a deity similar to Bran or Don, both giants'* (Norvill 1979, p. 102). This suggests that these deities may be one and the same.

The mightiest of the Celtic gods, Dagda, was described as a club-wielding giant (see p. 86). The Irish knew Stonehenge as the *Giants Round Dance* or *Ring* (Ashe 1990, p. 39) and it is associated with tales of Merlin, as shown in an early illustration (see image p. 22), where he is clearly a *'giant of a man'*. Merlin crops up again on the Isle of Man, which was inhabited by giants until he expelled them, although giants are said to be sleeping at Castle Rushen.

Giant's Cave is situated near the top of the Herefordshire Beacon on the Malvern Hills. Below the cave entrance is a boulder, locally called the Shew Stone or the Sacrificial Stone; every Midsummer Day the sun rises over the ridge and illuminates the stone.

The churchyard of St Andrews church at Penrith, Cumbria, is said to be the last resting place of a giant, possibly the one who inhabited a cave at Eamont Bridge, called Isis Parlis or Giant's Cave (Biltcliffe and Hoare 2012, p. 335-338). Two other Cumbrian caves at Grandtully and Tailburn Bridge also have giant folklore (op. cit. p. 377 & p. 441).

Cormoran, the Cornish giant, being slain by Jack. From a 19th century chapbook.

Many giants of English folklore were noted for their stupidity. A giant who had quarreled with the Mayor of Shrewsbury was intent on burying the city with dirt; however, on the way he met a shoemaker carrying shoes to repair, and the shoemaker convinced the giant that he had worn them all out coming from Shrewsbury, and that it was too far for the giant to travel. Other English stories tell of how giants threw stones at each other; this explained great boulders scattered across the landscape.

From Norfolk comes the tale of Tom Hickathrift, who was said to be 2.4m (8ft) tall, and defender of the Norfolk Marshlands. He defeated the fearful giant of Smeeth, and his gravestone can still be seen in the churchyard of Tilney All Saints.

In Hampshire, a legendary local colossus called Ascapart appears in a 13th century text. He was defeated by Sir Bevis of Hampton and both characters once adorned the Bar Gate in Southampton (image previous page); Sir Bevis himself was pretty huge, and was able to carry his wife and his horse under one arm. Ascapart was defeated after his club (made from a whole tree) was swung at Sir Bevis but became stuck in soft ground. Rather than slaying the giant, Sir Bevis decided to make him his squire; Bevis Mound is said to be the giant's final resting place. In neighbouring Sussex, folklore again speaks of Sir Bevis, but this time that he is buried in a mound near Arundel. Also in Sussex, we have already seen how the Long Man of Wilmington was regarded a giant who was slain by another, and that both giants were originally depicted on Windover Hill. A Sussex ogre named Brede was a child-eater, until some children sawed him in half whilst he lay drunk at Brede Park, where his ghost appeared for a long time after.

In Devon, legend says that the giant Hercules defeated other local giants to become King, and in fact Hartland Point was at one time called Hercules Point. In Somerset, a giant used to wade out to Lundy Island, and a tumulus near Combe St Nicholas is known as Giant's Grave. Further north, in the Midlands, giants are associated with Stokesay Castle, Brown Clee, Wenlock Edge and the Wrekin (all in Shropshire). Directly north of the Clifton Suspension Bridge at Bristol is an opening in the sheer limestone cliffs, about 75m (250ft) up the east side of the gorge. This natural karst cave, variously called Giants Cave, Ghyston Cave or Vincent's Cave, was named after giant brothers called Goram and Vincent (or Ghyston). The giants were said to have both courted the same woman, Avona, who gave them the task of draining a local lake. Vincent triumphed over his brother and won the hand of the lady, and created the Avon Gorge; Vincent Rocks, north of the bridge, is said to mark his burial. Romano-British pottery has been found in the cave, which was also used as a chapel in 305AD. Later known as St Vincent's Chapel, much of it later fell into the gorge below (Knight and Perrott 2008, p. 199-201).

The classic scene of the slaying of a giant or ogre by a hero on his noble steed.

A giant called Gorm was wandering the nearby Cotswolds, but tripped and dropped a spade full of earth into the Avon Valley, forming Maes Knoll. The chief astrologer of England, Idris, was said to have been a giant of a man. There is also a giant named Idris, perhaps one and the same, who gave his name to Cader Idris in Wales; a rock seat at the summit is said to have been his residence. But this tale is not in isolation, for a document written by Sion Dafydd Rhys, dated 1600, lists more than fifty Welsh giants and where they lived.

In Salisbury Museum there is an effigy of a giant, 3.6m (12ft) tall, known as St Christopher, which was periodically taken around the town at special times, particularly at mid-summer and Lughnasad (Lammas). It is known to date from at least the 15th century.

Trojans, Phoenicians and Dorset

In *The Chronicles of England, Scotland and Ireland* (1577), we read how the giant Albion, son of Neptune, defeated the Celts of Britain, renaming it after himself. His reign lasted until he was defeated by Hercules. Gary Biltcliffe surmises that, *'Perhaps the giant on the hill above Cerne Abbas, said to represent Hercules, was cut by locals inspired by this ancient folk tradition'* (Biltcliffe 2009, p.127). In the 12th century, Geoffrey of Monmouth wrote *The Historia Regum Britannie,* in which he related that Albion [Britain] was only inhabited *'by a few giants'* when Brutus and his fellow Trojans arrived following their defeat at Troy. Among these giants *'... was one detestable monster, named Goëmagot (Gogmagog), and of such prodigious strength that at one shake he pulled up an oak as if it had been a hazel wand'.*

The Brutus story goes something like this: whilst Brutus is holding a feast with his companions in Totnes, (or more likely Dartmouth, which is nearer the sea) some twenty giants led by Goëmagot descend on the company, *'... among whom he made a dreadful slaughter'.* At last the giants are routed and all are slain except for Goëmagot, who is taken alive so that Corineus can wrestle him. During the contest the giant breaks three of Corineus' ribs, which so enrages him that he, *'ran with him, as fast as the weight would allow him, to the next shore... getting upon the top of a high rock, hurled down the savage monster into the sea; where falling on the sides of craggy rocks, he was torn to pieces'.* The place where he fell, *'... is called Lam Goëmagot, that is, Goëmagot's Leap, to this day'.* According to Geoffrey of

Monmouth, Corineus was said to have, *'... experienced great pleasure in wrestling with giants, of whom there were far more there than in any other district'.* For his victory, Corineus was presented with Cornwall, to which he gave his name.

To this day, the Brutus Stone can be seen at Totnes. One version says that Brutus (or Brit) spared two of the captured giants, Gog and Magog, and had them stand guard over his new city of London, which was called Caer Troia, *'Seat of Troy',* or Nova Troia, *'New Troy'.* Effigies of them stood until the great fire of London of 1666. London has a long tradition linking giants with royaly and kingship. In Elizabethan times the figures were regarded as Gogmagog and Corineus; in 1413 Henry V was greeted by a effigy of a giant at London Bridge; two giants bowed to the same King at Tower

Gog and Magog, formerly displayed at the Guildhall, London, but destroyed during the Blitz.

Bridge in 1421; in 1522, Emperor Charles V was greeted by two giants, described as Hercules and Samson, at London Bridge. The present statues of Gog and Magog were set up in the Guildhall in 1953, replacing two former ones destroyed during the Blitz of 1940. Despite their negative depiction in the Bible, images or effigies of Gog and Magog have traditionally been paraded in the processions at the Lord Mayor's Show, as they have done since the days of King Henry V; they are the enduring guardians of the City of London.

Two other depictions of Gog and Magog can be seen on the outside of the old 'Sun Inn' at Saffron Walden. These depictions are in 16th century plasterwork; one holds a sword and shield, the other a long club. Interestingly, two oak trees just a few miles from Cerne Abbas were called Gog and Magog, as are two beech trees nearby on High Stoy (Biltcliffe 2009, p. 125). We located the latter on a field trip in February 2013, guided by local expert Gary Biltcliffe. The beeches are located in the eye of a landscape horse (see image p. 46).

This links nicely to *The Spirit of Portland,* in which Gary Biltcliffe suggests an alternative location for the landing site of Brutus and Corineus, as well as making convincing arguments connecting Portland with Cerne (Biltcliffe 2009, p. 127-132). Biltcliffe tells us that Melkart Hercules (Melcarth) was the first Phoenician King of

Tyre, who defeated Albion to become ruler of Britain. This idea was first championed by William Stukeley, who saw the Giant, '... to represent the famous and first Hercules, the Phoenician leader of the first colony to Britain when they came hither for Cornish tin'. Phoenician beads have been found in Dorset tumuli, and the famous golden plate from Clandon Barrow is in the style of Phoenician artwork. Biltcliffe asks the intriguing question as to whether Brutus landed not at Totnes, but at Portland. Surviving folklore speaks of giants on the Isle of Portland, and there are locations that fit the Brutus legends, including Giant's Castle. There is also the newly discovered landscape giant, whose raised right hand holds the weight of Verne Prison (site of an old hillfort). William Blake personified Albion (Britain) as a giant called Cronos, and according to the Greek Plutarch (AD 46-127) this giant lies sleeping beneath an island called Britain, and that he is bound in chains and guarded by another giant, Briaeus. Biltcliffe asks whether this could be the Portland landscape giant (Biltcliffe op. cit. p. 131).

Gary Biltcliffe also identifies an outcrop of rock on the north side of the island that resembles a giant's head, which he has shown me. This is just a short distance from a phallic pillar of rock called Nicodemus Knob. It is indeed a coincidence that these two features should be so close to one another: a giant and a phallus – now where have we seen that before? We shall come back to this subject later when, as Biltcliffe suggests, I will include Corineus in our line-up of the Cerne Giant's suspects.

Gary Biltcliffe's discoveries certainly warrant further investigation. According to Greek historians, the Phoenicians came to Britain to trade in tin, and would have undoubtedly been in Dorset (Biltcliffe 2009, p. 88). There is Crete Hill, for instance, at Godmanstone, suggesting that travellers came from that region of the Mediterranean.

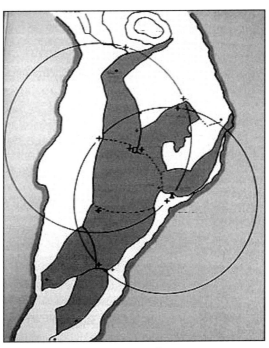

The Portland Giant.
(After Gary Biltcliffe, 2009)

Biltcliffe told me, 'Portland drew people in from afar. It was such a prominent landmark. In the Iron Age, Dorset had a flax rope making industry so seafarers came to buy rope for their ships. The Durotriges were not originally native, and were go-betweens for this trade' (pers. comm.).

As if to complement the Giant's head at Portland, many years ago I perceived huge facial features (large eyes, a nose and gaping mouth) on the north side of the Agglestone, near Swanage. This gigantic natural rock could formerly be rocked and there is Druidic folklore attached to it (Knight 1998, p. 190-1). Is this yet a further lost giant that has now been reinstated?

27

More Dorset giants

Dorset does not come up short (excuse the pun) as far as giants are concerned. I have discussed the county's giant folklore elsewhere (Knight 1998, p. 195-198), but I will recap briefly here.

There is a mound called Giant's Grave at Melcombe Bingham, not far from Cerne; on it a lonely sarsen stone marks where two giants held a rock-throwing contest between two local hills; the unfortunate loser was so mortified that he fell dead on the spot. Gary Biltcliffe speculates as to whether Melcombe and Melbury were named after the Phoenician god Melcarth. There is a similar tale of a giant, or the Devil, who played quoits by tossing rocks from Portland Pike; one of the stones he threw is the capstone of the Neolithic dolmen known as the Hellstone (Biltcliffe 2009, p. 82). The Valley of the Stones, nearby, is also said to be the result of more boulder throwing antics by giants.

Giants Grave and Giant's Trencher are two ancient earthen features near Swanage. At Brockhampton Green, just 5 miles NE of the Giant, a stone by the side of the road is said to be the one hauled up a hill to kill a giant (Knight 1996, p. 182). To the south of Cerne, the vast hillfort of Maiden Castle was said to have been built by giants. From Preston, near Weymouth, comes a 13th century record that speaks of Thursdyke, meaning *'ditch of Thyrs'*; a giant called Thyrs appears in the Viking/Anglo-Saxon Beowulf sagas.

Grim's Ditch is an old name for Bokerley Dyke, a huge Iron Age earthwork near the northern terminal of the Dorset Cursus, first named as *The Dyke of Grimr* in 1280; Grim is a pseudonym for the giant shaman Odin/Woden, who was later elevated to a god, and who also gave his name to Grimsby and Grimley.

The Hellstone, Dorset, which was thrown by either the Devil or a giant from Portland.

Folklore of the Cerne Giant

So finally we come to the Cerne Giant. Historian John Hutchins provides the following account: *'There is a tradition, that a giant who formerly did mischief, having made an excursion in the adjacent Vale of Blackmoor and devoured several sheep, lay down on the side of a hill to repose himself and digest his breakfast. Falling asleep, the people revitted him down and killed him and then cut his figure in the solid chalk. Fabulous as this story is, it is perhaps a proof of the great antiquity of this figure'* (Hutchins 1774, Vol 2, p. 292).

This may be a variant of a legend telling of a Danish Giant that terrorised locals and their sheep in Blackmoor Vale. Eventually, he was decapitated whilst he slept, and his outline was marked on the hill as a warning to other giants (Ashe 1990, p. 53).

One tale from 1901 speaks of the Giant devouring virgins. A variation on this comes from the 1930's, telling a similar story, but adding that the Trendle is the imprint of his frying pan (Harte 1986, p. 44). Ralph Wightman reports, *'It is said that a giant threatened Cerne and went to sleep on the hillside. A shepherd boy went up in the night and slew him, whereupon the people of Cerne carved around the outline of his body'* (Wightman 1977, p. 98). Jeremy Harte cites that these varying stories demonstrate how the basic myth has persisted alive and well in oral tradition (Harte 1986, p. 44).

Of the chalk figure himself, there are some modern tales. It is said that he comes down to the river to drink at night, or that he walks down to the mill stream to drink, this time more specifically at midnight. This is echoed by similar folklore from across Britain of how ancient stones move around of their own volition at specific times. Some local rivalry is suggested in the tale that the Giant was scoured by Cerne villagers to frighten people from neighbouring Sydling St Nicholas.

A tale from 1865 concerns the Giant lifting himself from the hillside when he heard that a cudgel-playing competition was being held between teams from Somerset and Wiltshire. The Giant called out, *'Fee-Fi-Fo-Fum, I sniff the blood of an Englishman'.* He then strode down the valley to where the contest was being held, offering himself as the 'stickler', or referee, to ensure that fair play ensued. His club rapped the ground when play was to begin, and the games were apparently a *'genial pastime to the giant'* (Cutler 1865, p. 65).

Cutler also records folklore that the Cerne Giant used to, *'stride over to the opposite hill, where Belchalwell nestles under Bulbarrow, and stretch himself out like a lazy shepherd boy on a summer's evening, and watch the golden light of the setting sun, claiming this district as part of his own domain, because they bear his own name'.* We shall return to this later, for it connects the Giant with the deity Bel.

In 1808, Dorset poet William Holloway published his poem *'The Giant of Trendle Hill'*, in which locals kill the Giant by piercing his heart. I have lifted some extracts from it, as they contain some informative lines:

The Giant of Trendle Hill
By William Holloway

Suffice it, that fair Dorset's vales
Where dark with forests deep,
Of many a cent'rys growth, and woods
O'erhung each shaggy sheep.

Amid this solemn pomp of shade,
The drear of vale and plain,
A Giant, of enormous brood,
Enjoy'd his lonely reign.

Stretch'd in a rock-pil'd cavern drear,
He snor'd the hours away;
Save when, with massy club he rang'd,
To forage for his prey.

The sturdiest bull that graz'd at large,
With single stroke he slew,
And, as a butcher would a lamb,
Across his back he threw.

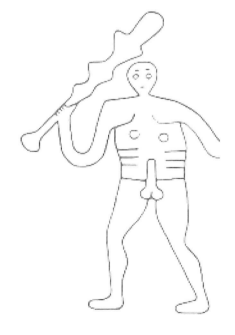

When forth he came, to walk his rounds
The crashing woods gave way
Beneath his steps; and herdsmen fled
With terror and dismay.

One day, the game lay far a-field –
Some twenty miles, or more;
And over vale and stream he strode,
In track untrod before.

When in the pastures of Blackness,
Fair beeves and sheep he spies,
And, rushing on the welcome spoils,
Secures them by surprise.

Then sits him down, by hunger press'd,
And, without aid of steel,
Like the fierce Lion of the wild,
Devours the living meal.

Now evening flung her yellow rays
Across the Cerne's calm flood,
When thirsty, stoop'd to drain the stream
The Monster, gorg'd with blood.

The night was cool, the turf was soft
On Trendle's verdant swell;
And on weary Glutton's lids
Oblivious slumber fell.

At length they form a bold resolve
To steal upon his rest,
With sure, but silent step, to rid
The country of its pest.

With cautious tread behold they move,
With wooden spear and dart,
And under covert of the night,
Deep pierce the Monster's heart.

Folklore of Giants is engrained in the
cultural memory of Britain.

Thrice he essays to rear his head,
And thrice to raise his arm;
But stronger death arrests his pow'rs,
And saves his foes from harm.

A reeking river, flow'd his blood,
Swift rushing down the steep;
His last groan shook the tall elm trees,
Like thunder loud and deep.

And thus he lay, the conquerors trac'd,
His figure on the green;
And his memorial of their deed,
May, to this day, be seen.

From here, when cheerful summer comes,
The swains, with annual care,
Clear all intruding weeds away,
And the chalk-trench repair.

Outstretch'd upon that hill he lay,
A moral cherish'd long:-
Heav'n's certain vengance will pursue
The sons of blood, and wrong'.

The poem speaks of the number three (the number of ribs showing on either side of the Giant's chest, and the number of broken ribs Corineus sustained), and of floods, lions and the Giant's heart. We shall return to these later, as they give us hidden clues as to the Giant's connection with the heavens.

We shall deal with the Giant's folklore specifically related to fertility in Chapter 6; he amassed plenty of myths which show us that rather than a giant to be feared, as we are told most giants should be, he was actively sought for his fertilising powers.

To this day the British landscape bears impressions and memories of giants that once walked the earth, most famously with the chalk figures that mark two hills of southern England – the Long Man of Wilmington and the Cerne Abbas Giant.

Chapter 4.
The Giant's landscape –
a walk through time and space

*'A legend is captured in the very outlines of the landscape…
living books in which the myths are inscribed'.
(Primitive Mythology, Lucien Lévy-Bruhl)*

Cerne Abbas is a picturesque village nestling in the rolling chalk downland north of Dorchester, in the heart of ancient Dorset. The Giant reclines on the SW slopes of Giant Hill, at grid ref. ST 666017, overseeing the valley of the River Cerne. The topography of the area is interesting; west of the valley are a series of E-W running hills cut by incised valleys, across the top of which runs an ancient ridgeway track. To the east is an upland region, from which a stream once flowed down Yelcombe Bottom. This now issues at Cerne's spring/well, due to long-term down-cutting, and possibly through glacial action. Between this former stream course and the River Cerne, the elongated ***phallic-shaped*** ridge of Giant Hill projects into the Cerne Valley.

The Cerne Giant strides northwards along this ridge, somehow separated by both time and space from the village below, as pioneer earth mysteries researcher John Michell observed: *'To stand on the hilltop at Cerne Abbas in Dorset above the head of the old naked giant, cut into the sloping turf, is to experience the definate sensation of a difference in quality between the wild elevated world of prehistoric habitation and the present village in the quiet secluded valley below with its pretty thatched cottages and medieval church'* (Michell 1969, p. 73).

The head of the Giant is 182m (597ft) above sea level, 60m (197ft) above the river below. The slope of the hill is around 40° mid-giant, but lessens when approaching the head and the tip of his club. The Giant is foreshortened when observed from below, appearing very compressed from the viewpoint car park. It has been noted that much better views can be obtained elsewhere, such as from Weam Common Hill and Rowden Hill (Darvill et al, 1999, p. 6), something I appreciated during my perambulations around the landscape. I shall return to this theme later, for certain facets of the Giant only become apparent when he is scrutinised in the context of the landscape he inhabits.

According to historian John Hutchins, names for Cerne Abbas have included *Cernel, Cerneli, Cernelium, Broad Cerne, Kern* and *Kernel.* The village originated as a small hamlet on a spring line, the waters of which well up into a valley that offers shelter from severe weather, as well as fertile soil. The area was visited by Mesolithic hunter-gatherers, and with the arrival of farming in the Neolithic, several burial mounds were constructed. Later on, Bronze Age barrows, or tumuli, were built to house the dead, and some of these still pepper the landscape.

Dorset was already a distinct region some 2,000 years ago, and the area's Iron Age clans were known collectively as the Durotriges. Their name gives us the root of the county name, as well as that of Dorchester. They were a cultured people, and long before the Romans arrived had their own roads, street plans and coinage, and used sophisticated earthenware made by skilled Purbeck potters. Their domain stretched west to the River Otter in Devon, north to beyond Lamyatt Temple, and east as far as the Avon Valley and the Iron Age port at Hengistbury. Cerne stood in its heartland, easily accessed via well-trodden ridgeway tracks, vital arteries of trade dating back to the Neolithic. The main chieftain towns were at Maiden Castle, Hod Hill and Cadbury, and Cerne is more or less central in relation to these.

The Iron Age was a period of uncertainty, as clans exchanged blows during inter-tribal disputes over land coveted for grazing and crops. It has been suggested that Cerne was a sacred place of ceremony, neutral ground for bickering chieftains, a meeting place for business and diplomacy, games and feasting. Is it possible that the Giant was etched onto the hillside when a truce or alliance was forged? The importance of Cerne during these times is aptly summed up by Rodney Castleden: '... the Cerne Giant springs into place as an important Iron Age nodal centre, at the crossroads of two major ridgeways' (Castleden 1996, p. 132): **Cerne was once major league.**

During this period, the Cerne Valley was rich in both small homesteads and larger settlements, some fortified with embankments. It was well populated by people who herded cattle, sheep and goats, and who farmed crops in the valleys and on gentler slopes. Iron Age settlements were situated on nearby Black Hill, Dickley Hill, Weam Common Hill, Smacam Down, and Seldon Hill. On Giant Hill itself, a large settlement thrived, with substantial earthworks, and to the south of it a cross-ridge bank straddled the hill. We should not be too hasty in assuming that this cross-bank is Iron Age, for the valley is rich is Bronze Age sites, including tumuli on Giant Hill. The Durotriges had moved into an

The landscape of the Giant. The two river valleys of the Cerne and the Sydling are separated by a ridge which is traversed by an ancient ridgeway. **S** = Iron Age settlement **+** = Bronze Age tumuli.

area already rich with older sacred places; the neighbourhood had been regarded as 'special' during earlier millennia. Traces of the cross dyke can be seen today, as well as the banks of a henge-like circular feature (see map below).

The Iron Age priests were of course the Druids. The earliest record of them comes from the Greeks c. 300BC, whilst Roman references date from 200BC. The oldest detailed description of the priesthood comes from the military general, later Emperor, Julius Caesar, in his *Commentarii de Bello Gallico* (c. 50BC). Whilst there is archaeological evidence of the religious practices of Iron Age people, Ronald Hutton observed that in Britain, '*... not one single artefact or image has been unearthed that can undoubtedly be connected with the ancient Druids'*.

Above the Giant is an enclosed earthwork known as the Trendle, or the Giant's Frying Pan, a site that has never been excavated. Because of how the Trendle is cut into the hillside, Prof Stuart Piggott regarded it as a temple (Piggott 1938, p. 328). However, the site may also have been a prehistoric burial mound, for it appears to have no entrance (Darvill et al 1999, p. 15).

We can state with some confidence that the Giant was closely associated with the Trendle. The latter is a rectangular enclosure comprising banks with ditches built on a carefully levelled, horizontal surface at the crest of the hill. There were other native Iron Age sanctuaries around Britain, such as at Pilsden Pen, Heathrow, Danebury, Hayling Island, and Queen Boudica's spectacular shrine at Thetford. We do not know if the Trendle ever contained a stone building, as did the sanctuary at Maiden Castle,

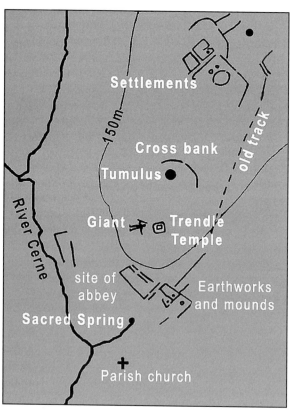

The key locations and monuments in the vicinity of the Giant.

as it is smaller than others of a similar date. It was but one element of a sacred ceremonial landscape that included the sacred spring and the Giant, replicating the link between the shrine at Pilsden Pen and the nearby spring at Sliding Hill.

The settlement on Giant Hill (grid ref: ST669022) is the nearest to the Giant, and is documented as an Iron Age / Romano-British community, with hut circles and a field system with pits. Vistas from here are truly inspiring and, amazingly, offer a view of Hardy's Monument to the south. Gary Biltcliffe has suggested that one of the features here may be the remains of a henge (pers. comm.). I have calculated that the two entrances of this feature are solstice-aligned. To the south of it is the Giant Hill Cross Ridge Dyke (ST667018), an elongated grass covered earthwork, consisting of a bank averaging 5m (16ft) wide and 1.2m (4ft) high, with a ditch on the north side averaging 0.5m (1½ft) deep.

The dyke might have been defensive, but might also have defined the southern end of Giant Hill as the sacred space of the Giant and the Trendle. Archaeologist Bill Putnam sees the dyke as a powerful argument for the Giant being an Iron Age monument (in Darvill 1999, p. 54).

Giant Hill Bowl Barrow (ST667018) is a gorse-covered Bronze Age burial mound, 9.2m x 10.2m (30ft x 33ft) wide and up to 1.1m (3½ft) high, but with no surviving ditch. The barrow demonstrates that the hill had a sacred status long before the Giant was forged; *'Giant hill is a special place... one to which people of several successive cultures have attached great significance'* (Castleden 1996, p. 16).

The Romans, led by Vespasian, subdued the local Durotriges tribes in their campaign of 43-44AD. The Imperial war machine rolled into a land occupied by people nowhere near unified enough to defend it. The Giant stood on the hillside, but its aggressive posture was unable to offer the protection needed against the interlopers: *'The threatening stance of the Giant – all bluster and exuberance – mirrored this instability as much as his primitive weaponry denoted the limitations of the Durotriges during the Roman invasion'* (Newman 2009, p. 96).

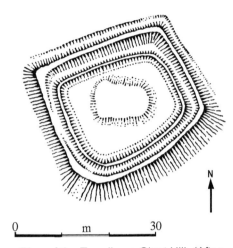

Plan of the Trendle on Giant Hill. (After RCHM 1952.) See also image p. 123.

After a few local clashes, the Durotriges were pacified by the Romans, who subsequently embraced local gods and goddesses. As they had done across Europe, they adopted shrines and sacred places, such as at Maiden Castle and Bath. Regarding smaller shrines, such as the Trendle, it is possible that, *'... small temples were dwellings for the gods rather than places to hold a congregation'* (Castleden 1996, p. 105). Perhaps carved totem poles were erected, a Celtic practice elsewhere.

One thing we know for certain is that the Trendle is visible from some distance away, and it may well have been at the heart of the valley's ceremonial practices. Gary Biltcliffe, author of *The Spirit of Portland,* concurs: *'The Trendle was where the rituals and ceremonies were carried out, not the Giant'* (pers. comm.). It has been suggested that the Giant may have been added as a sort of advertisement or marker for the *'Holy Hill where Helis's temple stood'* (Castleden 1996, p. 186). In other words, the Giant was only one element, and perhaps not even the most important, of an extended ceremonial landscape, with the Trendle and the spring at its heart. Over time, any wooden temple would have fallen into disuse and decayed away, whereas the Giant remained, looking timelessly across the valley to the Bellingstone, the stone of Bel/Helis.

Of the dozen or so place names in Dorset which owe their origins to the god Helis, all lie in central Dorset, in territory which came under Maiden Castle's influence; interestingly, the Giant stands practically north of the hillfort. There are at least seven Iron Age settlements known on higher ground within the parish of Cerne, although other stretches of land show signs of having been farmed (Putnam in Darvill et al 1996, p. 52); these clans might all have sworn allegiance to the chieftain at Maiden Castle. Even after the Roman conquest of 44AD, which lead to a major overhaul of political and social life, the people of the Cerne Valley continued to scour and worship their chalk icon. Although somewhat detached from the sophistication of Roman Dvrnovaria (Dorchester), the expansion of this thriving town would have brought new opportunities for trade. Later on, when the legions departed, times of greater uncertainty returned, and with it a revival of old practices, perhaps birthing a renaissance of the 'old ways'.

Cometh the Cross

At least one Pagan god was alive and kicking when missionary St Augustine arrived at Cerne in 603AD, and he may well have feasted his pious eyes on none other than the proud Giant himself, the 'Idol of Helis'.

Augustine is said to have struck the ground with his staff, at which point a spring gushed forth; in one classical myth, Mithras likewise performs the 'miracle' of striking a rock to open up a spring. Mithras was worshipped across Britain, so perhaps this myth had survived locally from Roman times, galvanising Augustine to 'upstage' it by supplanting an old 'miracle' with a new one. His description of, 'breaking the idol in two', could well be referring to the building of a small Christian construction between the Giant and the spring. He sought to separate these two Pagan places, as if to emulate Moses' parting of the Red Sea. The fact that the Giant was not destroyed at this time does suggest its adoption by an older brand of Christianity, where Nature was seen as part of God's creation. Although demoted, the Giant was nevertheless tolerated and not overtly censored. Perhaps he eventually became part of Christian propaganda.

Cerne Abbey was founded as a Benedictine monastery in 987AD by Æthelmær the Stout. Ælfric of Eynsham, a most prolific writer in Old English, was appointed its first abbot. Thomas Gerard, writing in the 1620's, spoke of the, '... fair and the rich abbey of the Black Monks'.

The order to build Christian foundations at Pagan centres, rather than destroy them, came right from the top, from Pope Gregory himself. There are several other examples of this in Wessex, notably at Knowlton (church inside henge), Toller Porcorum (church within stone circle), Glastonbury Tor (church on hilltop), and St Catherine's Hill at Abbotsbury (chapel on hill). By founding Cerne Abbey, the intention was that interest in the Giant would wane; the spring became associated with St Catherine, enabling local women to continue to visit it for 'miracles'.

King Canute is known to have plundered the monastery during an attack upon the town, but afterwards he became a benefactor of it. The last

The west front of the Abbey. From a 13th century seal.

abbot, Thomas Corton, was elected in 1524, but in 1539 it was his lot to surrender the Abbey following the Reformation. The buildings were mostly demolished and only parts of a gatehouse, and possibly a guesthouse, have endured to be incorporated into later buildings. Strangely, the very elaborate stone vaulted porch of the Abbot's Hall has also survived in a local property. Mysterious and unexcavated mounds in Beevor Field, to the east of the Abbey site, suggest a sanctuary may have existed near the spring. I have found astronomical alignments here (see p. 177-8).

It is a strange fact that local villagers must have been scouring the Giant right through the pious-riddled Middle Ages. That the Church could not stop the practice is in itself testament to the obstinacy of the locals and the importance of the Giant to them. Perhaps it was a case of the Abbey having to tolerate the situation, even turning it to their advantage. From the writings of Abbot Ælfric, it looks as if these more enlightened monks may have used the huge Pagan image as a teaching aid. The *'sins of the flesh'* were displayed quite literally for all to see: *'... temptation had to be there to make the choice of the right way valid'* (Castleden 1996, p. 194). The Abbey's own deer park was to the west of the Giant, offering one of the finest views of him. Although there is no supportive evidence, it would be ironic if the Abbey had been complicit in the Giant's survival.

It is not coincidence that Benedictine monasteries were founded under both the Giant of Cerne and the Long Man of Wilmington. It has been suggested that locals scoured, or reworked, the Giant to annoy and ridicule the Benedictines, especially in view of apparent sexual misdemeanours of the last Abbot, Thomas Corton. I don't think this is the case, however; the Benedictines were forward-thinking and more tolerant compared to other monastic orders.

Some of the Abbey's original ornately carved bench ends can be seen in Hilfield church, and feature various Biblical scenes. A selection of the Abbey floor tiles have been set into the flooring

The Giant brandishes his club on the exterior of St Mary's church.

at Glanvilles Wootton church, and include various hunting scenes, as well as Saltire Crosses (see page 159). Both churches are open daily.

St Mary's church stands south of the Abbey site and some interesting gargoyles adorn its exterior, including the Giant clutching his club (image above). Inside, there is an interesting display on the history of Cerne, as well as a six-petalled flower (a hexagram) that graces the wall near the altar. The church stands on a well-known alignment first suggested by Paul Devereux and Ian Thomson (1979), involving the church, the well, and the Trendle. Dowsing has shown that the church is a powerful place in terms of earth energies.

The Silver Well

Even today, with its crumbling monastic walls and modern concrete bench, Silver Well or St Augustine's Well is a magical place of meditation and contemplation. The spring has flowed here since prehistoric times, and was probably the original sacred site of the area. St Augustine rolled into town in an attempt to convert the locals and sought to Christianise the spring, which I suspect existed prior to his arrival!

For millennia the spring was vital to the people here, not only for drinking water, but for its spiritual potency and power; it was Helith's holy water, flowing out of the sacred hill to the north. The Norse, for instance, clearly regarded springs as key parts of their mythology, as this extract from the *Prose Edda* testifies:

'The third root of the Ash [the World Tree] stands in heaven and beneath it is a spring, very sacred, named the Well of Urdr. That is where the gods have their judgement seat'.

The spring bubbles up from the mysterious Underworld, where gods, goddesses, fairies and sprites reside and from where they forge the affairs of Men. As an entrance to the Underworld, it was a place where death might be encountered, but also where life was given. Many tons of votive

The Catherine Wheel on a stone at Silver Well, Cerne.

offerings were left at some springs, most notably at Bath, to appease the gods or to obtain healing or oracular vision. Castleden surmises that the relative isolation of the Cerne spring may have ensured it went largely unnoticed by the Romans, explaining why it did not develop into a major shrine (Castleden 1996, p. 116).

Because the flow issued from the body of the Earth Mother, such places usually had a goddess or female spirit attached to them, such as Sulis and Nemetona at Bath, and Coventia at Carrawburgh. However, spring deities were not always feminine. At Nettleton Shrub in Wiltshire, where a spring was upgraded by the Romans, the local Celtic god was transformed into Apollo Cunomaglos. Perhaps the Cerne spring *was* presided over by a male deity, especially considering its close proximity to the Giant. On the other hand, a resident spring goddess may have balanced the male Giant and the overtly phallic shaped hill - yin and yang harmonised. The spring may have already been an oracle centre when St Edwold founded a hermitage there around 875AD, for he experienced strange dreams and visions.

A Catherine wheel is inscribed onto one of the stones at the spring. A display board in the church shows a further stone, clearly a different one, also marked with an inscribed wheel. The carving at the spring has eight spokes, representing the so-called 'Celtic fire festivals' of the year. It is possible that the association with St Catherine gives us a clue that it may have been a *female* deity that was once revered here. Girls used to visit the well on May Day, midsummer and on St Catherine's Day (November 25th) and in a state of nudity would kneel, place their hands on the 'wishing stone', and recite the rhyme:

'St Catherine, St Catherine, O Lend me thine aid, and grant me that I never may die an old maid. A husband St Catherine, a good one St Catherine' (Newland & North 2007, p. 135).

They would then immerse themselves in the waters to consecrate the wish. Other surviving folklore tells women they should visit the well if seeking pregnancy, and that the waters also cure eye complaints and generally engender good health. It is still an oracle site, giving girls glimpses in the water of future husbands, as well as visions of those who will die in the coming year. It is also said that a wish will be granted if one drinks from a cup made of laurel leaves with one's back to the Giant.

The sacred spring is overlooked by the Giant; phalli have been linked with holy waters elsewhere, such as in the classical myth in which the woodland and fertility god Pan poured water upon his own member. In India, it was the custom to pour the waters of the Ganges onto a *Lingam*, a phallic symbol of Shiva (Scott 1996, p. 22).

There were two other wells at Cerne, both now lost, called Pil Well and Hel Well, the latter linking to the god Helis. Upwey Well, near Weymouth, was once known as Hele Well, and Hele Well Lane survives in the village. There was once a stream that issued from the foot of Giant Hill under the Giant called the River Silley, which fed a millpond and the Abbey Mill. *'Sil'* links to the sun, as does Seldon Hill (p. 42).

Maypoles were once erected in the village, possibly by the Town Pond, and/or, up at the Trendle, although the latter is now open to question. The maypole is ithyphallic, so was it put up for May Day rites associated with the Giant?

Local megaliths

Neolithic and Bronze Age burial mounds prove that Man's connection with the Cerne Valley is a long one. Although megaliths are notoriously difficult to date, some of the ones described here are almost certainly prehistoric.

To the north, in the Blackmoor Vale, a boundary stone once stood on Stone Ridge, to the NW of Hermitage, below High Stoy (*Stoys Hill* in the 16th century). In 1299/1300 it was known as La Ruweston (*the Rough Stone*), and as *'ancient boundstone'* in a survey of 1740; it has since been lost. The stone was of some importance as it marked an ancient route going north from the Giant to the Sherborne area, and may have been an object of veneration as late as the Middle Ages (Darvill et al 1999, p. 94). It was later procured as a medieval boundary marker, which has been the case elsewhere. Three other stones have fortunately fared better.

The Minterne Parva Cross (grid ref: 664034) is, in my opinion, a megalith mounted onto a medieval cross base. It stands on a small mound by the side of the lane one mile north of the Giant ('stone', top right on map p. 33). It is very rough and is probably a Christianised megalith, standing as it does at an ancient crossroads and aligned with other landscape features (Knight 1996, p. 172). It was in the 14-

Upper: Minterne Parva cross/stone. Lower: stone at Sydling St Nicholas crossroads. (After Knight 1996.)

15th century that the stone was mounted onto an octagonal base, a common enough practice elsewhere.

At Sydling St Nicholas, in the next valley west of Cerne, there is a classic example of the usurping of an ancient Pagan megalith by a Christian cross. At the crossroads stands a medieval cross, which has been dated as 15th century (Knight 1998, p. 257). On the opposite side of the road is a prone stone, an ancient way marker, which is located on an alignment involving Maiden Castle and the churches at Stratton, Chetnole and Yetminster (Knight 1996, p. 175-7).

The Cross and Hand (or Cross in Hand) Stone stands 3 miles NW of Cerne Abbas, by the minor road between Holywell and Minterne Magna (grid ref: 632038). The phallic-shaped pillar stands 1m (3½ft) tall and has been dated as pre-Conquest, and certainly resembles a Roman column. Kings are said to have forged contracts at the stone, and a *'pillar of fire'* was witnessed at the locality, an event retold in a story by Thomas Hardy. It marks a parish boundary and enjoys commanding views to the north - Glastonbury Tor can be seen on a clear day. The ithyphallic stone stands on an alignment involving Milton Abbas Abbey, the Minterne Parva Stone (above),

The ithyphallic Cross and Hand Stone, near Batcombe.

The author next to the Bellingstone, an ancient boundary stone and astronomical marker. (Image: Sue Wallace.)

Batcombe church, Holywell, and the Corscombe megaliths (Knight 1996, p. 165). The phallic nature of both the Cross in Hand and the Minterne Parva stones implies they may be relics of phallic-worship in the area.

On the crest of the ridge across the valley from the Giant stands the Bellingstone, the stone of Bel/Helis, a lonely sentinel guarding the north-south ridgeway track (grid ref: 647008). The stone has been described briefly by Rodney Castleden (Castleden 1996, p. 90) and myself (Knight 1998, p. 275). It was an important moot stone where the Hundred Court met, and was documented as an element of beating-the-bounds practices some 700 years ago. Today it still marks the Cerne-Sydling parish boundary, in keeping with countless other ancient stones across Britain.

Castleden stated that the 1.8m (5.5ft) stone, *'... would originally have been plainly visible up on the western skyline from the Cerne Giant'* (Castleden 1996, p. 90). More to the point, the Giant was visible from the stone! Rodney Legg comments that the stone is, *'... the point to which the Giant is looking... a viewing point for the people who are on the road [ridgeway track]'* (Darvill et al 1999, p. 132). From here, we look *down* on the Giant – he is not as foreshortened as from the valley (image p. 174).

Prior to 1998 I had visited the stone and felt it to be in some way connected with the Giant. But it wasn't until the Beltaine sunrise of 2007 that everything came to life as I observed the sun rising over the Giant from the vicinity of the stone (image p. 175). Psychic Marie Moon has informed me this was a place where ancient Beltaine Fires were lit. The stone also marks Imbolc sunsets when viewed from the Giant (image p.

176). I shall return to the Bellingstone later as it was a vital key to opening up the secrets of the Giant and his place in the greater landscape.

In 1842, John Sydenham published *Baal Durotrigensis,* in which he suggested that the sun was worshipped on a hill to the west of the Giant called Ellston Hill, at the foot of which was El-wood; El is an old name for the sun god El or Bel (p. 93-94); the hill may be the site of a prehistoric henge. From the vicinity of the Bellingstone, Ellston Hill marks the midsummer sunset.

The area was extensively farmed in the Iron Age and it may now be worth looking at the Iron Age settlements that were in the vicinity of Cerne Abbas, and the hills on which they stood; we shall see later that some are key localities concerning the Giant's connection with the skies.

The view from the Giant looking westwards. The Bellingstone and Weam Common Hill are important astronomically, as we shall see later (compare to p. 176). Image: Sue Wallace.

A womb with a view

Weam Common Hill rises to the west of the Giant, and provides the best vantage point from which to view him (Castleden 1996, p. 13). The hill has also been known as Weam Hill, and my initial investigations revealed that the name might have come from the Saxon *'Wamm',* meaning *'marshy or muddy place'.* But I soon discovered that *Weam* is an obsolete form of *'Wem',* which Webster's define as, *'abdomen, uterus, womb'.* I am amazed that the Giant, with his overtly male symbolism, stands opposite a rounded hill whose name derives from the female reproductive organs! Confirmation would seem to come from the Old Gaelic word *Wem,* meaning *cave.* Caves have long had feminine links, such as being the birthplaces of gods and heroes; they were the sacred openings of the Earth Mother. So, either side of the Cerne Valley, we have features representing the divine masculine and the divine feminine – perfectly balanced by equinox sunrises and sunsets!

In her poem *Boys will be Cerne Giants,* Jan Farquharson (in Clarkson and Tappenham 1998), insightfully and intuitively felt that the Giant was a vital component of the larger landscape, remarking on the relevance of Weam Common Hill:

'... I think this god points to the combe, with his arm, a womb,
Which lies along behind him in an arc... Crest to combe and cheek to spur,
Himself and her, surely she is that one, that breast of hill, who makes him swell?

41

A field system on Weam Common Hill (grid ref: ST652016) defines the remains of Iron Age/Romano British hut circles, the possible course of cross-ridge dyke, and later medieval field systems. We shall return to this important landscape location later, when we look at its astronomical alignments with the Giant. By a quirky coincidence, when you search for *Weam* on Google, the number one hit is the World's Erotic Art Museum, which seems sort of appropriate!

The Giant as viewed from Weam Common Hill. This view is in the direction of equinox sunrises, and stellar alignments (see Chapters 12-14). Image: Sue Wallace.

Seldon – *Hill of the Sun*

Seldon Hill rises to around 230m (754ft), and is a prominent feature that juts out into the Cerne Valley, about one mile to the NW of the Giant. From here the full length of Giant Hill can be seen, at the southern end of which stands the Giant.

The name may derive from the Old English *'sel-don'* meaning *'willow valley'*. Alternatively, its origins could lie with *Sil* or *Sol*, meaning *sun*. It is interesting that Michael Dames traces the name of Silbury Hill not to King Sil, but to a 17th century record of 'King Sel'; it was *Seleburgh* in the 13th century and *Selburi* in 1540 (Dames 2010, p. 77). Dames suggests that King Sel was the *'harvest monarch'*, who was annually, *'... delivered anew from beneath the hill'*. Viewed from the Giant, Seldon Hill marks sunsets from around midsummer to the time of the annual harvests. Interesting stellar and further solar alignments took place involving Seldon Hill in the Iron Age, which I shall detail in Chapters 12-14.

Seldon Hill Settlement (grid ref: ST651023) consists of earthworks and crop marks indicating cultivation terraces, field systems, a curvilinear enclosure, and pits, probably of later prehistoric and medieval/post medieval date.

High Cank Hill, NE of Seldon Hill, is the site of a henge (ST657031), a scheduled monument of the late Neolithic or early Bronze Age. The site comprises a circular ditch 2m (6½ft) wide and up to 0.4m (1½ft) deep, enclosing an area up to 10m (33ft) in diameter. The ditch is accompanied by an outer bank of flint nodules and which measures 3m (10ft) wide and up to 0.4m (1½ft) high. On the eastern side there is a break in the bank with a corresponding causeway, and traces of a slight mound have previously been recorded in the central area; however, all that is now visible is a depression, possibly resulting from excavation. The site has been described variously as a round barrow and a hengiform monument, while in the RCHM (1952) it is suggested that it might be of more recent origin.

To the south, there was an Iron Age farmstead at Black Hill, whilst at Smacam Down there is a Neolithic long barrow, tumuli, and signs of an extensive Iron Age farming landscape.

The view from Seldon Hill (near Sheriff's Wood) looking south-east
to the Giant and Cerne Abbas. Compare to image p. 151.

Gary Biltcliffe and Marie Moon both feel that Godmanstone, also to the south of Cerne, got its name from the Giant – he is the *'God Man'* (pers. comm.).

To the north, High Stoy and Dogbury Hill were two further ancient gathering places, which I shall return to regarding landscape and astronomical configurations.

The mythologized landscape

Myths and folklore are not static remnants of bygone ages, but are a fluid melting pot of stories to which new ingredients are periodically added. I suspect this has always been so: *'Myth in the landscape is both archaic and contemporary, and is always re-inventing itself in the context of the predominant cultural issues of the day'* (Thorley 2012, p. 12).

As long ago as 1872, W H Black looked at the Giant in relationship to its landscape. He thought that the figure was made by Roman surveyors as a landmark, and suggested several alignments running out from the Giant to both ancient and Roman sites, such as the Whiteleaf Oak, and St Catherine's Chapel at Abbotsbury. Black also saw the dimensions of the Giant to be relevant; the length of the club is 36.5m (120ft), which is the number of miles from the Giant to three sacred sites: a dolmen at Fishguard, Kit's Coty dolmen in Kent, and a lost megalith at Constantine, Cornwall.

This echoes the work of the late, great John Michell, who championed the concept that landscape features many miles apart might be linked by means of geometric configurations and mathematical proportion.

All this is of course heresy to most archaeologists, who have tended not to relate monuments to others outside the immediate vicinity. The idea of landscape alignments still sticks in the throats of many, some of who also see myths and the like as mere fiction and of no relevance to scientific study. But if we want to get to the true meaning of ancient monuments, surely we must try to get 'inside the heads' of the people who built them. Most ancient cultures I have studied have a universally connecting strand: **To ancient people, the landscape was alive with myth and meaning; they inhabited a dynamic and animated world where unseen forces forged the course of their lives.**

People once saw themselves as part of the land, not separate from it, seeing beyond the apparent physical nature of the world. The land *was* the myth, and they were part of the story: *'Every stream and pool was sacred, and the physical landscape as a whole became a theatre for a specific local tribal mythology'* (Castleden 1996, p. 120). Folklore and myths are a form of memory, which can give us glimpses into the hearts and minds of people in far off times. Forward-thinking Professor Barbara Bender comments that, *'Perhaps what we have begun to recognise today is that 'fact' and fiction are close bedfellows... the biography of the giant is ultimately bound up with the biography of the landscape and of the community'* (in Darvill et al, 1999).

Prof Bender continues that the Giant is, *'... in dialogue with what lies around him...'*, a sentiment to which Rodney Legg concurs: *'He's in an obvious dialogue with other features in the landscape...'* (op. cit. p. 132). Sue Clifford, of Common Ground, also asks if we might see the Giant as part of the greater landscape: *'Why is he here? Is there something about this place that we are missing because our attention is so focused upon the Giant himself? ... The land is the most elaborate storyboard'.* Nice one guys!

Giant Hill had been called a, *'noble-looking mount'* (Castleden 1996, p. 180). And I believe that the shape of Giant Hill itself may have attributed to why it became a sacred centre, and was chosen for the site of the Giant. I was first alerted to this by a digital map of the topography of the area produced

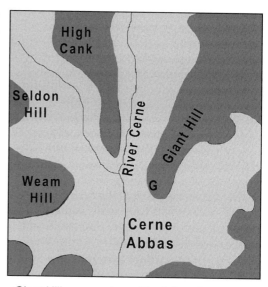

Giant Hill as a penis and testicles. G = Giant. Based on Ordnance Survey digital data. (After J Chartrand.)

by Jeffrey Chartrand, of Bournemouth University (Darvill et al 1999, p. 3). Giant Hill shows up as a long, **phallic-shaped** spur of chalk projecting into the Cerne Valley, complete with the semblance of testes at the north end!

There are plenty of precedents supporting the concept that topography is an integral component of a sacred landscape and its ancient monuments. These include the ithyphallic Waden Hill, which points to Avebury Henge, and the Paps of Anu in Ireland, which look like breasts when viewed from local sacred sites. The location of the Grey Mare and Her Colts chambered tomb was influenced by the intervisibility of

Pilsden Pen and Lamberts Castle which, when viewed from the barrow, resemble breasts, and which align with the midsummer sunset (Knight 1996, p. 33).

Phallic reference is made by Julian Cope, who comments that, *'I was amazed to descend onto Giant Hill as it thrust phallically out into the surrounding valley flatlands'* (Cope 1998, p. 207). I would also like to play with the idea that as the spring sits near the tip of the phallic hill, in line with it in fact, it is as if the Earth itself is issuing (ejaculating) the sacred elixir of life. Did the Ancients view it as such?

A thin ridge, from which rises High Cank, separates the two sources of the Cerne; the ridge resembles a serpent slithering south as if about to join the Giant to drink at the well. Cope also notes how the surrounding hills, *'... conspire to create a warm encircling around Giant Hill, though the OS map in no way suggests it'* (Cope op. cit.). I found a similar landscape encirclement at West Kennet Long Barrow, where the surrounding hills are higher than the ridge on which the barrow stands; the barrow *'... is not **on** the landscape, but rather **held within it**'* (Knight 2011, p. 23). The hills surrounding the Giant are amazingly similar in height, resulting in near-horizontal skylines that are very conducive to astronomical observation.

I believe that my previous comments on the relationship between the landscape, the monument of West Kennet, and its clans, apply equally to the Cerne Giant:

'The monument provided a central focus for a community that was scattered around the valleys and on the hills in small farmsteads. It provided continuity and a tangible connection, the glue that held a clan together and connected it to the ancestors, the seasons, the stars, and to the land itself' (Knight 2011, p. 23). This was a mythologized landscape, and as the people were part of the land, so they were participants of the landscape's myths.

Perhaps the Giant, like the long barrow at West Kennet, enabled people to lay claim to the land and its resources, and told interlopers, *'This is our land, not yours!'*

Possibly one of the reasons the Giant is on a reclining slope is not simply a matter of improving visibility, but that it **sets him into the hill**. He walks along Giant Hill, thus cementing his credentials as an emissary to the Otherworlds, those unknown and usually feared realms beneath the surface of the Earth. Man's spiritual history is rife with myths of gods, heroes and otherworldly beings associated with high places; Glastonbury Tor, Maiden Castle, Cader Idris, Mount Sinai and Uluru are just a small sample of elevated sacred places.

Lines on the landscape

As mentioned above, Paul Devereux and Ian Thomson (1979) plotted an alignment involving St Mary's church, Silver Well and the Trendle. I have extended this north to Holwell church, and down to Winterbourne Steepleton in the south, via Jackman's Cross, the Muckleford megalith and several tumuli (Knight 1996, p. 29). I have also described another alignment, first suggested by John Michell, which involves Cerne Abbey (op. cit. p. 184). This convincingly 'tight' alignment runs for about 50 miles from the Two Gates Stone, through the church at West Compton, Cerne Abbey, and via the churches at Mappowder, Belchalwell, Okeford Fitzpaine, Child Okeford, and Ashmore, finally ending at Old Sarum.

In terms of people travelling across the landscape, Castleden concluded: *'The Giant may even have had a subsidiary role as a signpost and waymark for travellers trying to find their way across Ancient Dorset'* (Castleden 1996, p. 132).

On Graham Hancock's website, William Glyn-Jones states: *'Now here is something to note: the villages of Cerne Abbas in Dorset, home of the Cerne giant, and Wilmington in East Sussex, home of the Long Man, are on the very same line of latitude, an East-West line stretching across the landscape. A dull mind ignores this. A lively mind wants to know why'*. This is one of many proposed alignments and landscape figures that are guaranteed to make academics squirm, and yet they are there none the less. That said, not long ago archaeologists regarded subjects such as acoustics, archaeoastronomy, and shamanism as not meriting much credence; how things have changed!

Another enthralling configuration is an alignment with the midsummer solstice running from the Giant at 51°; it takes in Banbury Hill, Melbury Hill, Old Wardour Castle, Castle Ditches Fort, Groveley Castle, Stonehenge, Inkpen and Watlington Hill. Mark Vidler has also proposed an isosceles triangle configuration involving Glastonbury, Stonehenge, and the Cerne Giant (Vidler 1998, p. 129).

Landscape Horse

Landscape zodiacs and figures have always been controversial, destined to be shunned by the academia. It must be admitted that whilst some seem to have credence, others may be little more than flights of fancy. However, a number of configurations are compelling, such as the one we shall now look at.

Gary Biltcliffe has informed me of a horse-like figure he discovered on the landscape north of Cerne. The horse is defined by roads and ancient tracks, field boundaries, woods, hills and the sources of the Sydling and the Cerne. Biltcliffe told me of his discovery: *'On the nose of the horse is a small triangular wood called Arthur's Copse, with mysterious steps leading up from the road where, according to a local author, King Arthur was born. The eye of the horse is marked by another triangular enclosure on the top of High Stoy Hill, where stand two ancient beeches called Gog and Magog, the giants of myth. The tip of the horse's ear is marked by Penn Wood (Penn meaning head). Her front hooves hover above the sources of the sacred River Cerne at Up Cerne and Lady Abingdon's Well, while her rear hooves stand firm upon the source of the River Sydling. At the centre of her back, marked out by the road from Batcombe to Minterne, is the Cross and Hand stone'* (pers. comm. 2013).

The horse echoes other, equally controversial, landscape figures, such as the London Unicorn, advocated by Chris Street (Thorley 2012, p. 58) and the most famous of them all, the Glastonbury Zodiac (Mann and Glasson 2007, p. 1).

The High Stoy Horse. This is configured by field boundaries, ancient tracks and topographical features. The horse's nose points to Dogbury Hill. The Cerne Giant is arrowed bottom right. (© Gary Biltcliffe, used with permission.)

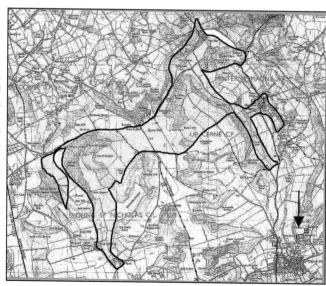

I found the High Stoy horse to be of great interest as I had already found astronomical alignments concerning Dogbury Hill, to where the horse is looking. When viewed from the 'eye' of the horse on High Stoy, the constellation Pegasus, the mythical winged horse, used to rise over Dogbury! The head and much of the body of Hydra, the mythical serpent, also rose over the hill when viewed from High Stoy: this reflects folklore that a dragon resides in Dogbury Hill. Regarding Dorset hills, I have described similar folklore elsewhere. Hod Hill and Hambledon Hill are said to protect local villages by supernatural forces; Lambert's Castle was haunted as long ago as 1630, and more paranormal phenomena are associated with Maiden Castle, Badbury Rings and Flower's Barrow hillfort (Knight 1998, and Newland & North 2007).

Two beech trees on High Stoy, known as Gog and Magog, were planted at the demise of two hollowed-out oaks bearing the same names near Glanvilles Wootton (Gary Biltcliffe, pers. comm.). On a site visit in February 2013 I believe we found the two ancient beeches - right in the eye of the horse. On a clear day one can see Glastonbury Tor from here, and a Neolithic track passes through the triangular copse. One of our party, Marie Moon, 'tuned in' and envisioned a cauldron; it was also here, many years ago, that local farmer John Beasley had a vision of a sword, which he took to be Excalibur. Folklore concerning Excalibur is also related to a pond at Trent Barrow, near Sherborne. So special was High Stoy to Thomas Hardy that he came here just prior his death.

Gary Biltcliffe has also kindly made available further work of his in the area:
'I discovered two circular alignments back in 1996 that include the three churches of Glanvilles Wootton, Buckland Newton and Holnest. The circles pivot from a point by Lyon's Hill where I found the source of the little River Cam (old English for 'battle'). This centre, or whatever was there, was buried by a huge landslide coming off High Stoy in Elizabethan times. There are many mysteries here' (pers. comm. 2013). Although I can hear academics groaning from here, the work is persuasive. The double circles involve the Giant Hill settlement, where Biltcliffe regards one circular feature to be a henge. Another site is Arthur's Copse at Dogbury, by local tradition the

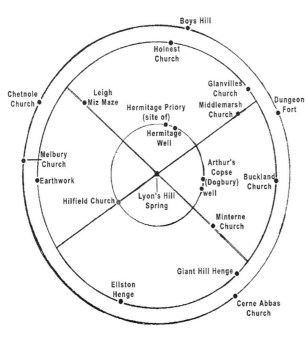

The landscape circles of the Cerne area, by Gary Biltcliffe. These involve accurate alignments with wells and springs, hillforts, churches, and possible henge sites. (© G Biltcliffe, used with permission.)

birthplace of King Arthur, and two of the 'spokes' of the circles are close to the azimuths of Beltaine and midwinter sunrises. Biltcliffe's classic exercise in 'ley hunting' demonstrates the hidden mysteries to be found within a landscape. More fieldwork needs to be done on these fascinating landscape enigmas.

Dorset resident Jonathan Harwood has shown that many of Dorset's churches are sited so as to form geometric landscape features, one of which involves our immediate area of study (Harwood 2000).

This is a hexagram involving the churches at Batcombe, Hermitage, Buckland Newton, Piddletrenthide, Nether Cerne, and Sydling St Nicholas. Another smaller hexagram is created inside, with Up Cerne at its hub. This complements other hexagrams that have been proposed in recent years by such researchers as Robert Coon, John Michell, Nicholas Mann, Tony Peart, Henry Lincoln and Michael Poynder. Two works involving Southern England include the beautifully complex *Earth Stars* of the London area (Chris Street 1990) and the *Wessex Astrum* (Knight and Perrott 2008).

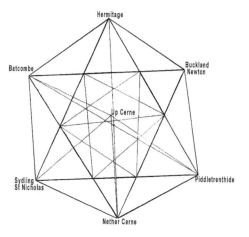

Landscape hexagram involving the Cerne area, after Jonathan Harwood ©. Used with permission.

In *Dorset Pilgrimages – A Millennium Handbook,* Mike Power and I advocate the need to walk Dorset's ancient landscapes as a means to truly connect with them on a deeper level. One of our walks is from the Nine Stones to Cerne Abbas, taking in the Bellingstone, the Cross in Hand Stone, other sites en route, and ending at Silver Well (Knight and Power 2000, p. 66-75); as I gazed across the valley to the Giant in the spring of 1999, my emotions inspired me to write a few words. What I felt then seems just as poignant today:

Silent Salute
'Oh man of the hill, wielder of mighty club,
Are you Hercules, Helith or Beelzebub?
Do you raise your club in anger, out of neglect,
Or in silent salute for the Earth you respect?
With proud member you fertilise the land, our Mother,
Remembering times past, Earth Goddess, no other.
You are Man of Mysteries and of Truth,
And hope to many a lass and youth.
You gaze across the vale, eternities roll by,
Oh Man of Cerne, I am a twinkling of your eye'.
(Peter Knight)

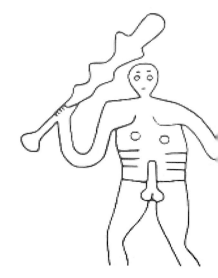

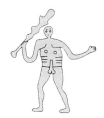

Chapter 5.
From god to cosmetic surgery –
the Giant through history

'The Cerne Giant is without question the most remarkable and the most outlandish hill figure in Britain'. (Rodney Castleden)

When we view the Giant today, it is difficult to comprehend the long history he has endured, and the physical alterations that were forced upon him. Considering the social, cultural, and religious upheavals that swept through Dorset during the past 2000 years, it is nothing less than a miracle that the Giant is still with us. We may never know what the Giant meant to the people who initially scoured him, or even ascertain how *subsequent* people related to him; did they in any way share the beliefs of their predecessors? The answer may well be that they did not: *'Generally speaking, if a community falls apart, so does the god, hero or beast emblematic of its unity'* (Newman 2009). This was particularly true when the Roman legions vacated Britain, which heralded wave upon wave of foreign invaders and settlers, who imported their own deities.

A walk through time
The contents of two excellent studies of the Giant (Castleden 1996 and Darvill et al 1999) need not be repeated in detail here. I offer just a brief overview for those less familiar with the history of research and debate.

The earliest record of the Giant is in a parish record of 1694, recording a payment for, *'... repairing of ye Giant 3s 0d'.* Subsequent letters between antiquarians produced some debate on the Giant, but it was not until September 1763, in the form of an anonymous letter in the *Royal Magazine,* that we have the first published description of the figure, which included twenty-nine measurements. In the same year a sketch of the Giant was destined to be the first illustration when it later appeared in the *Minute Book of the Society of Antiquaries of London (July 1762 - April 1795).* The letter that included it also contained some colourful lines: *'This monstrous figure viewed from the opposite hill appears almost erect, with a huge crab tree club in his hand, raised*

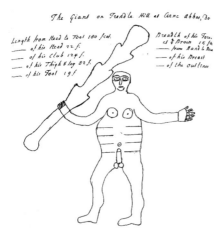

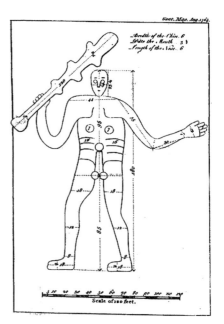

Above: 1763 sketch of the Giant.
Right: More accurate drawing with dimensions in the *Gentleman's Magazine* of 1764.

over his head, just going to strike a blow which seems sufficient, as it were, to overturn a mountain... some say it was cut by Ancient Britons and that they worshipped it; others believe it to be the work of Papists...'. The letter was later republished in the *Gentleman's Magazine* of 1764, this time accompanied by a more accurate drawing (above right).

In 1754, Dr Richard Pocoke visited the Giant: *'It is called the Giant and Hele, is about 150 feet long, a naked figure of genteel posture. It seems to be Hercules... the lord of the manor gives something once in 7 or 8 years to have the lines clear'd and kept*

An artistic drawing of an emasculated Giant, by Samuel H Grimm from 1790, which also shows earthworks on Giant Hill and the Trendle.

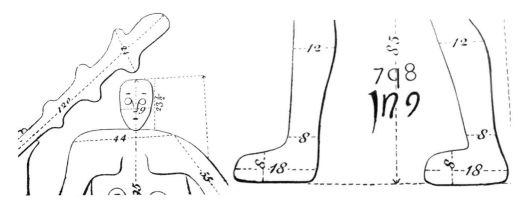

Left: Close-up of drawing in Hutchins, 1774.
Right: The letters that Hutchins describes in between the Giant's legs.

open'. Pocoke, who went on to become a bishop, describes the Giant as being *'of genteel posture'* and does not mention the phallus. Was this self-censorship, or was it that the publication of drawings of the Giant had unleashed a backlash from pious outsiders; the Giant was made more 'respectable'. A drawing from 1790 shows the Giant minus phallus (image previous page).

In his monumental work *History and Antiquities of the County of Dorset* (1774), John Hutchins showed the same illustration, also identifying some letters between the Giant's legs; *'God destroys Satan'* was his interpretation. Later, another writer thought the letters stood for *'God destroyed this'*. It now seems likely that the ciphers merely marked 18th century scourings. The Giant continued to be cleaned on a regular basis, as G A Cooke recorded in 1807: *'... it is repaired from time to time by the towns-people'*.

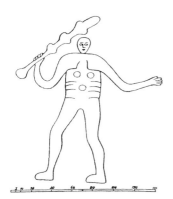

1842 drawing of the Giant, with a distinct lack of genitals!

In 1842, John Sydenham published his *Baal Durotrigensis*, in which he proposed that the Giant was a huge fertility prop, and the object of sun and serpent worship. He argued that the Giant would have had the status of a monument, rather than a mere idol, arguing that sun-worshippers did not bow down to idols, or 'graven images'. During the 19th century there were periods of 'cosmetic surgery', when the Giant's phallus was either allowed to become overgrown, or else was deliberately covered. Outsiders were now coming to Cerne to see the Giant due to the published drawings; the 'indecency' aspect of the figure was now in the wider public domain. Did this result in episodic losses of his manhood?

1885 drawing by Plenderleah – still minus phallus.

On occasions during the 1800's the Giant almost completely disappeared, shrouded by vegetation, but in 1868 it looks as if the Giant was cleaned up and his genitals reinstated; Lord Pitt-Rivers, local landowner and antiquarian, gave orders for the Giant to be cleaned up due to the fact that, '... it has for some years presented a shabby appearance... choked with weeds and rubbish'. But the local Reverend of Cerne Abbas was less enthusiastic, fearing that it might corrupt the morals of his parishioners! Local Historian Charles Warne visited the area just after this and commented (in *Ancient Dorset*, 1872) that: '... the eye is arrested by the apparition of a gigantic human figure rudely sculptured on the side of a lofty hill, which, to a person unaccustomed to the sight, is an astounding and probably a repulsive object... As to the anatomical proportions of the relative parts of his frame, we prefer to remain silent'. There may well have been more unrecorded scourings during this period: 'It is clear that when the figure is left unattended for more than 20 years the white lines disappear' (Castleden 1996, p. 30).

The former six-sided fencing was erected around the Giant at Pitt-Rivers' instructions to mark Queen Victoria's Jubilee. But by the early 1900's the Giant was again almost completely invisible, whereby a scouring was undertaken in 1906. It seems it was at this event that the original 4.8m (16ft) long phallus was lengthened by around 2.3m (7ft) by incorporating it into the Giant's navel, which sounds like a painful piece of cosmetic surgery to me! This mistake, if indeed it was one, has yet to be rectified; the National Trust retains this elongated phallus when it scours the Giant today.

In 1919, the Giant was presented to the National Trust by Pitt-Rivers' sons. Around this time, Egyptologist and pioneer archaeologist Sir Flinders Petrie did a fine job of surveying the Giant, employing his wife and son to hold tape measures, and plotting over 200 points around the figure. This was published in 1926, and showed a groove marking the previous separation of navel and penis (image below – lower centre). He draws the nose as a grassy hump; his survey has been the yardstick for subsequent conservation work.

In 1921, Walter Long of Gillingham objected to the giant's nudity and conducted a

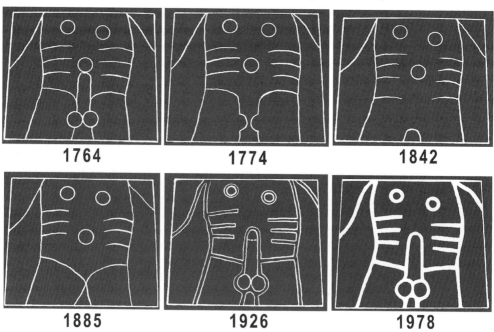

Now you see it – now you don't!
The episodic emasculation of the Giant. (After Grinsell 1980, with amendments.)

52

campaign to either convert it to a simple nude, or to cover its *'obscenity'* with a chalk leaf. Long's protest gained some attention, including the support of two bishops, and eventually the debate reached the Home Office. Dorset's Chief Constable responded by saying that it would not be possible to amend a protected monument. It seems that by 1934 the Giant was once again completely overgrown, marked out only by the V-shaped trenches. During the Second World War, it was ordered that the Giant be even more obscured by the addition of brushwood, so as not to be a landmark for German bombers endeavouring to find their way to Bristol.

After the war, the Giant had a major restoration lead by Stuart Piggott, the excavator of West Kennet Long Barrow. Even as late as 1956 the local vicar fought against the phallus being restored, and there were other protestations even later in the 20th century; one suggestion was that, *'Propriety demands that he don a loin-cloth'*, and another offended party queried why the Giant was allowed to expose himself and yet indecent books were forbidden. The situation was improved somewhat when Stuart Piggott announced that the Giant was a depiction of the god Hercules, and dated back to Romano-British times; after all, the exposure of a penis or two is an acceptable facet of classical art. Regular scourings have been undertaken since 1979, some requiring up to 4 tons of imported chalk to repair the effects of frost damage and sheep grazing; the enclosing fence is not just to discourage people, but is also rabbit-proof. The Giant was given more cosmetic surgery in 1993, when his nose was restored by the creation of a small mound of turfed-over chalk; the National Trust heralded this as, *'...restoring another important organ to prominence'*.

In recent decades the Giant has fallen victim, in my opinion, to some humiliating advertising campaigns, as well as other mockeries. I am not going to mention the companies responsible for using the Giant as an ad prop, as that would give them space here; however, the use of the figure by Durex for a 'safe sex' campaign may have had some merit. Businesses can in fact apply for permission to use the Giant in their campaigns, provided they donate a suitable sum towards its upkeep. Vandalism and publicity stunts periodically rear their ugly heads, including the placing of condoms on the phallus in 1988 and 1995. Nowadays the National Trust, who manage the Giant and the Trendle, permit local charities to use the figure to publicise their work; in 1993 the 'Great Dorset Clean-Up' campaign resulted in a logo of the

The head of the Giant, with facial features and reinstated nose. (Image: Sue Wallace.)

Giant holding a broom; in 1997 the Giant temporarily had a potential mate, when students from Bournemouth University added a female figure to Giant Hill; and in 2012 local children had the Giant grasping an Olympic Torch.

Anatomy of the Giant

I have described the periodic modifications made to the Giant's manhood, and how the 1906 cosmetic surgery has still to be resolved. Over many centuries he went from being a god to an embarrassment, from being highly revered to utterly loathed. Despite all this, he continues to show off his mighty and impressive physique.

To define the Giant, an estimated 25 tons of chalk had to be removed. Clearly some organisation was called for: '... a force must have been recruited under tribal direction' (Gibbons 1962, p. 9). Unlike the Uffington White Horse, which was created by the removal of topsoil and turf to reveal the white chalk, the Cerne Giant was defined by the cutting of trenches up to half a metre deep into the bedrock, which were then back-filled with chalk that was rammed in up to ground level.

The total height of the figure is 64.5m (211ft) from the bottom of his feet to the top of the club. His body length from heel to the top of the head is 55m (180ft) and the knobbled club he brandishes is 37m (121ft) long. He proudly displays his newly extended phallus, which attains a length of 7.2m (23½ft). Although he is not bashful, he is in fact just 'doing his own thing', as Rodney Legg expressed: 'He is no medieval or later hoax, Norman Hercules or Mars. Not even an Iron Age Cernunnos or Nodens. Our Giant is himself...' (Castleden 1996, p. 8). The phallus points towards an azimuth of 75° (North 1996, p. 219) and I have discovered that this marked some key astronomical alignments back in the Iron Age.

The Giant's head is about 7.3m (24ft) long, a noticeably rotund, somewhat baby-like, feature, typical of much Celtic artwork, and the neck is lacking. Although the rudeness, the child-like simplicity, and the uncomplicated manner of the Giant are sometimes commented on negatively, I find him functional, powerful, and to the point

The phallus of the Giant, which was extended into his navel early in the 20th century. On the skyline is the mound that forms the nose, which is not in line with the axis of the phallus.

54

(quite literally!). He is in fact the most detailed of all our hill figures, with plenty of internal features the others sadly lack. His knees are bent, one foot slightly raised, giving him inbuilt animation, like the Uffington White Horse. The side-on depiction of his feet is typical of Egyptian and Phoenician imagery. His feet both face northwards, and he appears as if about to stride off along the hillside. But where is the Giant heading off to – is it simply northwards? Or perhaps he is leading us into our history, into our collective cultural memory. I will show later how the Giant also strides to where the stars Deneb and Vega were setting in the Iron Age; it seems the big fellow also had one eye on the stars.

The Giant has three ribs on either side of his torso. I will later invite comparison with the myth involving Corineus, who sustained injury to three of his ribs. The Giant's left hand is open, as if waiting to receive something, or perhaps he points the way to somewhere. Let us take a closer look at this 'waving' hand and the extended arm that supports it.

Mystery of the lost head and cloak

Although the title of this section would suggest that we should call Sherlock Holmes immediately, there *is* a mystery here, one that even Sir Conan Doyle might find worthy of investigation.

Debate has flourished for some time as to why the left hand of the Giant is empty. But was it originally? In 1957, dowser Tom Lethbridge described finding, in an aerial photograph, what he thought to be a cloak hanging down from the outstretched hand, as well as a *'goddess-like'* figure to the south. The gods Mithras and Jupiter Dolichenus are sometimes shown with cloaks draped over their arm. A geophysical survey in 1979 hinted at disturbances under this extended left arm, which was hailed as proof that the Giant was Hercules; this hero often (but not always) carried a lion's skin over his arm, or held a lion's head (as does Orion I might add). The area in question was subject to a further geophysical study in 1989-90, carried out by Rodney Castleden, which seemed to confirm the presence of a feature that he took to be a cloak suspended below the arm.

Castleden did more resistivity surveys in 1995 which confirmed the faint survival of features that might be a severed head, which may have been part of the original hill figure (Castleden 1996, p. 156-165). In 1996, John Gale of Bournemouth University carried out a magnetometry and resistivity survey, but this failed to confirm these features.

Castleden has questioned whether the feature even represents a cloak at all. Would a severed head or some item of weaponry, such as a shield, not be more appropriate? A piece of Iron

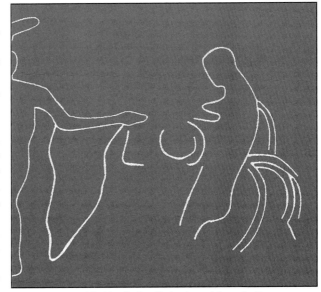

Tom Lethbridge's 'lost' cloak and female figure.
(After Lethbridge 1957.)

Age pottery found at Lothbury in London shows a naked figure displaying his genitals and ribs, has a cloak hanging over his left arm, *and* holds a shield. Some Iron Age warriors also used plaids, or cloak-shields, to deflect incoming blows. A carved bench-end at Christchurch Priory shows a *Wild Man* holding a club in his right hand and a shield in his left (image p. 86). Is this the Giant?

Was the Giant's left hand originally clenched, grasping the locks of hair of a severed head, as in depictions of a Pharaoh's conquest over his enemies? Although the Giant strides to his right, his other features, such as his head, torso and phallus, face directly towards us, similar to how people are illustrated on Greek vases or Egyptian temple paintings and bas-reliefs.

A small knoll has been noted, up to 40cm (15½ins) high, next to his left arm, which is visible in low sunlight. Is it a natural feature, or a dump from previous scourings, or is it the 'lost' severed head? Castleden produced a very fine contour map revealing what appear to be eyes, nose and a mouth – the haunting features of a decapitated head (Castleden 1996, p. 165). This feature, if a head, would have been hanging some 7-8m (23-26ft) below the hand. Dowser Guy Underwood detected a 'mound' in his dowsing survey, the southern part of which may coincide with Castleden's feature (images p. 72-73). Underwood asks if this mound is a second phallus, thus identifying the Giant as Cronos, who castrated his father Uranus. We shall look further into Underwood's dowsing results shortly.

So why might the Giant once have held a severed head? Decapitation of one's enemies was a common practice in the Iron Age, and appears in myths and sagas. The head of an important slain enemy would be mounted on a pole, a practice reflected in the detached heads of Celtic art. To many cultures, including the Celts, the skull was where the soul resided, so by decapitating and retaining the head of a defeated opponent, one held his spirit captive. One Gaulish coin from 60-50BC has the image of a warrior holding a severed head in his left hand. Coins found in Essex from the time of King Cunobelinus, dated 4-41AD, show a warrior god brandishing a club whilst clutching a severed head.

Water drunk from a skull was said to have miraculous powers. The magic of a severed head is of course epitomised by the story of Bran, whose head became an oracle in London.

Celtic and Romano-British sites at Steep Holm, Lamyatt and Cadbury have yielded stone heads. In Dorset we have several examples, such as those shown here from Portesham and Shipton Gorge, which display facial features and baldness, similar to the Cerne Giant, as well as ithyphallic noses. The infamous *Screaming Skull* of Bettiscombe is thought to be around 2000 years old and may to have come from an Iron Age sanctuary at Pilsden Pen. Severed heads appear on fonts at Toller Fratrum and Stoke Abbot, and solitary stone heads are plentiful in the North of England. Castleden concludes by calling this low mound *'severed*

Iron Age stone heads. Top: from Portesham. Bottom: from Shipton Gorge. Dorset County Museum. (After Knight 1998, p. 48)

head knoll', and I am inclined to think that this name might be appropriate.

There is also the possibility that any former severed head was added at a later date. It may be that this later addition was not executed as well as the original features, so it faired worse in terms of weathering and upkeep.

Certainly, any reinstatement of a severed head and cloak to the left arm makes sense as to why that limb is extended (as well as astronomical criteria I shall deal with later) and would give the Giant balance and a sense of equilibrium. Might he not also be representative of a triumphant returning warrior, displaying the severed head(s) of a defeated foe? This figure would be a clear warning to anyone thinking of messing with the local clan. The Giant was there, after all, to protect the valley clans from danger; his phallus acted in a similar manner to how a crucifix or garlic wards off evil – every home should have one!

I present here my vision of Castleden's restoration of what the Giant may have originally looked like, complete with a defined head, neck and navel, and carrying a cloak and a severed head. I have made slight allowances for recent work by Rodney Legg based on aerial photographs (in Darvill et al 1999); this indicates that the Giant's torso and legs have also changed over the years.

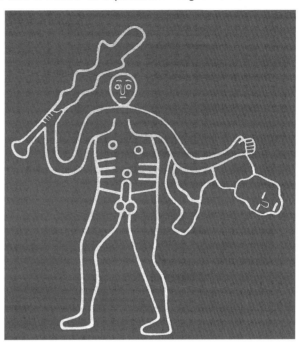

The Giant as he may have once appeared.
(After Castleden and Legg, with amendments.)

It is interesting that early depictions of the Giant show him with shoulder lines that join beneath the Giant's head – he had a chin and a clearly defined head. It demonstrated a clear demarcation between the sacred head, where the soul/spirit resided, and the rest of his body.

Spectral hound

It has been suggested that a canine companion once accompanied the Giant. In common with many ancient myths, a warrior or hunter often had a hunting dog - so did the Giant? In 1976, esteemed Dorset author Rodney Legg reported to have perceived the features of a large terrier-like dog, some 50m (164ft) long, immediately to the north of the Giant; the club in fact pointed down to the dog's nose. Legg proposed that the dog implied that the Giant might therefore be the god Nodens, who is often depicted with dogs (image p. 97). But I would suggest that this might also connect the Giant with the hunter Orion and his dog Sirius. In the sky, a line from Orion's raised arm and club projects back down to Sirius; of all the places on the hill that the dog might have been located, Legg's dog corresponds with configurations seen in our winter skies! (see image p. 151). The dog has proved elusive since Legg's claim, but much depends on light and ground conditions. It is interesting that psychic Marie Moon dreamed of two white dogs prior to meeting me at Cerne in February 2013.

An ancient Giant? The case for and against

Debate concerning the age of the Giant has raged for many years. Some scholars regard him as prehistoric or at least late Iron Age, whilst others see him as a post-medieval folly or political statement. Katherine Barker of Bournemouth University summarized the problem of dating: *'It is an image which is capable of demonstrating a continuum of meaning which, paradoxically, makes the hill-figure more difficult to date on stylistic grounds, not less'* (in Darvill 1999, p. 103).

On March 23, 1996, an 'Enquiry' was held at Cerne Abbas Village Hall under the auspices of Bournemouth University. Several speakers and 'expert witnesses' gave their views on whether they thought the Giant was an ancient or relatively modern construct. The day is detailed in the highly recommended book, *'The Cerne Giant – An Antiquity on Trial* (Darvill et al, 1999). I will here give a brief summary of the arguments for and against, as well as my views and those of my contemporaries.

The case against him being 'ancient' is based chiefly on two tenets; the lateness of documentation on the Giant, and how such an *'obscene'* feature could have survived from antiquity when situated next to a large Christian foundation.

It has been proposed that the Giant was made by Lord Holles during the upheavals of the Civil War, as a mockery of Oliver Cromwell. It is interesting that elsewhere Cromwell's supporters did depict him as Hercules, such as in the doorway to Highnam Court, Gloucestershire (op. cit. p. 85). This has echoes of the declaration of the Roman Emperor Commodus, who declared he was Hercules in the 2nd century AD. It was in 1645 that the *Clubmen of Dorset* were founded, who claimed to be neutral in the conflict between Parliament and the King, vowing to protect their homes and property against damage from both sides. It is worth looking at our record of the Holles premise in detail:

'There was once observed, in the possession of a pauper in the neighbourhood (since dead), an old thick folio volume, in the black letter, containing accounts of many antiquaries of the kingdom… in which book was an account of the abbey of Cerne and the giant; and in it was asserted that queen Emma in exile found an asylum in the abbey, and that the giant was cut in the hill at the dissolution of the monastery, in the derision of the abbot. That the indecent appearance of the figure was expressive of his lust; the uplifted club, of his meditated revenge; and the position of his feet, the necessity of his quitting the place' (Hutchins 1796-1814, Vol 3, p. 322).

Now, folklorist Jeremy Harte contests that 'black letters' ceased to be used for books (except Bibles) around 1600. This would seem to disprove the theory that the figure was cut by Lord Holles between 1654 and 1663 (Harte 1986, p. 44).

Even if the figure does represent Hercules, some have argued that this does not necessarily date him as Iron Age, as Hercules was still a popular figure after the arrival of Christianity. He often represents virtue, and as late as 1454 Philip the Good of Burgundy hung tapestries depicting the life of Hercules; Chaucer also wrote of a monk who spoke of Hercules. But it is a long way from the admiration of a strong and heroic mythical figure to creating a nude ithyphallic figure in rural Dorset. On the whole, Christianity's use of Pagan symbolism and mythical imagery was negatively used as a means of converting the populace.

It has been well cited by opponents of an ancient Giant that William Stukeley was the first person to give the giant 'antiquity' by calling him Helis. But what he actually says is: *'... the people there give the name of Helis to the figure'*. How would this name have even been on tongues of locals unless it was an old tradition? The names Hel,

Helis, and Helith would certainly have been circulated amongst antiquarians, learned gents who studied ancient history and classical myths. But how would local country folk have known of Helis if it were not part of an existent oral tradition?

Although the first documentation of the Giant was the account of 1694, *'... that does not stop it being middle or late - Iron Age in origin'* (Castleden 2000, p. 8). It shows us, if anything, the willingness of locals to take on the expense and effort of scouring the figure - **it must have been important to them.** The historian Gildas, writing around 540AD (around 60 years before the arrival of St Augustine), writes of *'devilish monstrosities... both within and without the deserted enclosures'*. Were these *'enclosures'* the hillforts and temple sites? It seems likely that Gildas spent time in Dorset, so one of the places he referred to might have been the Trendle.

There are numerous prehistoric sites that simply 'did not exist' until antiquarians came across them. Lack of documentation does not mean an ancient site was not there. After all, *'There are no title deeds for Stonehenge that provide either Mesolithic origin or its decommissioning in the Bronze Age, and no one would expect such documents to have been made'* (Castleden 2000, p. 102). Avebury stone circle, founded c. 3000BC, is the biggest in the world with hundreds of tons of stone *on full view*. Yet it was not described until 1649, when John Aubrey stumbled upon it whilst out hunting; he had no prior knowledge of it. Although the Domesday Book covers Avebury, it does not mention the stone circle.

The earliest record of the Wilmington Long Man seems to be 1704 (Darvill et al 1999, p. 138), even though Roman brick fragments have been found in the trenches. The first documented scouring of the Uffington White Horse was in 1859, yet its upkeep must have been carried out on a regular basis for over 2000 years! The first reference to the horse was made in 1180, and yet subsequent centuries came and went without a single mention. The list of prehistoric sites not documented until the 17th and 18th century is indeed a long one. This situation has recently been aptly commented on: *'An absence of evidence can never be taken as evidence of absence'* (op. cit. p. 30). How true!

1950 aerial photograph of the Giant, showing the old 'coffin' fencing. (Cambridge University. Public Domain)

It must be remembered that most of the population throughout the Iron Age and the Middle Ages was illiterate, so it is hardly surprising that landscape features got missed by the small number of literate gentlemen who travelled around the countryside. We must also bear in mind that these gents would have had to be passing by the Giant when it had recently been scoured; just a few years later it might well have been easy to miss, unless a local was there to point it out. The absence of the Giant in 17th and 18th century records may simply be down to people visiting the area when the Giant was overgrown, as it periodically would have been.

Having weighed up all the arguments myself, I have also concluded that the Giant is an Iron Age construct; this is largely because of the astronomical alignments I have discovered concerning the figure and other nearby sites. Although a few of the celestial events had long time ranges, spanning periods outside the Iron Age, most of the astronomy revealed to me does not extend beyond 500BC-500AD.

The Giant and the cross

The French Monk Gotselin wrote accounts of St Augustine around 1091, and mentions that the people of Cerne were carrying out, '... *things that were dreadful to the figure of Helia',* compelling Augustine to journey to Cerne. He had experienced conversion problems elsewhere, and at his first attempt was driven out by the people of Cerne. Not to be outdone, Augustine returned and cursed the local populace, and performed his 'miracle' of manifesting the spring, which he then used to baptise the poor converted sinners. You may recall that the order to Christianise Pagan centres came from Pope Gregory, as Bede recounts: *'The idol temples of this race should by no means be destroyed, but only the idols in them. Take holy water and sprinkle it in these shrines, build altars and place relics in them'.*

There are many examples of the take-over of Pagan sites by Christianity across Britain and elsewhere, good examples being Knowlton, Tara, Glastonbury, Rudstone and Winchester. Christianisation of such centres was common practice, and yet one which the advocates of a 17th century Giant are quite silent about. Christianity literally took possession of former Pagan cult centres; is this why the Giant survived throughout the period of the Abbey, due to the Papal edict? Cerne had two Pagan foci to supplant – the sacred spring and the Giant above, and this was achieved by the construction of the Abbey in between.

Ronald Hutton has argued that the sexual imagery of the Cerne colossus would not have been tolerated within sight of the Abbey (Darvill et al 1999, p. 105). But we have already mentioned that Ælfric, Abbot of Cerne 989-1005, was an enlightened man who may have been content to use the Giant as a teaching aid: *'... temptation had to be there to make the choice... of the right way valid'* (Castleden 1996, p. 194). The *'sins of the flesh'* were displayed quite literally for all to see. Are not churches adorned with phallicism, erotic imagery, sheela-na-gigs, green men, dragons and demons, all on show to its parishioners? These are not intended to encourage people to become salacious or licentious, but to warn of the evils that await them should they stray from *The Way;* they are intended to be objects of disgust not adoration. The widespread survival of giants in plays and ballads during the Middle Ages shows how deeply imbedded they were in the collective British psyche.

Perhaps the survival of an ithyphallic giant next to a Benedictine Abbey should not in itself be regarded as a mystery; Gary Biltcliffe informs me that, *'The Benedictines were more gentle than the Cistercians, and walked with Nature and the energies of the land. In Europe, for instance, Benedictines at Cluny in Burgundy taught geomancy, alchemy, herbal medicine, and astrology. They did not usually usurp pagan sites, but built next to them'* (pers. comm. See also Biltcliffe and Hoare 2012, p. 74-5).

If the Giant does have a pre-Christian origin, then the Abbey had to tolerate periodic scourings of the Giant throughout medieval times. It shows stoicism in the locals to maintain their hill figure, even when there were not always resident landowners around to oversee such projects. The Giant had no economic value, and was not on a boundary, explaining why it did not feature in medieval records, most of which were concerned with land, resources, rent, and ownership (Williamson, in Darvill et al 1999, p. 136).

Rather than being the result of an isolated, post-medieval gesture, Paul Newman argues that we are dealing with, '... *the inauguration of a continuous, arduous obligation to scour and maintain the figure down through the centuries. It is this prolonged effort that makes one assume that the figure arose from the collective concerns of the community rather than impulse or whim or playful prank'* (op. cit. p. 31). He also argues that the values needed to create such a brazen, phallic naked figure were not to be found during the Middle Ages or later, **but in prehistory**. Although created by human endeavour, perhaps one reason the Giant has survived is that he is otherworldly, a striding, shamanic emblem that is coaxing us to walk with him up the Cerne Valley.

It is good to see that the scales are now leaning towards an ancient Giant: '... *we can at last be satisfied that he belongs to the late Iron Age, having stood on this windswept Dorset escarpment since the time when Jesus walked in Palestine'* (Rodney Legg, in Castleden 1996, p. 9).

The last quote in this chapter is from Julian Cope, who makes a good point about people missing things right under their noses: *'Arguments have been raised as to the giant's genuine antiquity, since he was only recently recorded. But this seems far more likely to have been caused by prudery and sheer lack of belief by any who had not seen it with their own eyes... Discussing a chalk giant with a thirty-foot erection was not considered after-dinner conversation"* (Cope 1998, p. 207). True enough.

Amongst the background of arguments regarding the Giant's age, I decided to tackle the problem from a totally different angle, using a discipline that has gathered recognition in recent years. I set out with a view to see if there were any astronomical alignments involving the Giant and related sites, and what dates were most applicable. Later I shall let the sun and the stars do the talking – and the Giant of course.

Chapter 6.
Keeping it up –
phallicism and fertility folklore

'The study of phallicism is the study of religion.'
(George R Scott, *'Phallic Worship'*.)

Space does not permit me to delve too much into the weird and wonderful world of phallic worship and ancient fertility rites: some excellent works can be consulted on the subject (Scott 1966, Bord 1982, Hutton 1996). My aim in this chapter is threefold. First I wish to impress how important phallicism and fertility rites have been in the cultural and sociological history of Mankind; then I shall give evidence that such practices were common in Britain; and finally I will demonstrate that here in Dorset there are many examples of phallicism. We shall then be in a position to look at the fertility aspects of the Giant.

Worship of the male member is very ancient indeed, and is almost geographically universal. Perhaps this reverence for the phallus, and the belief that it has magical potency, began way back in the Palaeolithic; our distant ancestors frequented caves that were filled with stalagmites and stalactites, primal phalli growing rigid within the moist interior of the Earth Mother. Several ithyphallic paintings from these distant times have been found in deep underground caverns. The one shown here is from the 'Shaft Scene' at Lascaux, in the Dordogne region of France, and is thought to be around 17,000 years old!

Phallic symbolism, over 17,000 years old, from the caves of Lascaux in France.

Later, the Greeks, Romans, Hebrews, Babylonians, Egyptians, Chinese, and many other cultures (including the ancient British), all held the phallus to be representative of the fecundity of Nature and, as a consequence, of the ultimate well-being of *our* species. The name of the Sumerian god Iskur means *'erect'*. The Biblical phrase, *'Yahweh Sabaoth'* comes from SIPA-UD, meaning *'penis of the storm'* (Allegro 1970, p. 24); *'Yahweh was everywhere represented by images which were man-like in outline… All these images possessed, in comparison with their size, enormous phalli'* (Scott 1996, p. 110).

Bronze Age ithyphallic sun-men carvings from Scandinavia.
(After Gelling and Davidson 1969.)

Following the advent of Christianity, phallic worship was looked upon as something to be hidden, a taboo subject, and one that was subject to many ecclesiastical condemnations. Sex became sinful, and with it countless rites and ceremonies that had been carried out for thousands of years by King and rustic alike. Phallicism was isolated, suddenly seen as the cult of a minority of sexually obsessed deviants lead by the Devil. Although some phallic symbolism *is* connected with sex and pornography, most certainly is not, as Adrian Bailey observes: *'Is it not more likely that the source of any expression of the genitals in cult or religion comes from the analogy between human fecundity and the seasonal bounty of the natural world?'* (Bailey 1998, p. 26). Phallicism is more than titillation and penis adoration.

To ancient people life was often a struggle between life and death; the gods and goddesses who ruled over Mankind were all-powerful beings who were often sexually active, even promiscuous. Their myths echoed the forces at play in Nature, so to honour their sexual acts was to honour the deity. The sun in particular has been seen as the *'giver of life'* and as such connected with phallic fertility rites: *'There are clear associations between the sun and the image of phallic power and procreation'* (Bailey

Left: the Egyptian god Min. Above: papyrus showing Geb, the earth god, holding his phallus and directing it upwards to the sky goddess Nut.

63

1998, p. 86). Good examples of this can be found in Bronze Age rock engravings from Scandinavia, where well-endowed sun-men exuberantly wave axes, as the invinciblity of the sun is honoured (image previous page).

In Egyptian creation myth, the god Atum is feeling lonely as he sits on the primeval mound. So he grasps his phallus and ejaculates into his own mouth, from which issues Shu and Tefen/Tefnut, the first divine couple. Osiris was the god most associated with the phallus, as numerous obelisks built in his honour testify. He was the god of the dead, the afterlife and the Underworld agency that granted all life, including the sprouting of vegetation and the fertile flooding of the Nile. One Egyptian obelisk, the phallus of Osiris no less, can be seen in the grounds of Kingston Lacy, Dorset, brought back from the Isle of Philae on the Nile.

We shall return to Osiris in the next chapter concerning his association with the constellation Orion. But he was by no means the only Egyptian ithyphallic god; Min (or Khem/Khnum) was another, whose cult originated in the 4th millennium BC. He was worshipped in many temples as the god of regeneration and gardens, and as the deity who influenced procreation of the human species; he was later merged with the supreme deity Ammon-Ra. Min was represented in many different guises, but was often in male human form with an erect penis in his left hand and an upheld flail in the other (image above left and p. 79). As Khnum he was, '... *the maker of gods and men'.*

Geb was another Egyptian god who was usually depicted with an erect penis (image above right). Geb is the earth god, usually shown as a man reclining, sometimes with his phallus directing upwards to Nut, the sky goddess.

Kokopelli was a phallic, seed-carrying god of the Americas; there was an ithyphallic shrine near the Moqui village of Mushangnewy in Arizona, and at Colhuacan in California, phalli were said to be *'extremely prevalent'* (Allen 1966, p. 96). Further south, the Aztec fertility god Xopancale was represented by a pillar.

Across India, the phallic lingam is a pillar or post that is worshipped as the symbol of Shiva, whilst his wife Shakti is represented by the yoni, the divine opening. The shaft of the lingam is the axis mundi, the Tree of Life, connecting the heavens to earth. In Hindu tradition a white stone lingam is a symbol of a *Golden Age* long gone. Some temples in India are covered in sexual imagery, playing out myths of creation and regeneration, typical of ancient cultures from around the world, who saw no conflict between sexual imagery and religious faith: *'The failure to associate sex with obscenity sufficed to cause the ancients, and especially the Pagans, to enliven their temples with phallic images'* (Scott 1996, p. 43). The concept of obscenity and sin

Above: the phallic god Priapus at Pompeii, who holds a caduceus.
Right: Native American Indians in Virginia dance around carved phallic posts in a fertility ceremony.

was born of religious piety.

The association between phallic worship and serpents is well proven. Hercules kills a multi-headed serpent as one of his trials, and Bacchus, Thoth and Hermes are all associated with serpents. The staff of Hermes, the caduceus, was said to be the axis around which the whole universe revolved; he too is an ithyphallic god. The Knossos serpent goddess holds a snake in each hand, and Hermes / Mercury has two entwined serpents around his rod (itself a phallus). The fertility

The author has noted phallic-shaped stones at the Neolithic temples of Malta. This one is at Hagar Qim.

god Priapus deserves special mention here, as he is considered to be the Roman equivalent of both Hermes and Mercury. He is usually shown sporting a phallus, such as on Roman coinage, and orgiastic festivals were held in his honour. In Pompeii, his image was painted on the walls of brothels; the image above shows him also carrying a caduceus. He is known to have been worshipped by the Romans in Iron Age Britain (see below).

The Biblical story of Adam and Eve is a retelling of ancient procreation myths. All the elements are there: the god (Adam), the goddess (Eve), the Tree of Life, and the serpent. Moses turned the Aaron Rod into a snake and later called forth the Brazen Serpent, his guide and healer.

In terms of megalithic sites, many of the Neolithic megaliths of Brittany are decidedly phallic shaped, some of them over 5m (16ft) tall; many were later Christianised with inscribed crosses. Even in modern times French women seeking to have children were visiting such stones, as was the case at the Stone Mare of Locronon (Michell 1982, p. 162). I have also found phalli at some of the Neolithic temples on Malta, where at some sites, notably at Hagar Qim and Mnajdra, a single tall phallic stone was set into the temple walls (image above).

British phallic worship

The British Isles was not excluded from the ritualistic celebration of fertility, of which phallicism was often a central component. This is hardly surprising really: *'It was natural that the ancient Britons should worship stones and pillars, as emblems of the male principle, just as did the ancient Hebrews, Greeks, Romans, Egyptians, Japanese, et al'* (Scott 1966, p. 184).

The author standing at the foot of the gigantic Champ-Dolent Menhir, in Brittany. (Image: Sue Wallace.)

65

In Ireland, a hand-held phallic artefact was found at Knowth, a Neolithic tomb complex in the Boyne Valley. At the same site a 2.1m (7ft) pillar stone stands outside one of the entrances, marking the equinox (Brennan 1994, p. 104-5). Another ithyphallic stone, called the *Stone of Destiny,* stands at Tara, the sacred centre of the country.

Around Britain, phallic stones once stood in the centre of our towns and villages, right up until times when such objects caused offence (the one shown here is from Clackmannan near Stirling). Derek Bryce comments: *'The fact that stones of this kind survived through many centuries of the Christian era may indicate that they were not seen as offensive or embarrassing until the nineteenth century... most of them were quietly made to disappear'* (Bryce 1994, p. 15-16). This kind of thinking can also be applied to the Giant of course – it did not cause offence until relatively modern times.

Phallic megalith next to the village cross, Clackmannan, near Stirling. (From *Scottish Market Crosses* (1900) by J W Small.)

Bryce advocates that the high crosses of Christianity are the new phalli, replacing the ancient ones that were once an important element of a community.

The tallest stone known in Britain, the splendid 8.5m (28ft) Rudstone monolith, is ithyphallic, as was the Obelisk at Avebury (now destroyed). Much of my research in recent years has been in the Avebury area, and during my tours I frequently show people how many of the Neolithic megaliths were *intentionally selected* because of their phallic appearance. Some of the bluestones at Stonehenge are phallic, and might well have been selected, or shaped, to achieve this desired effect. On Dartmoor, the various tall *Longstones* are phalli, which rise suggestively out of the lonely moors. I found a stunning phallic stone inside the chambered tomb at Bryn-Celli-Ddu, on Anglesey (see Bord 1982, p. 58). Sometimes phalli are accompanied by the yoni of the Goddess, such as at Men-an-Tol in Cornwall.

Expanding this further, several chambered tombs (such as West Kennet, Newgrange and Stoney Littleton) were designed to enable thin beams of light to *penetrate* the dark interior, like a shaft or phallus penetrating the womb-tomb of the Earth Mother (Knight 2011). Today we speak of a *'shaft of light'*, and this term once had a quite literal meaning.

Roman phalli turn up in British excavations, from carved door lintels to pottery, from portable good luck amulets, to stone altars. Roman pottery found at Colchester had phalli

One of the ithyphallic megaliths at Avebury stone circle, Wiltshire.

around the necks of birds, and a carved phallus was also found at Wroxeter. It is known that Roman soldiers carried ithyphallic amulets, symbolising manhood and pride; the phallus was a good luck charm for soldiers stationed on Hadrian's Wall, and were carved into stone at the forts of Maryport and Chesters. At the Birrens fort, one inscription reads, *'the phallus of Priapus'* (Bédoyère 2002, p. 132), which demonstrates how legionnaires wished to associate with this virile god.

Celtic phallicism was a recurring theme, but not in a pornographic sense, or even in terms of representing the human sex act; it was all about the life-force of Nature. On the continent, ithyphallic warrior figures have been found at Val Camonica and Le Donon. Some of these bear swords, indicating a link between sex and aggression. Some nude war-gods of the Brigantia

Sheela-na-gig at Kilpeck, Herefordshire. (Image: S Wallace.)

of Northern England were both horned and phallic, as at High Rochester in Northumberland, *'... where a nude, horned, schematised god has large genitals, thus demonstrating the link between war and sexuality'* (Green 1989, p. 210).

The tenacious nature of phallic worship is proven by the numerous and widespread carvings of the phallus on Christian architecture, and hundreds of phallic images have been recorded across Europe; *Images of Lust* by Weir and Jerman (1999) is an excellent reference work on the subject.

Britain also has its fair share, with dozens of male exhibitionist carvings lurking in churches, to surprise and even shock the unsuspecting onlooker. These are complemented by female exhibitionist imagery, comprising nudes with exposed yoni, as at Kilpeck (above). Sometimes things were done in a more clandestine manner, proven by the number of phalli found inside pre-14th century church altars.

Old habits, it seems, were hard to break. In 1282, a priest in Fife had to appear before the Bishop to explain why he had lead a fertility dance around a phallic figure at an Easter dance (Bord 1982, p. 75). From 1786 we have a record of an unusual figure called *Jack of Hilton* (image left). In his left hand he holds his phallus, which is composed of a stump covered in oak leaves. Perhaps this is the origin of

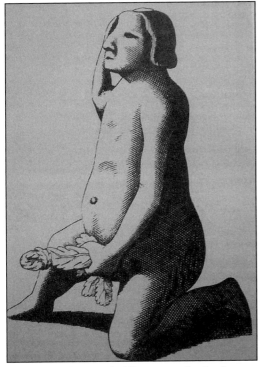

Jack of Hilton, holding a wooden/leafy phallus. From *'Natural History of Staffordshire'* (1786) by Robert Plot.

wood, the slang term for a phallus! This 30cm (12ins.) hollow brass statuette was believed to be Etruscan in origin and was used in a curious Staffordshire custom. Every New Year's Day hot water was poured into it, resulting in steam issuing from the phallus! A goose was circled around the figure seven times before being cooked for the table of Lord Hilton of Essington.

Two wooden phalli found during the demolition of a Welsh farmhouse were dated as late-17th century, whilst on the Isle of Eriska, phallic pillars were revered as late as the early 18th century (Scott 1966, p. 186). A male exhibitionist carving can be seen in the church at Whittlesford in Cambridgeshire and more phallic emblems have been identified in the Valley of the Fruin, Dumbartonshire,

Phallicism in Dorset

As an ithyphallic symbol, the Cerne Giant is not alone in Dorset - far from it. The county had a tradition of creating phalli at least two thousand years prior to the conception of the Giant. Neolithic chalk phalli, up to 25cm (10ins.) long, were found at Mount Pleasant Henge and Maumbury Henge, Dorchester. They were accompanied by chalk spheres, an association also found at Grimes Grave, Norfolk. Two more chalk phalli were also uncovered in a long barrow at Gussage St Michael; some of these had been damaged *prior to burial* suggesting that they may have been dragged

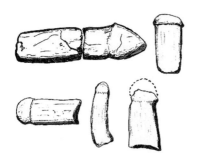

Dorset Neolithic chalk phalli. On display in County Museum.
(P Knight, *Sacred Dorset,* 1998.)

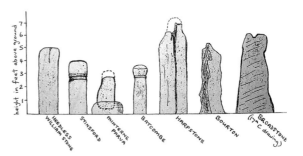

Dorset's ancient ithyphallic megaliths.
(From Knight, *Sacred Dorset,* 1998.)

along the ground as part of fertility rites. In 1987, a block of chalk found at Flagstones, Dorchester, was inscribed with markings that have been interpreted as a phallus and a yoni. I described Dorset's phallic megaliths in *Sacred Dorset* (image above).

But is there any evidence for phallic worship in Dorset later on, in the Iron Age? Indeed there is, and I give three examples (below) from central and west Dorset, all from the County Museum. The first is a head from a Roman pottery figurine from the Colliton Town House, Dorchester. It is 1st century AD, and has facial features that resemble a phallus and testes. The middle artefact is a fragment of carved red deer antler, from Romano-British layers in South St, Dorchester. The accompanying museum label states that it was probably connected with a *'fertility cult'*. The third object, on the right, is the most intriguing of the three. It is 15cm (6ins.) long, is made of local greensand, and is described as *'Celtic'*. It was found in 1935 in a garden in Eype, near Bridport. The stone is glans-shaped with an inscribed face on one side. The shape of the head and facial features are not unlike those of the Giant. Of added interest are the interlocking circles on the lower half, which are similar to the *mana* of Buddhists, and the vesica piscis of Christian symbolism (Knight 1998, p. 76-7).

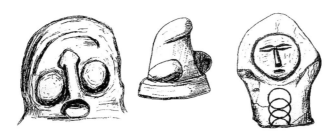

Iron Age phallic symbolism from Dorset. Left: Colliton Town House, Dorchester. Centre: South St, Dorchester. Right: Eype, near Bridport. County Museum, Dorchester. (After P Knight, *Sacred Dorset,* 1998.)

The Dorset Ooser is a peculiar survival of old Pagan rites. This carved wooden mask had bull-like horns, wild terrifying eyes, and a gaping mouth with gnashing teeth; his face is human yet he possesses horns, perhaps a distant memory of a shaman shape-shifting into a bull. He was said to instil fear in adults and children alike when paraded through villages on May Day and St George's Day, stopping at houses to demand kisses from the ladies! The original mask was last recorded in the early years of the last century in Melbury Osmond, only 11km (7 miles) from the Giant. In 1973 a new mask was made, closely modelled on the lost one using old photographs. The Ooser (pronounced *'wurser'*) is periodically paraded with the Wessex Morris, and was recently taken up Giant Hill (see image p. 178). Ralph Whitlock states that at one time, *'… almost every Dorset village and many other West Country shires had its ooser'* (Whitlock 1979, p. 51). Rodney Castleden regards the modern Ooser to be, *'… the last in a long line of replacements, intended to be worn with some special costume in ritual dances that may have originated in the Iron Age or earlier'* (Castleden 1996, p. 143). In Shillingstone, the Ooser was known as the Christmas Bull, no doubt connected with former midwinter Pagan rites intended to coax the sun back to life. The bull is of course an animal connected with ancient fertility rites and is remembered in Dorset in the names of the Iron Age hillforts of Bulbarrow and Bulbury. The Ooser used to issue smoke from its mouth, a sad testament to how a former deity had been reduced to a demonic figure; from such fearfulness comes the Dorset saying, *'Watch out or the Ooser 'ill get 'e'.*

I find it interesting that the old Ooser has an orb in his forehead, in the place that corresponds to the *third eye* chakra of Eastern religions.

The Dorset Ooser. Right: the modern Ooser with the Wessex Morris. Above: the old Ooser, drawn from a photograph (after Knight, *Sacred Dorset,* 1998.)

The maypole is another enduring memory of ancient Pagan rites that has survived to this day. The tall pole is clearly ithyphallic and is usually associated with agricultural celebrations in May, themselves relics of ancient Beltaine festivals. It was traditionally made from hawthorn, oak, birch or elm, and a new one was made each year. Maypoles date back to at least classical times; in Rome a pine tree was incorporated in processions to honour the god Attis, and the Romans may have brought the practice to Britain. We are left in no doubt that the maypole is a sexual/fertility symbol when we refer to this verse:

'Come lasses and lads,
take leave of your dads,
And away to the Maypole he;
For every he has got him a she,
With a minstrel standing by;
For willy has gotten his jill,
And Jonny has got his Jone,
To jig it, jig it, jig it, jig it,
Jig it up and down'.
(*May Song*, anon, 1672.)

The phallic maypole shaft is symbolic of the implanting of new seeds into the body of Mother Earth. On a deeper level, the pole is the Axis Mundi, the World Tree, and dancing around it celebrates the cycles of the sun, moon and the stars; during the dance participants gradually weave their way into the centre – the very heart of creation. Even today, there is usually a May Queen, who represents the Spring Maiden/Goddess, she who heralds the victory of the Summer King over his winter counterpart.

By tradition, a maypole was erected on Giant Hill, although it now seems more probable that it was in the village by the Town Pond (Harte 1986, p. 46). As I said, the Wessex Morris have recently been ascending the hill to dance at the rising of the sun on May Day, sometimes accompanied by the Ooser; I was fascinated by the fact that whilst I was observing the 2007 May Day sunrise from the Bellingstone (image p. 175), I could hear them making merry on the opposite side of the valley! The *Beating the Bounds* walk continues to this day in Cerne, and is also carried in May.

The fertile Giant

Rodney Castleden cautions us that the recorded fertility folklore in the area should not be taken as conclusive proof that the intention of the Giant's creators was to manufacture a fertility symbol (Castleden 1996, p. 17). However, it seems to me more than likely that this *was* their intention!

Complementing the Giant as a fertility symbol, there are many tales from around Britain of fertility practices associated with sacred monuments, places where it was advantageous for women to visit if trying to conceive. Amongst these are the Bride's Chair, a depression in a crag in Lancashire, the Kelpie Stane in the River Dee, and the Cradle Stone in Grampian. Some places were also said to help the fertilising power of men, such as the cross at Boho near Enniskillen, and the ancient cross shaft at Clonmacnoise in Ireland.

A parallel tale of phallus-engendering fertility comes from 18th century Scotland. In his *Description of the Western Islands of Scotland* (1716), M Martin tells us that, '*At Westerwood fort was found a remarkable Priapus or fallus… it may denote perhaps the continuance of some indisposition, upon the recovery from which this was erected; or else the time of barrenness, after which a child was obtained… decency forbids the saying of any more on this subject, as it obliges me to conceal the figure*'.

Male exhibitionism on the exterior of Sopley church, near Christchurch.

Folklore such as this should not be dismissed simply as 'old wives tales', but more as tools from which to glean information: '*So where local folklore refers to an early period, and speaks of Roman or prehistoric times, it is probably not so much an inherited tradition as a kind of folk archaeology*' (Harte 1986, p. 5).

That the Giant's phallus represents the male principle is a given; yet he balances the divine feminine yoni of the well/spring in the valley below. The one is erect on the hill and reaches to the heavens, the other issues water from the dark Underworld of the Earth Goddess.

It was said that if a girl sleeps upon the Giant she would become the mother of many children. This is confirmed by John Horsley in his *Britannia Romana* (1732): '*… the phallus was visited at times of barrenness, after which a child was obtained*'.

If a girl walks around the Giant the night before her wedding she will have a happy marriage. Another practice was for a barren woman to spend the night on the figure at new moon (Newland and North, 2007, p. 140).

Dorset folklorist John Udal commented on the Giant's lore, '*It is said to be the perfect cure for barrenness in women if they sit on the actual figure of the giant… some say that the married couple must actually consummate the marriage on the spot*'.

Even 20th century tales say that women about to get married would visit the Giant for good luck, as well as women in fear of losing their partners. F C Warren, writing in 1944, spoke of, '*… stories of girls entreating the aid of the Giant*'. New Moon was said to be a favourable time for them to do this. It seems that it is not always necessary to make love on the actual figure, as Ralph Wightman informs us: '*Several friends of mine have provided supporting evidence for the legend that sleeping within sight of the giant is a powerful fertility spell for women*' (Wightman 1977, p. 98). It makes one wonder if all this is the origin of the

This image of a phallic Devil, from 1865, demonstrates the final degradation of phallic gods into demons.

saying that a woman is *in the club!*

Modern couples seeking to have children have made love on the Giant, sometimes with a successful outcome. The Marquis of Bath, the flamboyant owner of Longleat House, *'... called upon its power after five years of childless marriage. His daughter arrived nine months later, and every year since the trio visit the Giant where, it is claimed, they talk at length about their problems'* (*Dorset Evening Echo*, April 28, 1982). The Marquis said, *'It worked for us and in gratitude we gave Cerne as Silvy's middle name, and made 'G Cerne' godfather at the Christening – the vicar never noticed.'* He used to make annual pilgrimages to the Giant with Silvy [his daughter], so she could tell her godfather what she had been up to since her last visit (Newland and North 2007, p. 140).

In 1998 a couple from Puddletown made love on the Giant after being told to do so by a white witch; after 5 years of failing to conceive she became pregnant. This story made the local press, and Monty Don and I had the pleasure of interviewing the couple and their son for a Channel 4 TV programme.

However, couples wishing to make love on the Giant need to beware, as Jeremy Harte warns: *'The bare slopes of Giant Hill - exposed to the elements, and still more exposed to the gaze of bystanders – would make an uncomfortable background on which to consummate a marriage...'* (Harte 1986, p. 43). Too true!

Turning on the Giant – earth energies

Master dowser Guy Underwood studied the Giant and found a remarkable coincidence between the Giant's trenches and outline, and the 'geodetic lines' that he dowsed (Underwood 1969). He found that there was not a perfect match, but that the currents he dowsed were close to, and usually just outside of, the Giant's features. He experienced a similar phenomenon at the Uffington White Horse: *'The fecundity of the local herds and fields were believed to depend upon the preservation of the hill figure'.* This echoes Gerard's account, written in the 1620's: *'The Saxon God Heile whom they honoured as the conferrer of their health'* (in Coker 1732).

Below the Giant's left hand Underwood noted, *'... a rough mound about 50ft [15.2m] long indicating disturbance of the ground'* (Underwood 1969), which he surmised covered some object associated with the figure. He noted that the obliteration of former trenches would have left a depression, not a mound: *'It would be interesting to show whether the tradition that St Augustine destroyed the local 'idol' in fact referred to this mound'* (op. cit. p. 154).

Underwood was excited by his findings at Cerne Abbas, seeing them as, *'... among the most exciting results of my practical researches'* (op. cit. p. 155).

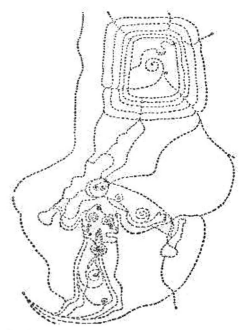

Guy Underwood's dowsing results, showing energies flowing between the figure and the Trendle. (After Underwood 1969.)

The energies Underwood dowsed seem to mark out the Giant's chalk features on the hillside, as he found at Uffington. These results are interesting as they show spiralling energy nodes inside each of the testes and at the tip of the phallus. The latter is exactly where the magic of fertility was granted to many a lass! Are these energy foci integral to the successes of these 'miracles'?

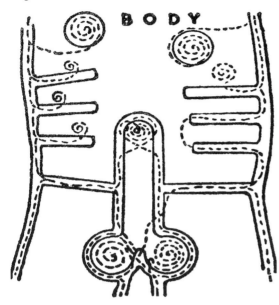

Guy Underwood's dowsing of the torso area of the Giant, with spiralling nodes at the tip of the phallus and at the testes. (Underwood 1969.)

Chris Thomas felt that walking around the Cerne Giant in a meditative manner, and stamping the ground at intervals, imprinted the energy of the figure into the very chalk itself (Thomas 1999). It confirms what dowsers have being saying for generations, and that I can confirm personally, that we *energetically interact* with sacred sites, and by attuning ourselves we can engender positive changes to their energy matrices.

In the forum pages of the website of the British Society of Dowsers, Lyndon Ronstadt posted that he had located an, *'Intercessory Portal… a square patch of ground above the head of the Cerne Abbas Giant'.*

Gary Biltcliffe has related a story to me about the power of Cerne: *'A lady with cancer was told by Maori elders in New Zealand that her condition would be healed if she moved to a valley in England called Cerne. She moved to the village and was subsequently cured'* (pers. comm.).

Keeping it up

It would seem that people are still interacting with the Giant today. Gerald Pitman was recently walking on the Giant when he found the photo of a woman on the phallus, fixed to the ground by a fragment of flint. On a trip to the site in 2012, I found a phallus constructed of small fragments of chalk and flint just outside the enclosing fence (image right). It made me smile and was ample proof to me that people are still coming here in the hope that the Giant will weave his magic for them.

Perhaps one reason we love the Giant's unabashed exhibitionism is that some part of us would like to unshackle the restraints of modern life, with its moral ethics and political correctness, that we

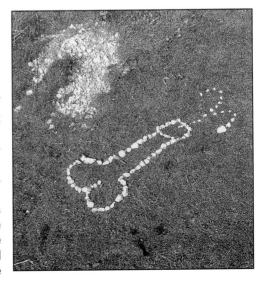

would occasionally like to run naked through the daisies, as Rodney Castleden concurs: *'We love him for his rampant shameless naughtiness, even though we may not dare to be naughty ourselves'* (Castleden 1996, p. 42). But the manacles of social morality are, at the end of the day, self-imposed. The Church has long sought to suppress the old ways, labelling nudity and fertility rites as *'sins of the flesh'*, warning us that the Devil lurks behind every standing stone to tempt us, and perhaps even on the Giant. The Victorians barely tolerated the Giant, and some did not even manage that. Perhaps the Giant remonstrates that we should rethink some of these issues, and make up our own minds as to what is right and wrong. This is exactly what people did for thousands of years right across our magical Isles.

'And Shillingstone, that on her height,
Shows up her tower to opening day,
And high-shot maypole, yearly dight,
With flowery wreaths of merry May.'
(William Barnes)

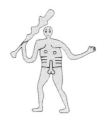

Chapter 7.
Who is the Giant?
Lining up the suspects

'Myth contains a kernel of deep wisdom
under a husk of extravagance'.
(Pausanius, Greek geographer/writer.)

The question of the Giant's identity has engaged people's curiosity for many generations. To this end, people have sought, as we have seen, to ascertain whether he is a modern folly or a genuine ancient monument. In 1808, when Dorset poet William Holloway published his poem, *'The Giant of Trendle Hill'*, he thought the Giant to be either Cudred King of Wessex, killed in 748AD, or else *'Heil or Eli The Great'*. It has been suggested that the Giant may merely be a mockery of Oliver Cromwell, or a portrait of Richard the Lion-heart, or even Dick Whittington heading off to London! I do not mock these forays into the sublime, as they show how the Giant has roused people, often in a romantic vein, to put pen to paper. People have sought to explain something that refuses to be identified, and even today the Giant declines our efforts to place him into an historical pigeonhole.

Dorset archaeologist Bill Putnam gives his opinion regarding the Giant's age: *'It is likely that the Cerne Giant was constructed by the Durotriges, whether during the Roman period or before. He should be regarded as a powerful symbol of tribal authority and beliefs... the Cerne Giant fits well into an Iron Age and Roman context'* (in Darvill et al 1999, p. 51 & 56). Professor Timothy Darvill, of Bournemouth University, is of the opinion that although the Giant had been cosmetically altered in recent centuries, *'... in its original form, the characteristics of the Giant conform to recognised iconography and show a 'warrior god' in an image common in many parts of Europe during later prehistory'* (op. cit. p. 63). As the majority of learned academics and researchers have now come down on the side of antiquity (although not all, by any means), we can consider here what Iron Age candidates fit the bill. The astronomy I have uncovered also allowed me to narrow the search to 500BC – 500AD. Admittedly, this is still a period of 1000 years, so we must tread carefully and with purpose, just like the Giant on the hillside.

Iron Age mythology is dominated by sagas of battle and war, of heroes and mighty warriors. Threats of immanent disaster and conflict created the impulse to be aggressive, to play out the lives of these new gods of war: *'War was regarded as natural and right, the royal road for a man to follow if he were to serve the gods, his king and his country'* (Baring and Cashford 1991, p. 286). The Celts, Vikings, Greeks and Romans all had remarkably similar war and solar deities, who were many in number, which now took preference over the once dominant goddesses of former times. The hero myth proliferated, wherein the participant goes off to slay dragons, giants and all manner of beasties. Perhaps having a warrior/hunter god as one's tribal guardian ensured hunting would be fruitful - a form of sympathetic magic. It should be noted, however, that the Cerne Giant displays both destructive powers (the club) and the power of regeneration (the phallus). Although seemingly contradictory elements, these dual qualities were the characteristics of many ancient deities.

Iron Age Egyptian figurine of a Gaulish warrior.
(After Castleden 1996.)

Is a specific identification necessarily an end goal in itself? Was the figure, from the very start, an all-encompassing icon, one that could accommodate everyone, regardless of their religious and cultural disparities? Is this why he survived Roman Imperialism, Saxon/Celtic settlers, and the dogma of the Church?

Celtic deities and heroes often evolved into others, and the Romans famously adopted local deities when they moved into a new area that fell under their control. The Giant may have been a universal icon, perhaps periodically re-modelled, that spoke to the various cultures that walked along the Cerne Valley; anyone could relate to him. Is this not the case today?

We cannot even take it for granted that the Giant was a fertility prop. The extension to his phallus is modern, and it has been estimated that prior to this, although still erect, it would have been the equivalent of 15cm (6ins.) on the average man. Perhaps the Giant's phallus was more of a frightener, a gesture that this god, and therefore the local tribe, was not to be messed with. A terracotta figurine crafted in Egypt, dated 3rd or 2nd century BC, depicts a Gaulish Celtic warrior. He holds a sword and shield, yet is naked but for a girdle, like the Giant. Importantly, he shows off his testicles and erect phallus. The warrior is very macho, displaying his proud manhood, and one would not expect him to show any fear in battle (image above).

A plaque from Slovenia, dated 450BC, shows two Celtic warriors in combat displaying their phalli (Castleden 1996, p. 150). Wooden figurines holding clubs and shields have been found in the British Isles, and stone warriors naked but for a belt or girdle have been found in NE England (Darvill et al 1999, p. 43). The Giant's nakedness seems to fit with the Celtic practice of going into battle naked, except for a girdle around their waist for holding weapons. These have a date range of 500-50BC, and it is his girdle that helps confirm the Giant's Iron Age status.

Hill figure authority Paul Newman sees the Giant as, *'... a mediator between the Bronze Age and the classical period... a hero-god, if you like, reflecting the concerns of warriors and cattle rearers'* (op. cit. p. 34). The early British and the Celts were great copiers of icons and myths, incorporating more and more of them into an ever-growing pantheon of gods and goddesses.

Regarding the Giant's basic wooden club, Rodney Castleden surmises that rather than illustrating a god or a member of a noble class, the Giant depicts the common man - a farmer or warrior: *'This is a god to inspire even the poorest and most disadvantaged in the community to fight on bravely... he is the god not of a ruling elite but of Iron Age Everyman'* (Darvill et al 1999, p. 50). Harking back to classical mythology, Hercules was not the result of a divine marriage, but of the union between Zeus and a mortal woman; Hercules was of the people for the people. So perhaps the Giant was not always seen as a god, but rather a local tribal guardian or spirit, protector and provider for the Durotriges clans. He may even be the motif of a particular local hero or warrior, who was responsible for some incredible feat, such as Corineus' slaying of a giant.

People were constantly attempting to explain their everyday world. As has already be stated, the spring is the oldest sacred site, nestling under the shadow of the ithyphallic contours of Giant Hill. But myths developed as people's belief systems evolved, including the modification of existing legends, and the creation of new ones: *'Once Cerne had become a sacred site, made sacred by the devotions at the spring, by the building of a sacred precinct, a mythic geography would have evolved to explain how the place came to be special'* (Castleden 1996, p. 120).

The interchange of deities between one ancient culture and another is well known. One Greek writer, Herodotus (c. 485-425BC) noted, *'The name of nearly all the gods came to Greece from Egypt'.* This is commented on by George Scott: *'The deity referred to in the Bible as Baal was the god of the Hamites and Ethiopians, a contemporary of Yahweh. In Egypt he was Osiris; in Rome Hercules; in Greece Dionysus'* (Scott 1996, p. 112). Inscribed text on a stone at the Mesopotamian temple of Arsameia reads, *'... It is thus that I have erected these statues in divine forms which you see, to Jupiter-Oromasde, to Apollo-Mithras-Helios-Hermes, to Artagnes-Hercules-Ares...'* (Gilbert 2005, p. 88). In the context of the Giant, Gardiner and Osborn make the following comparisons with Cernunnos, who is often shown with serpents: *'Cernunnos, the main figure of the Gunderstrup Cauldron... is none other than the 'Horned One' of much of the wider world, who is also Lugh, who is also*

The concept of the naked hero-warrior is epitomised in this
depiction of Hercules slaying the multi-headed Hydra.

Ophiuchus. And Ophiuchus is none other than Aesculapius, the Greek serpent healing god, and the Egyptian Imhotep' (Gardiner and Osborn 1997, p. 164).

Like the chalk on the floor at a crime scene, the white features of the Giant lack the finesse and realism of most Roman or Greek icons, as well as the anatomical precision. Perhaps this is because he belongs more to people we would class as the Ancient British and the Celts. The Giant is fairly abstract, akin to Celtic and Norse art, where it was the symbolism and the communication of the message that counted. Amongst the largely illiterate peoples of Northern Europe, any image had to have immediate impact, meaning and power.

With hundreds of gods to choose from, identifying the Giant may at first seem like a needle in a haystack challenge. But all is not lost, due to the fact that across many cultures, from Europe to Africa, from Britain to the Middle East, we find similar indigenous gods. This is because we are talking about **archetypes**. Carl Jung coined this word to describe inherited themes that exist within the 'collective consciousness' of cultures, indeed across all humanity, which manifest repeatedly in different societies who have had no contact with each other. Thus, all over the world, ancient cultures developed similar myths to explain natural forces, telling identical stories involving gods, goddesses, heroes, creation, and the afterlife.

Does the Giant's weapon, his long knobbled club, offer us any clues? Certainly we have several heroes and gods that carry such a weapon, such as Dagda, Orion and Hercules, as we shall soon see. The resemblance of the club to an oak leaf has already been commented on, but are we even looking at what was originally in the Giant's right hand? Perhaps not. Other possibilities are that the object was originally a throwing stick, or a sickle, mace, spear, axe, caduceus or a sword, and that one or more of these were later altered to a club. It is possible that the club may have appeared during the Roman occupation, to fit with Greco-Roman myths of Hercules and Orion.

I also noticed the similarity of the present club to a sistrum, which was a rattle used in rain-making and 4th level initations of Mithraism. It was a sacred percussional musical instrument, chiefly used by the ancient Minoans and the Egyptians; the latter used them in temples dedicated to Isis, particularly in the worship of Hathor, as a symbol of the Earth and fertility (Bailey 1998, p. 222); the U-shape of the sistrum's handle and frame was seen as resembling the face and horns of Isis as the cow goddess. In her role of mother and creatrix, Isis is sometimes depicted holding a sistrum, symbolizing the flooding of the Nile: *'It was one of the goddess's special symbols… shaped like a vulva'* (Scott 1966, p. 164); it is relevant that Scott links the sistrum to genitalia and fertility practices. I am not saying that a sistrum was ever the object held in the Giant's right hand, but the similarity of the club to this rattle may not have gone unnoticed by the Romans, and other people of a Mediterranean origin travelling through Dorset; one man's club was another man's sistrum!

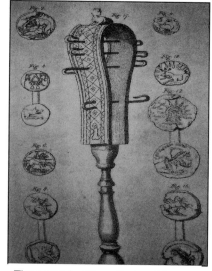

The sacred rattle called a sistrum. (From Payne Knight, *Worship of Priapus,* 1786.)

As we have discussed, many cultures believed that the skull housed the soul: *'The human head was recognised by the Celts as the most important part of the body'* (Green 1989, p. 211). This is reflected by the practice of head-hunting and the decapitation of sacrificial victims. So does the head of the Giant give us any clues as to his identity? Probably not in itself, but perhaps the style of it may help us speculate on a date. The head is bald and is slightly too small in relation to the rest of his body. We have already seen some of the Iron Age stone heads from Shipton Gorge, which are bald (p. 56). In Celtic/Romano art, the hunter gods depicted at Le Donon have disproportionately small heads. This is also the case with Mercury and Rosmerta at Chatenois, near Strasburg, and the 'Mars' figures at Bisley, Gloucestershire. And these are all bald! The Giant's round, googly-eyes, and the lack of ears and hair, are typical of Celtic art, as well as his nose, shown in older depictions as being long and slender. Referring to Celtic art, Miranda Green warns us not to take abstract style as being indicative of a lack of culture: *'Only by recognition that it is the cult, not art, that is of primary importance, may abstraction be judged for itself. Apparent simplicity may mask sophistication, and starkness, profound concepts'* (Green 1989, p. 223). Sometimes simple is best.

The suspects

Recurring threads and themes would suggest that cross-cultural archetypes are at work here. The suspects are often a hunter or a giant, possessing great strength, often wielding a club; they are usually nude and expose their phallus. At times, one or two of these criteria are met, sometimes all.

Although I have not strictly listed the possible contenders in order of my personal preference, I have left, in my opinion, the 'favourites' until towards the end. I start with two Egyptian gods, for although their names may never have been uttered in the Cerne Valley, they demonstrate ithyphallic features and were conceived when the very foundations of world mythologies were being forged. In fact, in the next chapter I shall return to Egypt, as I link the Giant to Orion, Osiris and the heavens.

Perhaps the original identity of the Giant is below, perhaps not. Maybe instead we might look for the **identities** of the Giant, plural, for I am reminded of a phrase said to me years ago as I was searching a plethora of deities for an archetype to connect with - *all gods are one god.*

Min

The cult of the Egyptian god Min originated in pre-dynastic times (4th millennium BC). He was represented in many different guises, but was often a human male, holding an erect penis in his left hand and a flail in his extended right hand. As Khem or Min, he was the god of reproduction; as Khnum, he was the creator of all things, *'the maker of gods and men'*.

One feature of Min worship was the wild prickly lettuce, of which the domestic version, *Lactuca sativa*, has aphrodisiac and opiate qualities; it produces latex when cut, which may have been regarded as Min's semen. As a god of male sexual potency, he was honoured during the coronation rites of the New Kingdom, when the

The Egyptian God Min (see also image on p. 63).

79

Pharaoh was expected to sow his seed - generally thought to have been by the actual planting of seeds; but it has also been proposed that the Pharaoh had to demonstrate that he could ejaculate, thus ensuring the annual flooding of the Nile. At the beginning of the harvest season, Min's image was taken out of the temple and brought into the fields in the *Festival of the Departure of Min*, when the harvest was blessed. Naked participants would play games in his honour, the most important of these being the climbing of a huge pole. Even some war *goddesses* were depicted with the body of Min (including the phallus), and some of these show him with the head of a lion. In the *Hymn to Min*, it is proclaimed: *'Min, Lord of the Processions, God of the High Plumes, Son of Osiris and Isis, Venerated in Ipu... '.* The fact that he was son of Isis and Osiris makes him a major Egyptian deity, whose influence would have spread to other lands via trade, conquest and pilgrimage; as the deity of fertility, whose festivities included orgiastic rites, the Greeks identified Min with Pan.

Geb

The Egyptian god Geb was an earth deity, the twin brother of Nut, the sky goddess. After being separated from his sister, his phallus rose up to join with her, and together they produced Isis and Osiris. He is described as the *'God of Earth'* and it was believed that earthquakes were Geb's laughter, and it was he who allowed crops to grow. In Egyptian mythology, Geb occurs as the primeval divine King of Egypt, from whom his son Osiris and his grandson Horus inherited the land after many altercations with the disruptive god Set, Osiris' brother.

Geb was personified as the fertile earth, but also the barren desert, the latter of which held the dead. Metaphorically described as *'the opener of jaws,'* he would release the souls of the dead from their tombs for rebirth. In this context, Geb was believed to have been engaged in eternal sex with Nut, and had to be separated from her by Shu, god of the air (see image p. 63). Consequently, Geb was often shown as a man reclining with his phallus pointing towards Nut. As an Underworld deity he (like Min) was associated with the earth and with vegetation; barley was said to grow upon his ribs, and he was often depicted with plants growing on his body. This description fits well with some Celtic gods, as we shall soon discover.

The Egyptian god Geb, pointing his phallus up to Nut, the sky goddess. The Papyrus of Tameniu, 102-952BC. (Compare to image p. 63.)

Silvanus/Sucellas

Silvanus, (or Sucellus, Sucellas, Sucellos) is from the Latin *'of the woods'*. He was a Roman deity of woods and fields, farmers and husbandmen; he was also a hunter god, as well as protector of forests (*sylvestris deus*). He especially presided over both plantations and trees growing in the wild; the Etruscan god Selvans may be the same deity. Silvanus is described as being fond of music, and is mentioned alongside Pan and nymphs. He was associated with the Roman god Mars, for he is sometimes known to as *Mars Silvanus*, and might therefore be '*... regarded as a rural version of Mars'* (Bédoyère 2002, p. 161).

The Gaulish/British equivalent was Sucellas, in the same vein as the Germanic god Donner. Both Dagda and Sucellos have been tentatively linked to Dis Pater, who Caesar regarded as the ancestor of the Gauls; Sucellas means *'good striker'* and his connection with thunder makes him a sky god; we shall see later that the Giant is very much connected to the heavens. Sucellas is usually (but not always) portrayed holding a mallet, sometimes with an extended left arm, the hand of which holds a drinking cup. Although not a club, '*... the mallet suggests kinship with the Giant's club'* (Castleden 1996, p. 140). He is usually depicted carrying a cloak, which can be draped over his left arm, which invites comparison with the 'lost cloak' of the Giant (p. 55). He is often accompanied by a tree or a dog, the latter suggesting hunting, although dogs can also represent healing; a dog has been perceived near the Giant (p. 57).

There is no evidence that Sucellas was ever a major deity in Britain, but his image does appear on a stone on the Fosse Way at East Stoke, and a silver ring found at York bears his name. The god is named on Romano-British inscriptions at Cirencester, Colchester and Rochester (Bédoyère 2002, p. 274). At Lydney Park (Gloucester) he is dedicated as *Nodens-Silvanus*, indicating cross-pollination between these two deities.

His consort was Nantosuelta, a goddess of streams, and Castleden makes a valid point that the *pairing* of a weapon-wielding god and a water goddess may have parallels at Cerne, even if only through their local equivalent deities.

Silvanus (Relief in Rom).

Upper: Latin god Silvanus;
Lower: Gaulish god Sucellos.
(Wikipedia Common Licence.)

Cronos

In Greek mythology, Cronos (Cronus or Kronos) was the leader of the Titans, the divine descendants of Gaia (the Earth) and Uranus (the sky god). This god should not be confused with the god *Chronos*, who was the personification of Time. Cronos is shown with a sickle, or else a crooked dagger, resembling a crow's beak. He overthrew his father Uranus, who had ruled during a mythological *Golden Age*. Dowsing by Guy Underwood revealed an elongated energy imprint near the left hand of the Giant that was longer than the low mound (image p. 72) and he thought that it might be a second phallus: *'This would identify the Giant as Cronus, who castrated his father Uranus with a sickle or billhook.'* Underwood goes on to imply that two spirals of energy, between his legs and over his left arm, might have been where a sickle had once been (Underwood 1969, p. 150-5).

In his poem *Hippolytus,* the Greek writer Euripides wrote of Cronos:

81

Great Heaven came,
And with him brought the night,
Longing for love, he lay upon the earth,
Spreading out fully. But the hidden boy
Stretched forth his left hand; in his right he took
The great long jagged sickle; eagerly
He harvest his father's genitals…
For all the bloody drops that leaped out
Were received by the earth… She gave birth
To the Furies, and the Giants, strong and huge'

Cronos/Saturn, holding his sickle.
(Wikipedia Common Licence.)

From the blood (or, by some accounts, semen) that flowed from Uranus and fell upon the earth, the *Gigantes* were created. This is all interesting on several levels - the *'long jagged sickle'*, the involvement of a phallus, the birthing of giants, and a character *'longing for love'* lying down on the earth. Some myths suggest that Cronos was banished by Zeus *'… to Britain, a land in the furthest west'*, and Druids do have a tradition of using ceremonial sickles. The Hebrews identified the Semitic god *El* with Cronus, an association recorded c.100AD by Philo of Byblos. In Britain, the Romans knew Cronos as Saturn.

Bran

Welsh mythology reveals Bran as a giant, who was a bard, King of Britain and god of the Underworld, who possessed a cauldron instilled with the power of restoring life. *Brân the Blessed* (or *Brân Fendigaidd*, literally *'Blessed Raven or Crow'*) appears in several of the Welsh Triads, but his most significant role is in the second branch of the Mabinogi, the *Branwen ferch Llŷr,* where he is the son of Llŷr and Penarddun.

British and Irish myth tells us that such was his size there was no house large enough to receive him. Bran's decapitated head was taken to White Hill (Tower of London) to save Britain, where it was a speaking oracle for 87 years. Legend says King Arthur later removed the head for fear of it falling into the hands of the Saxons. Bran gave his name to Brancaster and its Roman military base of Branadunnum, and some early Welsh chieftains were named Bran, to emulate their solar god (Biltcliffe and Hoare 2012, p. 377).

Some scholars regard Bran as the British equivalent of Cronos, in that the root word for Cronos in Latin and Greek means *crow*. This bird was consulted as an oracle, and links with both Bran's name and his oracular head.

There are Dorset connections with the god Bran, or at least Kings named after him. Bran is apparently a common surname on

Bran lowering the dead into his *cauldron of rejuvenation*. The Gunderstrup Cauldron.
(Wikipedia Common Licence.)

Portland, where Gary Biltcliffe found associations with giants, as well as relevant place names; Bran's Barrow was once a landmark for shipping, and Branscombe Hill rises between Portland Bill and Southwell. A headland opposite Portland on the Dorset coast is called Bran's Point (Biltcliffe 2009, p. 20).

Biltcliffe speculates as to whether the giant landscape figure he perceived on Portland (image p. 27) is in fact Bran: *'Perhaps the giant male figure represents Bran, and therefore Bran is the Genius Loci, the Spirit of Portland'* (op. cit. p. 132).

A further link to Bran and the Cerne Giant may come from the chakra system of Eastern spiritualities. The root chakra is associated with the sexual organs, which are certainly well represented on the Giant. Peter Dawkins advocates that a chakra system is laid out within the ancient city of London, and he places the root chakra at the Tower of London, the very location traditionally associated with the oracle head of Bran (Thorley 2012, p. 41).

Images of Bran are very rare, but he is thought to be depicted at least once on the Gunderstrup Cauldron found in Denmark, dated 4th – 2nd century BC (image above). The figure is clearly a giant, judging by the size of the adjacent riders and horses, and shows the god lowering the deceased into his cauldron of rebirth.

Pan

Although I do not really regard Pan as a serious contender, he warrants inclusion as a 'rank outsider' by virtue of his connection to fecundity, and for his legendary sex drive! His name originates from the ancient Greek word *paein*, meaning *'to pasture'*. In Greek mythology Pan is the god of the wild, of shepherds and flocks, nature, mountains, hunting and rustic music, and he is companion to the nymphs. He has the hindquarters, legs, and horns of a goat, in the same manner as a faun or satyr. His homeland is in rustic Arcadia (in Greece), where

An ithyphallic Pan chasing a shepherd boy; Greek vase, dated 470BC.

he is recorded in the 6th century BC. As the god of fields, flocks and wooded glens, he is akin to Cernunnos; because of this, Pan is connected to spring, when he played his *pan-pipes*; he is also the origin of the word *panic*, from his practice of scaring forest travellers. Pan may be a child of Cronos, and is also connected with Hermes, who had sex with a goat! As well as an ancient fertility god who assisted hunters, Pan also possessed the gift of prophecy, which in one myth was coaxed from him by Apollo. He disliked clothing and is usually nude, as were the participants at his rites. The image above is from a Greek vase, dated 470BC, and shows a goat-headed Pan, with erect member, pursuing a young shepherd boy. Behind him stands a Herm, a rustic fertility statue of the god Hermes (see image p. 98).

Speaking of Egyptian mythology, Herodotus tells us, *'Pan is very ancient, and once one of the eight gods that existed before the rest'*. Some scholars have suggested a link between Pan and Sirius, the Dog Star, and the Greek poet Pindar called Pan, *'the shape-shifting dog of the Goddess'*.

Liber/Bacchus

This is another 'long shot' contender, which I am including simply because this deity is often described in a sexual context, or displays his phallus, and that he was also the focus at springtime fertility rites. In ancient Rome, Liber ('*the free one*'), was also known as Liber Pater (*'Free Father'*) and was a god of viticulture and wine, fertility and freedom. The festival of Liberalia (on March 17th) became associated with free speech and coming of age rites. His cult and functions were increasingly associated with Bacchus and his Greek equivalent Dionysus, whose myths he shared. The god was a personification of male/yang procreative power, a force that issued as the 'soft seed' of human and animal semen; at the Dionysian Temple at Delos, several columns crowned with phalli were erected. Liber's temple at Lavinium was the principal focus for a month-long festival; according to St. Augustine a '*dishonourable member'* was taken in procession around local crossroad shrines, before ending up at the forum for its crowning by an honourable matron. The rites ensured the growth of seeds and repelled any malicious enchantment (*fascinatus*) from their fields. Liber's festivals were timed to the springtime awakening, the renewal of fertility in the agricultural cycle, and the god was interchangable with Bacchus. An effigy of Liber-Bacchus was wheeled around Roman cities, '*... with such obscene licence that male phalluses were made the objects of worship in Liber's honour'*.

The Cult of Bacchus was widespread and was associated with drunken, frenetic orgies. His name comes from the Greek *bak-khos*, which is a shortened version of the Sumerian 'BALAG-USH', meaning '*erect penis'* (Allegro 1970, p. 86). The image shown here is from a Greek vase, and shows an erect Dionysus/Bacchus with a dead deer over his shoulder, as he is a hunter. He was born on December 25th to a virgin mother, and heralded as a saviour sun god. Early Christians moved the birth of Jesus to December 25th to replace the birthday of both Bacchus and Mithras, as well as to usurp the festival of Saturnia, held on December 24-25th. Bacchus also has celestial connections, for the constellation of Crater was known as the '*Bowl of Bacchus'*.

Dionysus/Bacchus, sporting a phallus, on a Greek vase (Louvre Museum).

The Temple of Bacchus was one of the main temples in a large complex at Baalbek in Lebanon, and neoclassical visitors referred it as the '*Temple of the Sun'*. It is considered one of the best preserved classical temples in the world and is larger than the Parthenon in Greece, though much less famous.

Bacchus was certainly revered in Roman Britain. A marble nude figure of him was found at a villa at Spoonly Wood (Gloucestershire), and at Cirencester he was depicted on an altar with a drinking horn (Bédoyère 2002).

A record from 1282 speaks of a Scottish parish priest gathering up the local lasses at Easter, encouraging them to '*... dance around in circles to the honour of Father Bacchus',* proceedings that included parading an image of genitalia on a pole! It would seem that old practices die hard (no pun intended!). Bacchus was particuarly associated with drunken orgies, and such practices may have surivived in Dorset until St Augustine arrived, explaining why he took such offence at Cerne.

Cernunnos/the Wild Man

Cernunnos was a European Iron Age god, typically portrayed as the *'Lord of the Forest'*, with resplendent antlers, often with attendant animals including stags and serpents. Associated symbolism confirms that the god was related to fertility, crops, prosperity, and human well-being. He is sometimes depicted alongside Mercury and Apollo, confirming his solar attributes. We find him in the Welsh Mabinogion: *'And he [Cernunnos] took his club and struck a stag, which loudly brayed, and all the animals came together… and they bowed their heads and did homage as vassals to their lord'*. The sole written archaeological record of his name is from Nôtre Dame, where an inscription is accompanied by his image, which is shown below. It was found in 1711 below the Cathedral, and is dated 17AD. Like the Giant, he is curiously shown bald. Another depiction of him from Bourey (Seine-et-Oise) shows him naked *without antlers*. Removable antlers are an element of some carvings, suggesting that he only donned them for seasonal rites and was not antlered himself - he was more humanlike.

Iron Age depiction of Cernunnos, along with an inscription, found under Nôtre Dame Cathedral in 1711.

On the famous Gunderstrup Cauldron, Cernunnos sits cross-legged, and is without the typical long hair and animalistic appearance of much contemporary art; he is clean-shaven, perhaps even bald, and wears a 'cap' or headdress of some kind, onto which deer antlers appear to be attached.

Cernunnos is the *'Green Lord'* of the forest. As Michael Hodges has reminded us, the grassy infill of the Cerne Giant is green - he is eternally a *'green man'*. Hodges makes a convincing argument that a Wild Man depicted in the choir area of Christchurch Priory is both Helis *and* the Cerne Giant (Hodges 1998, p. 12). This Wild Man (image below) brandishes a club in his right hand, is naked but for a girdle, and in his left hand holds a shield depicting a green man. Did the Giant once hold a shield?

Prof Stuart Piggott linked the Cerne Giant to French medieval stories about Hierlekin or Helequin, a wild huntsman and god of the Underworld - who bore a club (Piggott 1932 & 1938). The Dorset Ooser shows us that horned Pagan gods were once worshipped in central Dorset; the mask is surely the survival of distant memories of shamans shape-shifting into horned creatures, or of sympathetic magic involving the spirit of the bull.

It is somewhat sad to witness how deities and nature spirits from one age are subsequently denigrated, as H Dewar (in 1968) summed up in *The Dorset Ooser: 'It is not difficult to trace the evolution of a god of an early cult, or a fertility spirit with attendant ritual, to the Devil of a succeeding religion'*.

85

So it would seem that Cernunnos-like fertility deities could be bald, like the giant. On a Gaulish depiction of Cernunnos at Reims, a bull is seen below him, confirming his fertility aspects. Although Cernunnos is not named anywhere in Britain, Romano-British fertility gods have been found; the god Jupiter Dolichenus stands on the back of a bull whilst brandishing an axe, and his cult spread from Wales to Northumberland. From Benwell, on Hadrian's Wall, comes a Roman bust displaying a hairless male head sporting horns. A further stag-headed god was found at Cirencester, and the bust of yet another horned deity was excavated at Moresby, Cumbria (Bédoyère 2002, p. 152).

Not far from Cerne, at Yellowham near Dorchester, a *'Wild Man'* was said to kidnap local girls and get them pregnant (Newland and North, 2007, p. 141). A vestige of old beliefs comes in the form of a horned head hidden at the base of the church tower at Charminster, just south of Cerne. I found it

Bench end at Christchurch Priory, showing a *Wild Man* brandishing a club, like the Giant, and a shield on which is a green man. (From Knight, 1998.)

some years ago, but it can be difficult to find and photograph (image below).

Rodney Castleden sees the Giant's lack of torc, stags, antlers and serpents as an indication that the Cerne figure is not Cernunnos, and resistivity studies have failed to show any signs of horns above his head (Castleden 1996, p. 143 & 172).

Perhaps we are splitting hairs that need not be split, as many different hunting-fertility gods were in fact one and the same archetype, each filling a particular local niche in the pantheon of clan gods.

Dagda

In British/Irish mythology, Dagda was the King of the Tuatha de Danann. His name means *'Father of the Gods'* and *'The Good God'*, and he is also *Dag dae, 'good hand'*, or *Daeg dia 'god of fire'*. Along with Lugh and Ogma, he was one of the three gods of art, as well as the patron of war and magic. According to legend, he was King of Ireland for eighty years until defeated by the invading Fomorians. He was a mighty warrior, protector of the tribe, who is associated with the festival of Samhain, which was when he mated with the war goddess Morrigan. He had an *'eight-pronged war-club'*, that required the effort of 8-9 men to lift, and which was *'... drew after him on a wheel'* (Squire 2000, p. 46); the tracks left by it were taken as the territorial boundary ditches, known as *'The Tracks of the Dagda's Club'*. It was said that this club could take life at one end, yet its handle could give or restore life; so Dagda,

Horned head with deer- or elf-like ears hidden in a corner of Charminster Church.

like the Giant, could end life and be the benefactor of fertility. His fertilising attributes are confirmed by the fact that his genitals dragged on the ground! Descriptions of Dagda's *'enormous pronged club'* fit well with the Giant's club, which is suitably 'knobbly'. The god was the protector of corn and milk and, according to *The Wooing of Etain*, was the controller of weather and crops. He possessed a cape/tunic of horse hide, and had a bottomless cauldron that *'left no man unsatisfied'*, indicating he was a god of abundance.

The resemblance of the Giant's club to an oak leaf may be relevant, as we will see later with Orion and Thor. Dagda's Greek equivalent was Zeus, who once incarnated as an oak spirit. Rodney Castleden suggests that the club may be the uprooted Tree

The Celtic god Dagda, depicted on the Gunderstrup Cauldron. (Wikipedia Common Licence.)

of Life, with partly trimmed branches, making it, *'... half nature, half artefact'* (Castleden 1996, p. 135). His name may also refer to the oak, *dair*, and the association of *duir* and *dair* appears in ogham texts. Comparing Dagda to an oak would also lend credence to the interpretation of him as a thunder god (see below), as oaks are frequently struck during lightning storms. An inscription found at Hadrian's Wall in 1848 said *'Fulgur Div(or)um'*, meaning *'Thunderbolt of the gods'*. Scholars have connected him with Sucellos, the *'good striker'* of the Gauls, because of his hammer/club and bowl, which is similar to Dagda's staff and cauldron.

Dagda was said to be responsible for the turning of the heavenly bodies by means of playing his magic harp, called *Coir-cethar-chuir*, which means *'Four-angled music'*, referring to the four seasons (Squire 2000, p. 46). He made the sun stand still for nine months so that his son, Oengus, could be conceived and born in a single day. Dagda's daughter, Brigid, is traditionally associated with the ancient spring festivals of Imbolc and Beltaine.

Dagda is connected with Newgrange passage grave in Ireland, as in the following verse, written in the *Book of Ballymote*:

'Behold the Sidh before your eyes,
It is manifest to you that it is a king's mansion,
Which was built by the firm Dagda,
It was a wonder, a court, an admirable hill.'

Another mound close to Newgrange is called *'The Tomb of Dagda'*. In Albion, one local deity, Hiccafrith, worshipped by the Iceni tribe, has been identified with Dagda, according to Ralph Whitlock; he also notes that the qualities of most giants, *'... can almost certainly be identified with him'* (Whitlock 1979, p. 45).

Freyr/Frey

Freyr comes from *'frawjaz'*, meaning *'lord'*, and is one of the most important gods of the Pagan Norse, and from whom we derive a day of the week - Friday. Featuring in many Scandinavian and Icelandic sagas, Freyr was associated with sacred kingship, virility and prosperity, sunshine and fair weather. He was sometimes a phallic fertility god, said to, *'bestow peace and pleasure on mortals'*. He was fierce in battle and is associated with a boar, which was forged by the dwarves to be his formidable ally, as this Nordic verse tells:

'The battle-bold Freyr rideth
First on the golden-bristled
Barrow-boar to the bale-fire
Of Baldr, and leads the people'.

In his role as a fertility god, Freyr needed a female counterpart to complete a divine couple, and fell for a female giantess called Gerð; He bargained away his sword to aquire her, so had to fight another giant, Beli, without it; he nevertheless slew his opponent with an antler. Eventually, Freyr was fated to fight the fire-giant Surtr, still without his sword, but this time he was defeated. The sword with which Surtr slew Freyr was the *'Sword of the Gods'* which Freyr had earlier bargained away to obtain Gerð. Is this sword a metaphor for the phallus, the shaft of life itself?

Norse god Freyr, with the *'Sword of the Gods'*. (Jacques Reich, 1901.)

It was said that Freyr's spirit entered the body of each King after death, leaving it when they were returned to the Earth. This mirrors the myths of Osiris and the Kings of Egypt; the Pharaohs were regarded as half man/half god, and after death would be transported to the stars by Osiris.

In 1904, a Viking statuette identified as Freyr was discovered on a farm at Lunda, in the province of Södermanland, Sweden. It features a cross-legged, bearded male with an **erect penis**. He is wearing a pointed cap and stroking his triangular beard. The statue is 9cm (3½ins.) tall and is displayed at the Swedish Museum of National Antiquities.

Fryer's link to the Giant is not just because Freyr was a phallic warrior god, but also because both his mother and wife were giants; keep it in the family, it would seem.

Odin/Wodin

Odin or Wodin was King of the Norse gods, who gave his name to Wednesday - *Woden's Day*. He was a shaman-like figure who envisioned the runes and carried fallen warriors to the Otherworld, known as Valhalla or Odin's Great Hall. He was the god of battle and magic, who ruled over the Berserkers, an elite band of devotional warriors who went naked into battle. As well as consulting the runes, Odin also used the decapitated head of a slain colossus, Mimor, for divination, reminding us of the oracular head of Bran (p. 82). He was a shape-shifter, who could change his form at will, which made him invincible in battle. Odin had only one eye, having pledged the other at the Well of Mimir in exchange for a knowledge-giving elixir. Such was his status that huge statues of him were erected at Uppsala in Sweden.

Odin does have links with giants, such as Suttung, who held a magical mead drink stolen from Odin by dwarves; later in the tale Odin seduces the giant's daughter, Gunnlod, to retrieve the mead. But when she agrees to him sipping a little, he drinks it all, changes into an eagle, and flies away. It was said that Odin needed no food and lived purely on mead and wine.

Instead of hunting dogs, Odin had two wolves and two raven familiars, the latter of which gifted him wisdom. Ravens and wolves are traditionally linked with battles and death. His other animal companion was his eight-legged horse Sleipnir, whom he prized highly as it carried him over both land and sea.

There are many sites in Britain linked to Odin/Wodin, such as Wainsdyke (*Woden's Dyke*) and Waden's Hill (*Woden's Hill*) in Wiltshire, and Wednesbury, in the West Midlands. Links have been suggested between Odin and the Long Man of Wilmington; the Finglesham Buckle shows Odin holding two spears (p. 11-12).

Norse god Odin, with his ravens and wolves, by Johannes Gehrts, 1901.

If the Cerne Giant does not depict Odin himself, then perhaps it is one of his famed Berserker warriors. Odin was certainly associated with hills and the sun, linking him to Mercury, as this 10th century poem concurs:

'Once there was a man who is Mercury.
The heathens had made him the highest of their gods…
And to the high hills brought him victims to slay.
The god was most honoured among all the heathen;
His name when translated to Danish is Odinn.'

This is fitting when discussing Odin, as he was the god of poetry, and in fact spoke only in verse. Memories of Odin echo in the name that the Saxons gave to the three stars of Orion's Belt - *'Frigg's Distaff'*. Frigg was Odin's wife and this is a rather humorous reference to his phallus. A link to the god Mithras is suggested as Odin came down to earth wearing a cloak. Odin is closely related to the World Ash, Yggdrasil, on which he hung in great pain for nine days until visioning the runes. The third root of the tree stood in heaven and beneath was the Well of Urdr, where the gods had their *'Judgement Seat'* (Knight 1998, p. 106). The spring at Cerne Abbas flows out of the surrounding hills, so perhaps Viking traders or raiders, who might not have created the Giant, nevertheless regarded the warrior scoured into the hill as their supreme god - Odin.

Linking with the World Tree theme, Paul Screeton relates the Giant to Yesod, one of the stations of the Qabbalah, the Tree of Life of Hebrew tradition, '... *whose image is of a beautiful, strong, naked man. What other than this is the Cerne Abbas giant? Yesod's correspondence in microcosm is the fertilising, reproductive organs, so handsomely displayed at Cerne Abbas'* (Screeton 1977, p. 201).

Thor/Taranis

This deity, who gives his name to Thursday (*Thor's Day),* is another example of the interaction between the Romans and the Celts, resulting in a hybrid sky-god (Green 1989, p. 117). Taranis (or Tanarus) is the local Celtic equal of Jupiter, the great sky god. As a thunder god he equates to Thor of Norse myths, and possesses similar symbols such as the wheel and thunderbolt; the wheel also represents the sun in Norse mythology (Green 1989, p. 116). Thor was colossal, with flaming red hair and fierce flashing eyes, whose main preoccupation was to protect both the gods and humans from giants.

Thor's hammer, the crashing of which gave rise to thunder, was called Mjölnir or Mjölner, and was distinctively shaped and one of the most fearsome weapons of Norse myth, capable of leveling mountains. Amulets in the shape of the hammer were worn for good fortune, and Germanic Iron Age people took to wearing Roman *'Hercules' Clubs'* as symbols of Donar, their equivilent of Thor. Athough generally recognized and depicted as a hammer, Mjölnir is sometimes referred to as an axe or *club* (Orchard 2002, p. 255).

In Britain, Thor is depicted on a pottery mould at the Roman military depot at Corbridge (image upper left), and on an altar at Chester is named as *Jupiter Optimus Maximus Tanarus* (Bédoyère 2002, p. 260). The lower image here is from Roman Gaul, and shows the god about to launch a flash of lightning. Thurshole, or *Thor's Hole,* in Staffordshire is named after the Norse god, as is Thurlaston, Thurmaston and Thurcaston, all in Leicestershire (Trubshaw 2011, p. 89). Thurstable, in Essex, literally means *'Thor's Pillar'.*

Mars

Although Mars was the Roman god of war, second only in importance to Jupiter, I discovered that he was initially associated with fertility and vegetation. The old Latin form is the word *Māworts,* however this name is from the Etruscan *Maris,* a god of vegetation not of war. The importance of Mars in establishing religious and cultural identity within the Roman Empire is indicated by the vast number of inscriptions identifying him with local deities, particularly in the western provinces. Virility as a kind of life force *(vis)* or virtue *(virtus)* is an essential characteristic of Mars.

Upper: Taranis/Thor, Corbridge, Northumberland.
Lower: Taranis/Jupiter, Roman Gaul, from Le Chatelet.

90

Mars' potential for savagery is expressed in his obscure connections to woodlands, and he may even have originated as a god of the wild, beyond the boundaries set by humans. In his book on farming, the Roman Cato invokes *Mars Silvanus* for a ritual to be carried out *in silva*, in the woods, an uncultivated place that if not held back could overtake land needed for crops. In peace times Mars was worshipped at springs and was guardian of a clan's culture. A group of statues that stood along the Appian Way showed Mars in the company of wolves, like Odin. Most gods received castrated male animals as sacrifices, just as goddesses took female victims; Mars, however, was one of the few male deities who regularly received fully intact male animals, usually bulls. In Roman art, Mars is shown as either bearded and mature, or else young, nude and clean-shaven. Even if naked, he often wears a helmet and a military cloak, and carries a spear as an emblem of his warrior nature.

The Celts readily adopted Mars, as he possessed qualities they admired, such as skill and bravery in battle. Mars and Nerine (his consort) were celebrated together at a festival held on March 23rd, around the spring equinox. Mars is named on innumerable Romano-British inscriptions and statues, in varying guises, such as at Bath, West Coker, Cirencester, Colchester Hastings, Chedworth, London, and Lydney Park (as Mars Nodens). Mars was blended with local gods, and epithets were attached. Thus we have Mars Teutatis, a fusion of Mars with the Celtic god Teutates/Toutatis, a deity worshipped in ancient Britain and Gaul, who is widely interpreted to be a tribal protector. In 2005 and 2012, silver rings inscribed with the letters *'TOT'* were discovered at Hallaton and Hockliffe, both in Bedfordshire; these inscriptions confirmed that the god being referred to was Toutatis/Totatis.

A statuette of the Roman god Mars, from Gaul. Now in Lyon Museum. (Wikipedia Common Licence.)

Mars Rigisamus means *'Greatest King'* or *'King of Kings'*. At West Coker in Somerset, a bronze figurine and an inscribed plaque dedicated to the god were found in a field, along with the remains of a building, perhaps a shrine. The figurine depicts a standing naked male figure with a close-fitting helmet; his right hand may have once held a weapon, and he probably also had a shield (both are now lost).

Mars Lenus is a god that makes an appearance at the Roman healing spa at Chedworth, in Gloucestershire, where two drawings, if crude, give us an insight of how the natives pictured Lenus in their minds; in one he displays his penis, in the other he holds a spear and an axe/club.

Mars Cocidius was a blending of the Celtic hunter/war god Cocidius with both Mars and Silvanus. He is referenced in Cumbria and at Hadrian's Wall.

Mars Smertrius/Smertrios is interesting as he appears and is named alongside Cernunnos on the Boatman's Pillar at Nôtre Dame (image below), dated 17AD. Here he is shown exuding power and strength as he wields a raised club! The god also appears at a spring sanctuary at Mohn, north of Tier, dedicated to Mars Smertrius.

This gives us an additional link between warrior gods and sacred springs, an association that may have existed at Cerne. The name Smertrius can be interpreted as *'Provider of Abundance',* taking us back again to divine fertility attributes.

The Gaulish god Smertrius, wielding a club, on the Boatman's Pillar, Nôtre Dame in Paris, dated 17AD.

Corineus

The story of Corineus is very much bound up wih Brutus, or Brute of Troy, the legendary Trojan hero known as the eponymous founder and first King of Britain. This legend first appears in *Historia Britonum*, a 9th-century historical compilation attributed to Nennius. Corineus comes across as Brutus' champion, a figure of great strength, who lacks fear and loves fighting giants. The Trojans win most of their battles as they make their way across Gaul, but are conscious that the Gauls have the advantage of numbers, so eventually retreat and set sail for Britain, then called Albion, where they land at Totnes. However, one early antiquarian considered that Portland, just 17 miles south of the Giant, was where Brutus and Corineus landed in 1149BC (a date that may possibly be too old).

Gary Biltcliffe speculates that the Cerne Giant may be Corineus: *'Perhaps the giant is a depiction of Corineus, his name later corrupted to Cerne, cut as a memorial to his famous battle on Portland'* (Biltcliffe 2009, p. 123). The name Cerne/Cernel may indeed be derived from Corineus, for in the Welsh language he is *'Ceryn'* (op. cit. p. 115). An early name for Rufus Castle on Portland is Giant's Castle, and the locality of the contest between Gogmagog and Corineus may have been close by, according to Biltcliffe. Portland has giant folklore, as do some other local sites, such as Maiden Castle, Badbury Rings and Spetisbury Rings. Portland folklore speaks of giant skeletons, over-sized coffins, and the island's inhabitants are known to be of large stature. It may be recalled that during his battle with the giant, three of Corineus' ribs were broken. This invites comparison with the Cerne Giant, who displays three ribs on either side of his chest.

Helis/Hel/Helith

The Helis, Hel, and Helith group of gods, and those including Bel, El and Belinus, may well be variations on a theme, local versions of the universal urge to deify the sun. It seems worthwhile, however, to look at these individually, if only in an effort to try and make sense of it all! This solar deity was known by many names: Helios, Helius, Ra, Apollo, Horus and Sol, and, in ancient Britain, variations of Helis/Helith and Hel, the local solar protector god. In Greece, the cult of Helios was widespread. The Island of Rhodes was sacred to him, where there stood the Colossus, a gigantic statue of a naked, Hercules-like god, through whose legs ships could sail. As the god of light, it was said that he saw everything and knew everything, and that nothing escaped his gaze.

You may recall that in 1754 Dr Richard Pocoke visited the Giant, identifying it thus: *'It is called the Giant and Hele',* and in 1764 William Stukeley reported that the Giant was known as Helis or Helith. In 1842, John Sydenham published his work *Baal Durotrigensis* in which he proposed that the name for Cerne in the Domesday Book, *Cernell*, could derive from *Cern He, 'the hill of Helis'.* He also noted that the sun was worshipped not far west of the Giant at Ellston Hill, at the foot of which was El Wood, El being an old name for the sun god: *'But God's messenger according to the precept of the Lord and the example of the apostles… cast upon them* [the people of Cerne Abbas] *a judgement they richly deserved, not by the prayer of an evil-speaker who desired the safety of all, but by divine justice and by way of things that were dreadful to the figure of Helia'.* This shows, at the very least, that Cerne was identified with the Pagan sun god *Helia*, who was almost certainly Helith or Helis. Historian John Hutchins stated that the Giant had previously been regarded as the idol Heil or Hegle, and that Heil was the Romano-British equivalent of Aesculapius, the *Preserver of Health.* This Roman god is depicted and named at Carlisle (Cumbria) and Binchester (Durham). It has been suggested that Helith was just a Dorset version of Hercules, whom we shall look at soon.

The god Helis may have been incorporated into French medieval stories about the Hierlekin or Helequin, a wild huntsman and god of the Underworld - *who bore a club*: *'… which may explain the use of Helith for the spectral club-wielding giant'* (Castleden 1996, p. 94).

So important was this solar deity that several British 'kings' and chieftains were named after him, such as Elanius, Elidure, Eldred, and Elihud (Biltcliffe 2009, p. 155-158). This list could also include Queen Eleanor of Aquitaine, who is associated with some sacred sites on the Belinus Line (Biltcliffe and Hoare 2012).

The Hellstone, the Bellingstone, the Hel Stone, Ellston Hill, Elwood, and Ellingstone, may all be Dorset relics of the worship of the solar god Hel/Helis/Bel/El – they were one and the same. Writing in 1921, V L Oliver, confirmed a tradition that the Bellingstone was once called the Hell or Hel Stone. A former well at Cerne was called Hel Well, and Upwey Well, near Weymouth, was once known as Hele Well. Of the dozen or so place names in Dorset that owe their origins to Helis, all lie within territory that would have fallen under the control of Maiden Castle.

From the 12th and 13th centuries we know that Helis, Hel, Helia or Helith was worshipped in the area, and this folklore has persisted to this day. Seeking an origin to this name also offers some alternatives to *sun*; in Cornish, *hellys* means *'hunted'*; in Welsh, *hel or hela* means *'to hunt',* whilst *helwyr* or *heliwr* translates as *'hunter'* or *'huntsman'.* Also in Welsh, the word *helw* means *'protection',* indicating that the god was the totem guardian of local clans, which is a role he may have fulfilled for the Durotriges. Perhaps when the Romans rolled up, he become Mars Helis or the local equivalent of Hercules: *'Roman Gods and their Greek equivalents, were identified with native Durotriges gods according to their characteristics'* (Putnam in Darvill et al 1996, p. 55). This local Durotriges fertility god, whatever his original name, was identified as Hercules or Mars by the Romans, just as the local goddess Sulis became Sulis-Minerva at Bath.

Writing in 1872, W Black attributed a Roman origin to Helis and the Giant: *'This remarkable object appears to me to be one of the ancient landmarks made by the Roman surveyors in Britain, serving uses analogous to the stones or circles of stones, and to the mounds...'.* Castleden concludes that the identity of the Iron Age god represented by the Giant, *'... has been under our noses all the time... he was Helis'* (Castleden 1996, p. 145).

Baal/Belinus/Bel

The cult of this major Assyrian, Babylonian and Phoenician god was already flourishing in the 3rd millennium BC, and was to have a big influence on the religious beliefs of many subsequent cultures. Myths speak of Baal as a *'storm god'*, the *'Rider in the Clouds'*; like Odin, Thor and Orion, Baal was associated with thunder, lightning and storms, and is often shown bearing a club or mace. Baal derives from the Sumerian verb AL, *'to bore'*, and when combined with the element BA, gives us the Latin words for *'drill'* and *'penis'*, and the word *'phallus'* (Allegro 1970, p. 24).

Paul Newman noted how the shape of the club, *'... mimics the shape of an oak leaf* (Newman 2009, p. 112). Baal once incarnated as an oak spirit, linking him to the tree stump-like club of the Giant.

The main creator god of the ancient Middle Eastern cultures was Bel, Beli or El, the father of Baal. The Assyrian and Phoenician god Beli was synonymous with Apollo of the Greeks and Horus in Egypt. Many temples around Europe had joint Belinus/Apollo dedications, and in

The god Baal on a Phoenician stela from Ras Shamrah, in the Middle East. He brandishes a club.

Britain Apollo was worshipped under the name of Belinus or Belus. The name of Apollo comes from the Greek *Apollymi (to destroy)* and, rather suggestively, *aeiballon (ever-shooting)*. He was a hunter and solar deity, some of his epithets being *'the sun'*, *'giver or bringer of light'*, and simply *'light'*. In his role as a hunter and god of archery, he is Apollo Aphetor *(to let loose)* and Apollo Argyrotoxus *(with silver bow)*. A temple to Apollo was erected at Pagan's Hill on the Mendips, not far from Cerne.

Bel was the Celtic sun god that had shrines from Aquileia on the Adriatic to Kirkby Lonsdale in England. A shrine dedicated to Belinus was built at Essarois near Châtillon-sur-Seine, in Burgundy, where a sanctuary was centred on a curative spring. This association of shrine and spring is relevant in relation to Cerne. Bel gave his name to Belgium, as well as the Belgae or Belgares tribe: *'They were a seafaring race and at Winchester the Romans renamed the British settlement Venta Belgarum, meaning 'Capital of the Belgares'... they were followers of Bel...'* (Biltcliffe and Hoare 2012, p. 81).

Variations on the Bel theme are numerous, such as Beli, the mythical ancestor and King of Britain, and the name of a Celtic thunder and lightning god. This god gave his name to many Kings and heroes, such as Beligius and, of course, King Belinus himself (op. cit. p. 155-158). Belinus was a great builder and erected London's first embankments of the Thames. The former southern gateway into the city was called Belinus' or Belin's Gate (Dawkins in Thorley 2012, p. 41). Some coins from the time of King Cunobelinus, dated 4-41AD, show a warrior god brandishing a club and holding a severed head from an extended arm; Cunobelinus clearly took his name from either the god Bel, or Belinus, the previous King. But why would Cunobelinus use a figure holding a club and a severed head unless it was an image he was familiar with? *Do these coins depict the Cerne Giant?*

So Belinus or Belenos (the solar god) derived from the Phoenician and Assyrian sun god Beli, Bel or Baal. He was a deity later worshipped in Gaul and Italy, where he is named in some 30 inscriptions, and across the Celtic areas of Austria, Spain and Britain. He is particularly associated with Cornwall, the ancient name for West Cornwall being Belerion *(Place of Bel)*. Sydenham suggests that the incoming Belgae introduced El or Bel to the Durotriges, the natives of Iron Age Dorset.

Beltaine was the god's festival, Bel-tene meaning *'good fire'*. It was a time when cattle and bulls were purified, giving us a link with Taurus, the constellation the sun occupies at Beltaine. Despite the cross fertilisation of deities, some see the gods Bel/El and Baal as having distinct core qualities: ' *... El means 'god', and Baal meant 'Lord'... the principle god El is almighty, but his son Baal (the Lord) takes up the dominant position... as 'Lord of the Earth'* (Knight and Lomas 1999).

Bel and Lugh were the most popular Celtic deities of hilltop temples and sanctuaries, later to be usurped by St Michael and St George, the Christian dragon slayers. Originally, the idea was not to slay the dragons, but to direct the fertilising powers of the land to the fields in summer; St George, in fact, means *'earth tiller'* (Mann, 2002, p. 86). This conflict between hero and dragon, good and evil, was an update of ancient myths telling of the sun's annual passage between summer and winter.

The Belinus Line is the name of the north-south British alignment recently studied in great detail by Biltcliffe and Hoare (2012); along the line Bel's worship was widespread. Biltcliffe and Hoare point out the confusion that has existed amongst researchers, who have confused sites connected with King Belinus and those of the sun god Bel or Belinus (op. cit. p. 12). As far north as Peebles in Scotland, a standing stone at the aptly named Bellanrigg marks a cult centre to Bel (op. cit. p. 382-3).

In Dorset, places derived from the god are Belchalwell, Elworth and Belstone. Concerning the Cerne Giant in particular, an account of 1865 records folklore that the Cerne Giant used to, *'... stride over to the opposite hill, where Belchalwell nestles under Bulbarrow... claiming this district as part of his own domains, because they bear his own name'* (Cutler 1865, p. 65). These are probably places where Bel or a variant of this god was once worshipped.

Beelzebub/Ogmios

The name Beelzebub comes from the Hebrew *Ba'al and the* Arabic *Ba'al az-Zubab*, and means *'Lord of the Flies'* or *'Lord of Heavenly Dwellings'*. He was a Semitic deity that was worshiped in the Philistine city of Ekron, but later, in Christian and Biblical texts, Beelzebub appears as a pseudonym for Satan. In the *Testament of Solomon*, a Hellenistic Jewish text with Christian corruptions, *Beelzebul* was one of the demons whom Solomon tackled; he appeared as the demons' prince, but was said to have formerly been a leading heavenly angel, associated with Hesperus, the Greek name for the planet Venus. According to 16th century occultist Johann Weyer, Beelzebub opposed evil and led a revolt against Satan. Interestingly, he survives today in German folklore as Rubezaal, a character *who brandishes an oak tree as a club*. This connects with the oak-leaved shape of the club already discussed concerning Dagda and Baal/Bel.

It may well be that the Cerne Giant was *later* regarded as Beelzebub, for a character bearing that name features in medieval literature. This Beelzebub makes an appearance in medieval Christmas mumming plays, the Iron Age god now denigrated into a club-wielding demon, as in this local verse:

'Here comes I, Beelzebub,
Under my arm I carries my club,
And in my hand a frying pan –
Don't you think I'm a jolly old man'

Rodney Castleden surmises that the local mummers may have had Beelzebub in mind when the Trendle was named the *Frying Pan*: *'... and that the four lines were meant as a specific reference to the Cerne Giant'* (Castleden 1996, p. 83). Not far away, local villagers at Burton Bradstock annually performed mumming plays that involved a Beelzebub, which had four legs, a reptilian tail, and puffed smoke!

Is this Iron Age club-wielder, from Gaul, the god Ogmios, or is it Beelzebub? (Wikipedia Common Licence.)

The mention of a club not only links him to Hercules, but also to Ogmios, or Ognion, a Celtic hero-figure. But whereas Hercules was a mortal man with superhuman powers, Ogmios seems to have been a god. He might have derived from Ogma, a champion of the Tuatha de Danann in Irish mythology, and the 'Og' element may also link him with Gogmagog, and Dogbury Hill near Cerne. The image shown above is a Gaulish carving from the Museum Aix-en-Provence.

Lud/Lugh/Nodens

The god Lud is a solar deity, the *'Light Bearer'*, also known variously as Lugh, Llew, Lug, Lugus, or Lludd. He first appears in Portugal around 700BC and was replaced by Mercury or Nodens as the Romans spread across Europe. Root words concerning his name suggest *lightning* and *raven,* an association we have seen with other deities. Lugh is the god of the harvest, metalwork and blacksmiths; he is known as *'Lugh of the Long Arm'* or *'long-handed'* and in Wales as *'Llew of the skilled hand'*.

Two early British Kings, Lud and Lugdus, took their name from the god and place names connected with him are widespread across Europe and Britain, including Lothians, Louth and Luton. London (*Caer Lud - Lud's Town*) was named after either King Lud or the god Lud; Ludgate Hill is a remnant of these times, where once stood a sanctuary associated with Arianrhod (aka Ariadni), the feminine counterpart of Lud (Dawkins in Thorley 2012, p. 39). The River Lea in London is Lugh's River, and it rises from springs at Waulid's Bank, a Neolithic site where tradition says Lugh took the waters to receive his divine powers (Louise Coe, op. cit. p. 126). It is interesting that this site stands on the famous St Michael Line. This Cornwall to East Anglia alignment is usually described as lining up with sunrise on Beltaine (the festival of Brigid). However, the annual cycle of the sun ensures that it also aligns with sunrise in early August, which is the old festival of Lughnasad – Lugh or Lud's festival (later Christianised into Lammas). Anthony Thorley reminds us that the St Michael sites that define the line would previously have been associated with Lugh, and he proposes that we might rename it the *'Lugh-Brigid Line'* (op. cit. p. 118).

Lughnasad festivals were later taken over by those of St James and St Anne, held during the last week in July. It was by an incredible 'coincidence' that the Olympic Games of 2012 were held July 27th – Aug 12th, during Lughnasad.

The Milky Way was known as *'Lugh's Chain';* concerning his name *'Lugh of the Long Arm',* was Lud/Lugh once seen as the constellation Orion, whose stellar arm stretches upwards? Is Lud therefore the Giant at Cerne, whom I shall demonstrate later is aligned with the rising of an ancient Stargate in Orion (see Chapter 13). Paul Newman, the knowledgeable writer on hill figures, states that, *'... the Long Man's origins are essentially Celtic, like those of the Cerne Giant, and relate to the cult of Lugh or Lugus...'*

Nodens/Nudd has been proposed as an equivalent to Lud. In Glastonbury, the local deity Gwyn ap Nudd means *'Gwyn, son of Nudd',* whilst the Romans knew the god as

Nodens-Cunomaglos, with hunting dog, Southwark Cathedral, London.

Nodens *'the catcher',* signifying he was a hunter. Like Lud, Nodens/Nudd was the Romano-British god of the harvest. Today, we still have a vestige of Nodens worship with the saying that we journey to the *'Land of Nod'* when we sleep.

During WWII a skillet handle depicting Nodens was ploughed up at Hod Hill, to the east of the Giant. The image shows him with a hare in one hand and a knobbled **club** in the other, with his feet turned sideways – just like the Giant! This scene suggests that it may not have been a cloak or severed head that formerly hung from the Giant's left hand, but a hare, and would therefore identify him as the god Nodens. Later we shall discuss the association of the Giant with the constellation Orion; in the winter night sky Orion, like Nodens, is accompanied by a hare, the constellation Lepus. Nodens may also mean *'the cloud-maker',* further connecting him with Orion, who was seen to instigate storms and the rainy winter season.

The Temple of Nodens at Lydney Park, in Gloucestershire, was a major Roman centre of worship, where he was revered as Nodens-Mars and Nodens-Silvanus. Nodens may also have been associated with healing, because his dogs, as well as helping his hunting activities, may have aided in other ways, *'... because dogs were considered to help in healing by licking afflicted wounds'* (Bédoyère 2002, p. 200).

As already touched upon, local Dorset author Rodney Legg made out a large dog immediately to the north of the Giant in 1976; the axis of the club in fact pointed down to him and Legg indicated that the Giant may represent Nodens. Chris Street has identified *Noden's Well* at Trent Park in Enfield, North London (Street 2009), and in Southwark Cathedral is a wonderful carving of Nodens, or possibly his local equivalent Cunomaglos (image above). He is also mentioned on an altar stone found at Nettleton Shrub, Wiltshire, where a spring shrine was built by the Romans, and the local Celtic god transformed into Apollo Cunomaglos, which means *'Hound Lord'.*

Nearby is the massive 58m (190ft) long Lugbury chambered long barrow, surely named after the same god. You may recall the rock-throwing contest between two giants involving Norden Hill, which may be a corruption of *Nodens Hill*.

Priapus/Hermes

These deities have been regarded as one and the same by many scholars (Westropp and Wake, 1875, p. 50). Priapus is usually shown with an oversized phallus, and at Pompeii amorous images of him were painted on the walls of brothels. His fertilising aspect also made him an agricultural god (Bédoyère 2002, p. 26).

In Britain, Priapus is named on an inscription at the Roman fort at Birrens, near Hadrian's Wall, where a relief depicts a horned god and the words: *'The phallus of Priapus'*.

Dr Richard Pococke visited the Giant in 1754 stating, *'It seems to be Hercules... but it is with such indecent circumstances as to make one conclude it was also Priapus. It is to be supposed that this was an ancient figure of worship and one would imagine that the*

The phallic god Priapus, on a painting at Pompeii. (Wikipedia Common Licence.)

people would not permit the monks to destroy it'. Dowser Guy Underwood noted: *'No scholar appears to have suggested identification with Priapus, whom the Orphics identified with Helios, and whom was regarded as the promoter of fertility'* (Underwood 1969, p. 153). Paul Newman concurs: *'The qualities exhibited by Priapus may be applied to the Cerne Giant. His massive oak-leaf club protects and defends the fertile vale of Cerne'* (Newman 2009, p. 87).

In Greek mythology, the equivalent of Priapus was Hermes, god of boundaries and exchange (popularly the *messenger* god), considered to be a phallic deity by his association with wayside pillars called Herms, which feature phalli. This image (left) is from Siphnos, dated c. 520BC, whilst another is shown with Pan on p. 83. The staff or rod of Hermes, the caduceus, usually has two entwined serpents, and is said to be the axis around which the universe revolved. As Hermes was a phallic god, we must ask the question as to whether the Giant's club is a reshaping of a caduceus, symbol of Hermes and Mercury. He occurs on Romano-British inscriptions at several sites (Bédoyère 2002, p. 266) and the caduceus usually points to the heavens, like the Giant's club. The caduceus is also found in ancient cultures in Mesopotamia, Europe, India and in the Americas. Whereas the rod of Hermes usually had two serpents,

A Greek boundary stone called a Herm, named after the god Hermes. (Wikipedia Common Licence.)

that of the god Aesculapius had only one. Hermes is also considered to be comparable to the Egyptian god Thoth (Gilbert 2005, p. 30).

If these connections might be thought to be too far-fetched, too alien to Britain, let me add that Aesculapius/Askelpios is named on Romano-British altars at Binchester, Carlisle, Chester, Lanchester and Maryport (Bédoyère 2002, p. 243). Images of Mercury were found at the temple at Lamyatt Beacon (Somerset), some holding a caduceus; this is only a few miles north of Cerne.

Greek statue of Hercules, 5th century BC.

Hercules

Scholars and antiquarians have long regarded this great and popular hero of Greek mythology as one of the leading candidates for the Giant. Worshipped by the Phoenicians as the sea-god Melkarth, he was first recorded as Heracles around 500BC by the Greek poet Panyasis, and later became Hercules to the Roman Empire. In Greek art and literature Heracles was presented as an enormously strong man of moderate height, his characteristic weapons being the bow and the club. Vase paintings demonstrate the unparalleled popularity of Heracles, his fight with a lion being depicted many hundreds of times. Writing around 44BC, the Greek Herodotus wrote, *'The result of these researches is a plain proof that the worship of Heracles is very ancient'*. Even though images of the strongman rarely show an erect phallus, John Allegro says that Hercules was in fact named after the size of his phallus, as the Greek *'Ura-Gal-Us'* translates as, *'large, erect, penis'* (Allegro 1970, p. 218).

Hercules had to partake twelve labours, which included slaying a lion, a bull and a multi-headed serpent (the Hydra), all with the help of a two-headed dog, Orthus; these twelve adventures represent the sun's annual passage through the zodiacal signs. We shall return soon to the two-headed dog, as this may possibly represent the constellations Canis Major and Canis Minor.

Hercules was the favourite son of Zeus, and in one myth the pair defeat a tribe of earth-born giants threatening Olympus. In another tale, as he was being suckled by his mother Hera, she spilt some of her milk, which formed the Milky Way; we shall see later how the Milky Way rises out of Cerne Giant at certain times of the year. Hercules is associated with the sun, as he is described as fiery, with golden hair and glowing eyes. He was certainly an amorous hero, as he slept with the 50 daughters of King Thespios in a single night. This number comes up again with Orion, who sired 50 sons with Kephisides. Such vitality would certainly link Hercules with the Giant, who always appears 'ready for action' and quite capable of such a feat.

The so-called *Hercules' Clubs* are Iron Age amulets, which appear from 2nd - 3rd century AD, and from whence spread over

The Willingham Fen Mace, an Iron Age votive object.

99

the Roman Empire (including Britain); they are mostly made of gold, 3-5cm (1-2ins.) long, and shaped like clubs. A specimen found in Germany bears the inscription 'DEO HERCULI'. Indeed, Tacitus mentions a special affinity of the Germans for Hercules, stating, *'... they say that Hercules, too, once visited them; and when going into battle, they sing of him first of all heroes'.*

Hercules is named on several Romano-British inscriptions, such as at Silchester, Carlisle and York (Bédoyère 2002, p. 255) and he was cast in bronze at South Shields. Some of the stone carvings of Hercules certainly resemble the Giant. One at Corbridge shows his legs spread apart as he holds a club over his head (below left). A knobbled bronze votive mace found in 1857 at Willingham Fen in Cambridgeshire follows a Roman design, with added indigenous iconography, such as animal heads,

Romano-British carvings of Hercules. Left: from Corbridge, Northumberland (after Ross, 1967). Right: Hercules with the Hydra, on an altar at Whitley Castle.

anthropomorphic figures and a wheel at the club's base (image previous page).

In a letter to the Society of Antiquities, dated 1764, antiquarian William Stukeley thought the Giant to be a figure of, *'... an Hercules'*, and speculated that this particular Hercules was a Phoenician chieftain who led the first colonial expedition to Britain in search of tin. And it was Pitt-Rivers, archaeologist and former owner of the Giant, who commented that figures of Hercules in the British Museum, *'... have always the club in the right hand; it is usually knotted. The left hand is usually turned out like the Cerne Giant but it nearly always has the lion skin hanging on it. The private parts are always shown'* (Thompson 1977, p. 72).

Prof Stuart Piggott was a strong advocate that the Giant represented Hercules (Piggott 1932). He thought it to be part of a cult promoted by Emperor Commodus; following his victory in Northern Britain in 187AD, the Emperor declared himself to be Hercules incarnate, and coinage minted during his reign depicts the hero. Piggott suggested that Roman soldiers might have carved the Giant as a tribute to him, to direct people up to the Trendle, the Romano-British temple on the hilltop. However, this would date the Giant 187-193AD, the year Commodus was assassinated. There was of course the nearby Roman town of Durnovaria (Dorchester), and several

Roman villas and shrines across Dorset, where Hercules would have been a household name.

It has been suggested that anomalies detected under the Giant's left hand may be remnants of Hercules' missing lion skin. But Castleden does make the valid point that the Romans did not make hill figures at any of their other shrines in Britain or on mainland Europe, and concludes that *'... it is likely that they had nothing to do with the creation of the hill figure in Dorset'* (Castleden 1996, p. 95). It is more likely that the Giant was the image of an indigenous god, a construct of the local Iron Age tribe, the Durotriges.

As a potential candidate, one problem with Hercules is that he is never shown with an erection. If anything, he is generally depicted with small genitals, in keeping with classical tradition. Rodney Castleden comments on this: *'The Giant could therefore only be Hercules if the erect phallus was added later, but to argue that would be desperate'* (in Darvill et al 1999, p. 45).

Roman statuette from Tunis showing a suggestive Hercules holding his penis.

However, archaeologist Bill Putnam reminds us of the changes at Uffington: *'... it is important to remember that recent study of the Uffington White Horse shows that substantial changes may have taken place to the Giant's appearance over the centuries'* (op. cit. p. 55). John North also raises the issue of the lack of a lion skin, which Hercules often holds, but he does not see this as a critical issue, as some have done: *'... for in some early representations [of Hercules] he carries neither club nor skin. This is so on the stone star sphere known as the Farnese Globe'* (North 1996, p. 219). This globe, at present in Naples, dates from the 1st or 2nd century AD, and is a Roman copy of a Greek original. Also, in the two images on the previous page, both attributed as being Hercules, he carries neither a lion's head nor a lion's skin. It is possible that the 'lost' cloak of Hercules, which may have been under the Giant's left arm, was added to the figure by the Romans, and when the legions departed

Britain it was, *'... left to heal over'* (Newman 2009, p. 94).

One last possible link between the Giant and a sexually proactive Hercules is a Roman statuette from Tunis, which has the strongman holding his penis in a very suggestive manner (image above). Hercules was a man's man, it would seem, explaining why he was so popular with Roman legionnaires. This also confirms the ancient association between aggression/battle and displays of genitalia. Hercules was not adverse to sexual activities, as told in various myths: he seduced Auge, a priestess of Athene; he obtained the hand in marriage of Deianeira, daughter of Oceanus; he bore nearly eighty sons; and he captured the Minos Bull, a symbol of virility and fertility. Although Hercules/Heracles was the personification of strength, his chief role was that of protector, someone to be called upon when danger threatened. This 'tribal protector' role has been assigned to the Cerne Giant.

To summarise, Paul Newman, Rodney Legg and Rodney Castleden see the Giant not as Hercules, but as an indigenous Celtic god, to whom Hercules was identified with following the arrival of the Romans. As I have shown, the ithyphallic symbolism of the Giant was part of a tradition of phallic worship that was already thousands of years old prior to the arrival of Imperial Rome.

Gary Biltcliffe concurs: *'The Giant was placed there by people who displaced those of the Bronze Age. But the Durotriges were unlike the neighbouring tribes in that they wanted to remain separate and not lose their identity'* (Gary Biltcliffe, pers. comm.). Perhaps the Giant was an icon that gave them their identity.

I will describe next, in some detail, the exciting concept that the Giant has links with Orion and his local manifestation in Britain, Gwyn ap Nudd.

*'A great thought begins by seeing something differently,
with a shift of a mind's eye.'*
(Albert Einstein)

102

Chapter 8.
Orion, Osiris
and Gwyn ap Nudd

*'Myth is a traditional tale with secondary, partial reference
to something of collective importance'.*
(Walter Burkett.)

In this chapter I shall attempt to weave together the myths of three different deities, in an effort to tell the story of an archetypal character who, I believe, is vital to understanding the hidden meanings of the Cerne Giant. We shall look at three prime suspects in our quest to identify him: Osiris, god of the Egyptians; Orion, the giant hunter of Greek and Roman myths; and Gwyn ap Nudd, the mythical deity closely associated with Glastonbury. This is a necessary study in order to appreciate the discoveries I will reveal in subsequent chapters concerning the hitherto shrouded secrets of the Giant's links to the heavens.

Once again we shall call upon legends, some of which go back over 3000 years. Myths were once science made manifest, anecdotes that contained knowledge of how people related to the universe around them. Cultural knowledge was once collected and extolled through myth: *'Manifold dimensions of the phenomenal world were brought into relation with human feeling, and the mystic bond that unified humanity with nature could be explored'* (Baring and Cashford 1991, p. 233).

Osiris/Orion

Orion is the well-known constellation that adorns our winter skies, and his association with Man's mythology goes back to prehistory. He has been positively identified with the Egyptian god Osiris, and George Scott concluded that, *'... it is impossible to overestimate the importance of this particular deity in Egyptian mythology'* (Scott 1966, p. 135). Adrian Gilbert considers that, *'The story of Orion the Hunter, an archetype deeply rooted within the human subconscious, goes back to the very origins of civilisation'* (Gilbert 2005, p. 181).

Egyptians believed that Pharaohs went up to the heavens after death and that their guide to the afterlife, Osiris, was the constellation Orion, sometimes called Sahu. In sacred Egyptian writings called the Pyramid Texts, we read:

'O King, you are this Great Star, the Companion of Orion, who traverses the sky with Orion, who navigates the Duat [Other worlds] with Osiris... In your name of Dweller in Orion, with a season in the sky and a season on the earth, O Osiris, turn your face and look upon this King, for your seed which issued from you is effective... O King, the sky conceives you with Orion... behold he (the king) has come Orion, behold Osiris has become Orion'. This connects fertility with Orion in its manifestation as Osiris. The appearance of Orion marked the changing of the seasons, as a further Eqyptian text demonstrates:

'Osiris! You went away, but you have returned,
you fell asleep, but you have awakened,
you died, but you live again.'

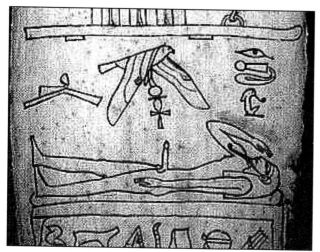

Papyrus showing Isis, in the form of a bird, resurrecting an ithyphallic Osiris.

As they are both phallic gods, we must make a distinction between Min and Osiris (p. 79). The former is the god of the harvest, the giver of the vitality of life. Osiris' gift is revitalization and resurrection; they are related, however, as the crops begin to flourish when Osiris/Orion becomes visible.

The relevant story regarding Osiris (god and creator) and Isis, his wife and universal mother, needs to be told, as it is the origin of the association between phalli and Osiris. After killing Osiris, his brother Typhon dismembered his body and the evil usurper Set scattered the parts across the land. Isis set out to recover the portions of her husband's body and she succeeded in her task, all except his penis, which had been cast into the Nile and swallowed by a fish. One story says that she founded a temple to Osiris wherever she found a missing body part, and that the most sacred of these, at Abydos (dated 1291-1278BC), was built where Isis found his head. As the phallus was never recovered, Isis ordered that ithyphallic images should take pride of place in temples; the magnificently elevated Egyptian obelisks represent the phallus of Osiris. It was later left to Osiris' son, Horus, to obtain justice against Set, who was banished by the Council of Gods. Through divine magic, and with the help of Thoth, Anubis and Horus, Isis later restored her husband's body back to life. Osiris festivals were often orgiastic, and were the origin of the famed Greek Dionysian orgies.

Because of this myth, Osiris became the Egyptian god of the dead, who stood in the Hall of Judgement, deciding whether people were worthy of journeying to the Afterworld. We shall look at this aspect in more detail in Chapter 13, regarding Osiris' key role of guiding the departed into the Stargate. Because of his association with the afterlife, Osiris is also the god of rebirth and fertility, and he is often depicted with a green face – he is the Egyptian green man! This links him to the Celtic god

Cernunnos, as well as to Pan and other nature spirits. Osiris was also known as 'the good king', mirroring the British god Dagda, who was 'the good god'.

According to the Greek Diodorus, writing in the 1st century BC, Osiris was the eldest son of Chronos. This god was the 'Lord of Time', the Grim Reaper, who comes to claim us all. Gilbert suggests that he was originally Orion. The feast of Saturnalia was held on December 25th, just as Orion is rising at sunset, and the staff that Orion carries could easily be seen as a Chronos' scythe. This date is also the birthday of both Bacchus and Mithras, and the date on which the Phoenician god Melkarth woke from winter hibernation in a sacred cave.

In terms of Orion the constellation, the Egyptians sometimes referred to it as Sahu, such as in the tomb of Nakhi and in the *Book of the Dead*. In all the Egyptian depictions I have seen of Orion, he is walking with legs slightly bent – as is the Cerne Giant! Orion-Sahu is shown on the western wall at Teotuhuacan, brandishing a mace- or club-like weapon (images p. 143 & 158).

Osiris was originally a nature/vegetation god, often worshipped in the form of Apis, the fertility bull. The story of his resurrection takes him full circle, as he represents the annual demise of vegetation and its subsequent rebirth. Inscriptions to Serapis, the Romano-British equivalent of Apis, were found at York and Kirkby Thore (Bédoyère 2002). The importance of Apis the bull in British mysticism is confirmed by its depiction in the grounds of the former Rosicrucian centre at Biddulph Grange, in Staffordshire (Biltcliffe & Hoare 2012, p. 227-8).

It is not so outlandish to suggest that the cult of Osiris, and therefore veneration of Orion, could have made it to Dorset. Many units of the Roman army and cavalry were posted to Egypt, some of which later spent time in Britain (Bédoyère 2002, p.170-1). The first mounted cohort of the Thracians, for instance, was in Britain several times between 122-208AD; this unit was also posted in Egypt, and in fact Egyptians were recruited into the Roman army. The cult of Isis came over with the Romans, proven by the fact that she is named on a stone found in London bearing the inscription: LONDINI AD FANVM ISIDIS or 'From London at the temple of Isis'. Small artefacts had hinted at Isis worship in Roman London, but it was not until the mid-1970's that two altars bearing 3rd century AD inscriptions, celebrating the restoration of an Isis temple, were found at Blackfriars: 'London will have been the home to the sacred procession of Isis in which her devotees scattered the road with flowers and perfume' (Bédoyère 2002, p. 173). Even today a stretch of the Thames is called the Isis.

I am indebted to Bob Trubshaw, who drew my attention the image of Osiris below, in his book *Singing up the Country* (Trubshaw 2012). It comes from the Hor-Uben B Papyrus, dated c.1000BC, and shows a resurrected ithyphallic Osiris reclining on the slopes of the hill of Khepri, a primeval mound linked with creation myths. A phallic god

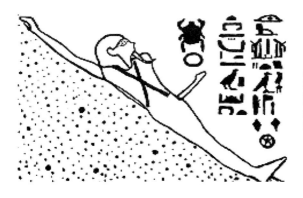

A resurrected ithyphallic Osiris reclining on a hillside, from a papyrus dated c.1000BC.
(After Mysliwiec 1998).

exposing himself, reclining on a hillside - now where have we seen that before!

In Greek myths, Orion was a giant huntsman, the son of Zeus and Gaia, and is mentioned in the oldest surviving works of Greek writing, c. 7-8th century BC. In Homer's *Odyssey,* Odysseus has an Underworld encounter with Orion, a great slayer of beasts who hunted with a bronze club and a bow. Hesiod speaks of Orion as a constellation that was used to mark out the year, and also tells a story of Orion the hunter-hero walking on the waves of the Aegean Sea; he wades shoulder deep in another myth. I wonder if this is due to the brightness of Orion's stars, which were literally seen to rise from the sea – Orion walks on water! The constellation was clearly invaluable for sea navigation: *'To people sailing in northern latitudes in winter, Orion was so important'* (Gary Biltcliffe, pers comm.).

Recklessness and virility are characteristics attached to Orion. In *Dionysus* (1976), Karl Kerenyi portrays Orion as a shamanic hunter, who had survived from Minoan times, whilst others have seen him as a violent lover of the Divine Huntress. Orion was said to have sired 50 sons by Kephisides, which mirrors Hercules, who slept with the 50 daughters of King Thespios. One myth says Orion chased Pleione, the mother of the Pleiades, for seven years until Zeus placed them all in the sky. In another account, Orion is said to have raped Artemis, as well as Opis, one of her band of huntresses. In yet a further tale, Orion breaks into the bedroom of Oenopion's daughter, Aero, and rapes her, although justice is swift when he is blinded.

Detail from Nicholas Poussin's painting *'Landscape with blind Orion seeking the sun'.* Cedalion stands on the giant's shoulders, guiding him towards the sun. (Wikipedia Common Licence.)

During a journey to Crete, Orion threatened to hunt down all the creatures of the world, but Mother Earth objected, and sent the goddess Artemis to stop him; the goddess killed him with an arrow from her bow, although another version says she sent a giant scorpion to kill him. Afterwards, she pleaded with Zeus to have him placed amongst the stars as a memorial to his death, which he did, along with the scorpion.

The close association of Orion to Taurus (to which it is adjacent to in the sky) is born out by one version of Orion's birth; the gods ejaculate into the hide of a bull and then bury it in the earth. Ten months later it is dug up and Orion is found within - he is therefore earthborn. In another version, it was Dionysus (an ithyphallic god) who sent satyrs to put Orion in a deep sleep so he could be blinded. To regain his sight, Orion was told he had to travel to the east, and did so with the help of Cedalion (or Cyclops in one variation), who sits on his shoulders to guide him. They eventually meet Helios, the sun, who restores his vision. This may refer to the invisibility of Orion during summer months; the Greek Corina sang of Orion, *'... conquering all the land of the dawn',* surely referring to the reappearance of its stars in dawn skies in the autumn.

A Roman copy of a Greek statute of Orion. He holds a bird, a deer and antlers around his waist.

Regarding the above story, Adrian Gilbert links Orion with St Christopher, a 'wild man' and a giant of a human being. Carrying Jesus (the solar god) across the river on his shoulders is mirrored by Orion carrying Cedalion; Orion seemingly 'carries' the sun when it is over the constellation in May. Orion's outstretched hand steadies the sun, just as St Christopher held the infant Jesus. It is appropriate that Orion is 'sandwiched' by the path of the sun and the Milky Way on one side, and on the other the constellation Eridanus, *the River*. It will be shown how Eridanus rises out of Cerne's sacred spring just as Orion rises!

In his work, *Greek Myths* (1955), Robert Graves views Oenopion, the character who blinded Orion, as the perennial 'Year-King' who, at the stage where the King pretends to die at the end of his term, appoints Orion as his substitute to die in his place. Thus the solar hero is caught up in a daily cycle, blinded by his enemies at dusk only to regain his sight at dawn. To the Greeks, Orion reached the status of a heroic cult figure, the super hero of his day. Homer calls him, *'... illustrious Orion, the tallest and most beautiful of men'*. Even though he hunts animals, he respects them and is their lord, and in some Sumerian myths even releases some from his snares. The name Orion probably came from the Greek *ouron,* meaning *'to make water'*, which relates to the constellation heralding the rainy season, and Orion was regarded as the personification of a storm by the Roman poet Statius. The Phoenicians and Hittites

The Roman-Egyptian Manze Globe; Orion (right centre) faces up to Taurus with a club.

had a weather-god that held lightning bolts in his left hand and was carried along on a chariot pulled by bulls. This links Orion with the European weather/thunder gods, and with Taurus.

In yet another myth, Orion is stung by a scorpion. This no doubt arose from observations that the constellation Orion dominates the winter skies when the sun is in Scorpio. This extract is from the Greek astronomical poem *Aratus Phaenomena* (3rd century BC): *'The winding River will straightaway sink in fair flowing ocean at the coming of Scorpios, whose rising puts to flight even the mighty Orion'*. Orion's death at the hands of the moon goddess Artemis was said to be the cause of winter storms. This is just one of many myths demonstrating how people were linking the Underworld,

Mankind and the heavens; 19th century scholar Erwin Rodhe viewed Orion as an example of how the Greeks erased the boundaries between the gods and humankind; if mortal Orion could reach the stars, then perhaps they could.

Orion was a major cult in many parts of Greece. A temple said to be the tomb of Orion was built at Mount Tanagra, where his festival was held, and his image appears on a tomb frieze at Taranto (c. 300BC). Romans also related to the heroic tales of Orion, and in Greece, especially, the hero continued to be revered after the rise of the Roman Empire. A temple at Messina in Sicily was dedicated to Orion, who was said to have built some of the island's cities and temples, as well as being responsible for the shape of the Straits of Sicily; a fountain depicting Orion can be found in Messina (image right).

Orion's Fountain at Messina, Sicily.

Surviving Greek images of Orion are rare, and sometimes difficult to identify, as a club-wielding figure might be Hercules. This link to Orion is furthered by the fact that accounts tell us that Hercules had a shield on which were images of Perseus, Draco, and Orion with his two dogs. Roman art yields a few good examples, such as a 4th century bas-relief on a wall in the Porto region of Naples, and on Underworld scenes at Esquiline Hill (50-40BC).

The *Manze Globe* is a small bronze-brass celestial globe, 11cms (4ins.) in diameter, and dated c.150-220 AD (image above). It is believed to have originated in Roman Egypt and shows Orion bearing a club or sword. It is currently in the Römisch-Germanischen Zentral Museum in Manze (Germany). I shall return to this later, concerning the Orion Stargate.

The Giant as Orion/Osiris

I have been an amateur astronomer since childhood, and early on in my studies into the Giant I was already considering the possibility that he might be a representation of the constellation Orion. Research revealed that I was not alone in my suspicions, and that others had been thinking along similar lines.

I had already formulated these ideas when I found an extract from *Dorset Magazine* (1978, 54, p. 32), which contains a letter from Philip J Grant of Bournemouth, in which he noted, almost in passing, the similarity between the shape of the Giant and the constellation Orion.

On Graham Hancock's website, William Glyn-Jones states, *'Of all the figures of mythology there is none that matches the Cerne Giant half so well as Orion the Hunter... Cerne's feet point sideways while his shoulders point forwards, and in this respect his image conforms to the Egyptian artistic rules.'* He continues, *'The role of Orion in British folk tales is played out by Herne the Hunter but in Celtic mythology he becomes Mabon, the deity of the winter sun who is the only god who can handle the hunting dog Drudwyn'.*

The *English Movement* website proclaims*: 'The figure of Herne the Hunter (Orion) can be found in the Cerne Abbas Giant, the name 'Cerne' being an equivalent to the English 'Herne' and which means 'Horn'.* On his *Hidden Record* website, Wayne Hershel also links the Giant with Orion. On the blog *'Elphin of Angleland',* the blogger likewise sees the Giant as Orion; he also overlays the Great Pyramid over Southern England, with the Giant at the end of the Orion Shaft. Also online, Robin Allott has noted the similarity of Orion with both the Giant and the Wilmington Long Man.

Perhaps way back in 1808, Dorset poet William Holloway was giving us a clue when he published his poem *'The Giant of Trendle Hill'* (see page 29). In one section he describes the Giant's arrival: *'Now evening flung her yellow rays, across the Cerne's calm flood'.* The river was in flood, which would link with autumnal-winter storms, traditionally associated with the appearance of the constellation, and link with the

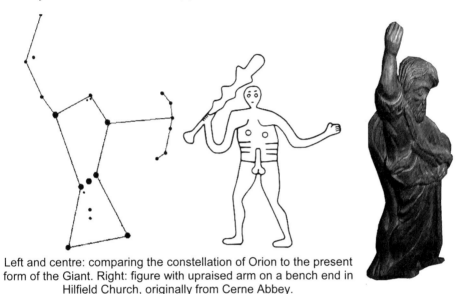

Left and centre: comparing the constellation of Orion to the present form of the Giant. Right: figure with upraised arm on a bench end in Hilfield Church, originally from Cerne Abbey.

tales of the mythical hero.

One direct comparison between the Giant and Orion *in print* is in Adrian Bailey's excellent book, *The Caves of the Sun*. I came across it, by the way, *after* I had already spoken of my theory at my 2012 *Convention of Alternative Archaeology* in Wiltshire; it was indeed encouraging to see that someone else had independently arrived at the same conclusion: *'What is interesting is that the Giant closely resembles the outline of Orion, the constellation that rules the sky in winter, during the months of rain, and which in ancient times was associated with springs'* (Bailey 1998, p. 234). Bailey is implying a link between Orion, the Giant and the spring at Cerne, an association I touched upon previously. Bailey also notes the myth regarding Hercules and the springs of Lerna, as part of his underlying premise that mythic solar gods are linked with the creation/appearance of water.

Gary Biltcliffe has pointed out to me that traditional Boxing Day hunts, as well as the annual pheasant shoots, occur when Orion the Hunter is prominent in our night skies: *'The hunting season coincides with the visibility of Orion and the ancient people in the valleys were great hunters. The hunt was a sacred act, akin to the hunt for the Grail, a mystical journey. The hunt represented the struggle of life and death to those people and the god of the hunt was very powerful'* (pers. comm.).

Gwyn ap Nudd

Yuri Leitch has given a scholarly treatise on the myths associated with Glastonbury (Leitch 2007). He discusses the stories concerning Gwyn ap Nudd, who he sees as more than the *'King of the Fairies'* of popular folklore. Rather he is, *'... the Hunter God and the psychopompos of the native Britons, their Lord of the Golden Realms, whose name means, 'blessed, white' and when extended to 'Gwynfa' - 'Paradise''* (op. cit. *Introduction*). We have already met this name, in the guise of Nodens or Nudd (p. 97). Gwyn was introduced to Glastonbury from Wales, where in Welsh tradition he is *'Lord of the Otherworld'*. Gwyn leads the Wild Hunt that takes souls to the Otherworld. He is the, *'... door-keeper, a Guardian of the Threshold, a ferryman... a 'conductor of souls' to the realms of the dead'* (Mann 2004, p. 40). Gwyn is the Winter King, who rides out in the form of the stars of Orion around Samhain/Halloween; Mann and Glasson have proposed that at Glastonbury the stars of Orion were once

'Gwyn ap Nudd' by Yuri Leitch. Detail from the Covenstead Murals at Glastonbury, (© Yuri Leitch, used with permission.)

seen as Gwyn ap Nudd. Leitch agrees and regards him to be closely connected to Herne of the Saxons and Cernunnos of the Gauls. Gwyn's association with whiteness may be a link to snow-covered winter landscapes, when Orion dominates the sky and rises out of the Tor: *'The event could well have seemed symbolic of some great Lord of the Underworld, a psychopomp, riding out with his hounds, to hunt and throw down all his rivals'* (Mann and Glasson, 2007, p. 67). Like Orion, Gwyn has a dog, Dormarth, which means *Death's Door*, the relevance of which I shall return to in Chapter 13.

Gwyn's father, Nudd, was known as *'Nudd of the Silver Hand'*. He is interchangeable with Lud/Lugh, whose arm was said to reach across the whole land. The Gwyn of Glastonbury may have a direct link with Cerne Abbas, via the Iron Age Durotriges clans, whose lands extended from Dorset into Somerset.

The first reference to Gwyn is in the *'Black Book of Carmarthen'* written around 1250AD; he is celebrated as a mighty warrior, a war god, who takes the souls of the fallen to his Underworld. In Welsh folklore, to hear the baying of Gwyn's hounds was a portent of an imminent death in the family. Linking to Orion, Gwyn also announces, *'I come from battle and conflict, with a shield in my hand'*, as well as, *'... handsome my dog, and round-bodied, and truly the best of dogs, Dormarth was he...'* Yuri Leitch does not hesitate linking Gwyn with Orion: *'... he is the constellation Orion 'The Wild Hunter'. This great constellation is also the 'Winter King' because it appears in the sky from October.'* (Leitch 2007, p. 32). Nicholas Mann adds: *'As a Serpent God of the Waning Year, Gwynn returns to earth at Beltaine in a boat-shaped coffin. He re-emerges six months later at Samhain'* (Mann 2002, p. 17). This echoes Osiris taking the dead down the Nile in a boat on their journey to the Otherworld.

Returning to the *'Black Book of Carmarthen'*, Gwyn's skill in combat is extolled in a poem in which he is described as, *'the hope of armies'* and the *'hero of hosts'* and, when asked from which region he comes, he simply replies: *'I come from battle and conflict'.* The poem ends with Gwyn's proclamation:

'I have been where the warriors of Britain were slain
I am the escort of the grave.
I have been where the warriors of Britain were slain.
From the east to the south
I am alive, they in death!'

Old drawing of the Wild Hunt as it charges across the sky collecting the souls of the dead.

This shows clear parallels with Odin and Osiris, both of whom lead the dead over to Otherworldly realms.

Just as Orion rises out of the Glastonbury Tor when viewed from St Edmund's Hill, I shall demonstrate how it also rises out of Giant Hill; Orion climbs out of the earth to go a-hunting across the sky. British star-lore divides the heavens into two regions, two seasons - winter, which is dominated by Orion, and summer, which is ruled by Scorpio. This was played out, you may remember, with Orion's death by the sting of the scorpion, a metaphor for this celestial battle.

So do we dismiss the folklore and myths we have discussed as mere fiction? I believe that we should acknowledge that Hercules, Helis, Orion, Osiris, and Gwyn, might have played just as an important role in the Giant's history as the white lines that define him. Myths can be brought to life today, every time we stare across the valley to the Giant, or see the stars rise above his head; we can bring the Giant back to life. Perhaps the question of the Giant's age has been our focus for far too long, to the detriment of all else. We could be thinking of him more as part of our history, of our present, and, more than that, the stuff of future legend.

The Giant was an ever-present component in an ever-changing and often fearful world. To the Iron Age people of the Cerne Valley he would have been a mighty and fearsome ally, one that would help them overcome sickness, famine, attack, and would instil strength and belief into its warriors. He also represented the laws of Nature; death (the club) is followed by renewal (the phallus). He upheld the principle that death is a vital part of the continuation of all life.

111

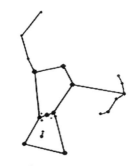

Chapter 9.
Starry, starry night -
the Giant and the heavens

*'We shall show them our portents upon the horizons and within
themselves, until it manifests unto them that it is the Truth.'*
(The Koran, XLI: 53)

Watching the heavens has always been a worthwhile activity. Celestial objects can tell you of impending changes to the seasons, or when high and low tide are due, even which direction north is. Like music, the stars speak to us in a universal language, enabling them to be ordered, mythologized, and interpreted regardless of millennia, religion, language, and geographical location. Way back in prehistory, once the stars, planets, sun and moon were named and myths attached to them, they were promoted in status; they now possessed the very energies and supernatural powers of the gods they represented.

Our ancient ancestors had a spiritual mindset and the foundation of their science was myth-based; their knowledge was passed on orally through storytelling. Myths incorporated not only natural phenomena they observed in their landscape, but also in the skies above. They watched attentively for any signs in the heavens that held meaning, omens that could be interpreted. When looking to the heavens, they saw gods and goddesses, giants and heroes, animals and mythical creatures, all interacting in a constant but ever-changing celestial ballet.

Ancient Egyptians and Babylonians, in the 3rd millennium BC, were studying the motions of their sky gods, relating them to issues such as creation, the continuity of human life, and as explanations for what they observed in Nature. They were trying to make sense out of apparent chaos, as they strove to find Mankind's place in their cosmology; all natural forces were seen as products of the will, actions and conflicts of gods and goddesses, and of giants. Science and religion were inseparably bound together, and would remain so until the 16-17th century, as John North observed: *'There is no sharp distinction between primitive myth and primitive science'* (North 1996, p. 533).

The familiar images of the prominent constellations and the zodiac signs are an inheritance passed down to us from cultures such as the Sumerians in the Indus Valley, some 5,500 years ago; the stars not only influenced people's lives, but political and social order was celestially based. In 419BC, Aristotle wrote to Alexander the Great that, *'Heaven is full of gods to whom we give the names of stars'*. As George Scott observed: *'It was but a small step from the personification of an object or force to the deification of that same object or force. Thus the moon, the sun, the stars, the heavens, became deities'* (Scott 1966, p. 11). The belief that the sun, the moon, and the planets influence our lives is ancient, and one that persists to this day. The Dendera Zodiac is a complex map of the heavens seen through Egyptians eyes in the 1st millennium BC. It was found in 1799 on the ceiling of the Ptolemaic temple of Hathor at Dendera, and shows constellations, stars and planets portrayed as mythic gods, goddesses and animals (image below); the Greek word for *zodiac* simply means, *'house of the animals'*.

Pliny, writing in 270BC, mentions 45 constellations, whilst Ptolemy listed 48, made up of 1028 stars; the Romans themselves acknowledged the Greeks to be superior astronomers. Aristotle stated, with some vigour, that the gods were originally stars, and that all the forces that control Man's destiny resided in the starry vaults, whilst Plato spoke of *archaic myths* as he constructed the first tenets of philosophy. Today we make a clear distinction between mythology and science, and perhaps our world is the poorer for it. As early as the 6th century, writer Gregoire de Tours sadly concluded that, *'The mind has lost its cutting edge, we hardly understand the Ancients'* (Santillana and von Dechend 1977, p. 10). Even in ancient times, this state

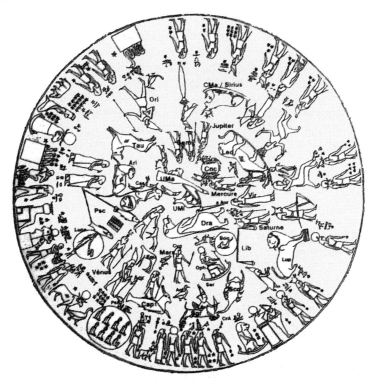

The Dendera Zodiac, 1st century BC from Egypt, showing
mythical figures and animals representing the constellations
and planets. (After Collins 2006.)

113

of affairs was already rearing its head, as Aristotle observed: *'We tend to think of the stars as mere bodies or items arranged in order, without soul or Life. We ought rather to regard them as possessed of Life and activity.'*

Much later, the lives of Iron Age people were controlled as much by the stars as they were by the sun. The herb Vervain was used by Druids for divination and it was vital that it be picked just as Sirius rose. The images on the Iron Age Gunderstrup Cauldron have recently been reinterpreted by F Graham Millar, of the Royal Astronomical Society of Canada, who sees astronomical significance in the characters: *'... the 'Horned One' was resident in the constellation of Menat, which is Hercules plus Ophiuchus... snakes were used to mark important circles on the celestial sphere... Hydra marked the equator... the autumn equinox by Serpens Caput, the snake in the hand of Menat'* (in Gardiner and Osborn 2005, p. 164).

At Hod Hill, Dorset, an image was found of the god Nodens, naked and holding a knobbled club and accompanied by a hare, symbolising his role as a hunter. Hares were sacred animals to the Celts, and one story tells that as Boudica was amassing her army against the Romans, she let loose a hare from under her cloak and regarded the way it ran off as a good omen. As we have seen, Orion is accompanied by a hare, Lepus, immediately beneath him in the sky. Nodens was the *'cloud-maker'*, just as Orion was the instigator of the rainy season.

In the past, archaeologists were guilty of not necessarily taking the trouble to look up from the ground. When Alexander Thom accurately surveyed hundreds of British prehistoric sites and found precise alignments with the sun, moon and the stars, the reception from academics was cold and cynical. Only recently has it been acknowledged that astronomy had indeed played an important role in the lives of prehistoric people; a missing piece of the jigsaw of our heritage has been retrieved. Robin Heath concluded that, *'Once this missing sky component is restored, the reason for the nature and locality of a sacred place often reveals itself in a dramatic fashion...'* (in Mann and Glasson 2007). Recent work has been done by Martin Brennan in Ireland (1994), Nicholas Mann and Philippa Glasson at Glastonbury (2007), Mann at Avebury (2011), and by John North (1996) and myself (Knight 2011); these have convincingly argued the case that **intentional** astronomical alignments are an integral component of many Neolithic and Bronze Age sites. My work on the megalithic sites of Dorset revealed many more astronomical alignments than had previously been known for the county (Knight 1996).

David Furlong has suggested that the famous St Michael Line may have been laid out by marking where one star of Orion's belt, Mintaka, rose during the Neolithic (Biltcliffe and Hoare 2012, p. 19). It is the first star of the belt to rise, and ancient astrologers saw it's rising as a portent of good fortune (Allen 1899, p. 314).

It has taken many decades for astro-archaeology to get established, and one of its champions was, ironically, *'one of their own'*. Professor John North (1934 - 2008) was primarily a historian, but one who had an interest in the history of astronomy, which led him to delve into the subject ever deeper. This resulted in his 653-page classic, *Stonehenge: Neolithic Man and the Cosmos* (North 1996). North meticulously reinterpreted the early history of science and astronomy, establishing that the midwinter sunset at Stonehenge was at least as important as the famous midsummer sunrise. As Paul Newman tells us: *'John North's book is technical, authoritative and - he is a professor of the Exact Sciences - diagrammatically ravishing... the detail and evidence he accrues are formidable...'* (Newman 2009, p. 183). Paul, I wholeheartedly agree. North changed forever the way I looked at sacred sites and their place in the greater landscape, and inspired me to do work of this nature in Dorset and Wiltshire (Knight 1996, 2001, 2011); I was primed to discover any hidden astronomical alignments that might involve the Giant.

We should not be surprised that Neolithic and Bronze Age people were building megalithic structures to align with the movements of stars, planets, sun and the moon. This celestial knowledge had been handed down by the 'hunter-gatherers' for thousands of years. It was just as important for a Mesolithic nomad to know of an impending season change, or which direction north was, or the tide times, as it was in later millennia. Nicholas Mann astutely notes that star-gazing is indeed ancient: *'... it is likely that Neolithic peoples' knowledge of the stars had been accumulating for millennia. Their Mesolithic and Palaeolithic forebears would surely have named the stars, and no doubt, developed and retold their stories'* (Mann 2011, p. 16).

A 9th century depiction of Orion.
(Wikipedia Common Licence.)

In light of Man's long and close relationship with the heavens, we should not be surprised that Iron Age people living in Dorset continued the ancient tradition of watching the stars, recording their movements with some accuracy. In many ways the Iron Age was a golden age of mathematics and astronomy, with the Greeks at its cutting edge.

By the time the Giant was created, star-lore and accurate astronomical observation in Dorset was already at least 3,000 years old, proven by the Neolithic and Bronze Age sites aligned with the of the stars, sun, and the moon. For instance, in Dorset and Wiltshire I noted how Sirius and the midwinter sun both rose at the same azimuth for a time in the Neolithic, which may account for the abundance of alignments I found in that direction (Knight 2001, 2011).

Britain's indigenous Iron Age astronomers, philosophers and mathematicians were of course the Druids. Julius Caesar wrote of them: 'They hold long discussions about the heavenly bodies and their movements, the size of the Universe and of the earth… and the power and properties of their gods'. These were uncertain times, an age of metal and men, of war gods and possession, and people looked to the skies for stability and solace: *'The fixed stars are the essence of Being, their assembly stands for the hidden counsels and the unspoken laws that rule the Whole. The planets, seen as gods, represent the Forces and the Will'* (Santillana and von Dechend 1977, p. 151).

It may be remembered that academic John North had advocated alignments with the constellation Orion for both the Long Man of Wilmington and the Uffington White Horse, as well as for the Whiteleaf Cross and Bledlow Cross figures. These were important pieces in the jigsaw, as they gave me the impetus to seek out any possible astronomical secrets concealed in the Giant's landscape; this was pioneering ground, for no one in modern times had trodden this path with any purpose before.

The Giant and the stars

As throughout previous millennia, the cycles of the sun, moon, and stars not only enabled Iron Age people to order their lives, but also underpinned their cosmology and their spiritual beliefs. The gods not only guided them but were always on the move, being responsible for the cyclical seasonal changes. Time itself was a sacred concept; the awareness of *sacred time*, or the harmonious concordance between heaven and earth, was vital to all ancient indigenous societies.

The Durotriges of the Cerne Valley were first and foremost farmers, and the landscape was seen as the abode of spirits and otherworldly beings, to be revered and contacted at various stages of the agricultural cycle. The weather and the changing seasons were as important to Durotriges farmers as they are to our farmers today, and it was to the sun and stars they turned to for order and guidance, as we shall see. The relationship cultivated between Man and the stars could hardly be better articulated than here by Paul Newman: *'Stars conserved – perhaps reanimated – the energies of those who had passed on. Their shifting positions spelt out messages to priests and scryers, and in time became personalised until each self-contained point held a power charge of myth and heroism'* (Newman 2009, p. 184). By aligning the Giant with the heavens, the Durotriges drew power from Otherworldy realms down to the earth to imbue themselves and their fields.

Neolithic and Bronze Age people were enticed into the Cerne Valley by the appeal of fresh water from rivers and springs, coupled with sheltered valleys and rich soil, and shaman/astronomers were an element of these clans. There are Bronze Age tumuli on Giant Hill, and a Neolithic long barrow on Smacam Down to the south. And the unusual topography must also have played its part; many hills and ridges in the area are of a very similar height – ideal for astronomical observation. The astronomer-priests standing on top of Giant Hill saw Orion, Sirius and the other stars rise and set into distant, almost level horizons all through the year. This applied equally to sunrises and sunsets, and to lunar events.

John North has suggested that the slope gradient at the Giant's head, 1 in 5, is a *'Neolithic signature'* and that some other marker may have existed on the hill before the Iron Age. This might have later been amended or abandoned because it no longer functioned as it had previously, perhaps due to the precession of the stars. A tumulus and a possible henge monument are still visible on the hilltop.

The height of Giant Hill immediately above the Giant is around 200m above sea level. The ridgeway hill to the west is remarkably level, the sections visible from Giant Hill being between 214–250m; the Bellingstone stands around 232m, whilst Seldon Hill sunsets occur over the 225m mark. From Seldon Hill the sun rises in line with the Giant out of a more distant skyline that is around 240m. To the south both Dickey Hill and Black Hill rise to 213m. From the Trendle there are near-horizontal skylines from the NE all the way around to the south and beyond; to the east the skyline is a flat ridge that only varies between 240-250m and is sufficiently distant for the slight height difference to be negligible.

Amidst this magical and mythic landscape, a spot was chosen with great care to be the home of the Cerne Giant, that it might complement and help play out their views of the Universe. Speaking of the hills on the opposite side of the valley, Rodney Castleden insightfully observed that: *'... it is as if the Giant was made with the intention that it should be viewed from them...'* (Castleden 1996, p. 13). This is pivotal to our study, as I shall soon explain.

John North makes the point that we must distinguish between the *form* of the Giant and its *placement* in the landscape; he concluded that, *'On both scores the Cerne image seems to belong to classical antiquity [i.e. Iron Age] or later, rather than to [earlier] prehistory'* (North 1996, p. 219).

North gives the axis of the Giant to be an azimuth of 75° (op. cit. p. 219), and I agree that it is very close to this. However, I do not think it is possible to be truly exact, for we do not know all the past amendments that were undertaken. There is also the fact that the phallus does not point directly towards the centre of the head, but to his left side, south of the axis. So what do we take as the axis, crotch to the nose, or the direction of the phallus? For now, I shall work with North's azimuth of 75° - the axis of the phallus.

Other local features are also important regarding astronomical alignments. For instance, Dogbury Hill is visible from the river below the Giant; High Cank and High Stoy are visible from the Giant; the Bellingstone and the Giant were at one time intervisible.

Matters of time and place

Where the sun, moon, or a star rises and sets depends very much on latitude and longitude, but also on the height of the horizon. The higher the skyline above the observer, the later the object will appear to rise, because it has to first clear the skyline as it moves upwards and to the south (to the right). So too with setting objects, which will set earlier and further to the south (left) if the skyline is above the observer. That said, I have already commented how the skylines around Cerne are remarkably similar in height, making the landscape ideal for astronomical observation. Weather conditions and the brightness of a star will also determine when and where it will become visible to the naked eye. The brighter the star, the lower it will be seen. The point at which an object becomes visible is known as its 'extinction angle', measured in degrees of altitude above a horizontal skyline. Sirius, for instance becomes visible less than 1° above the horizon in clear conditions, due to its brilliance, whereas Deneb will not be visible until at least 2.35°.

The latitude and longitude co-ordinates for the Giant are Lat 50° 48' 49" N, Long 2° 28' 28" W, based on OS maps and Google Earth. The height above sea level was calculated into each individual astronomical event I explored, dependant on where observations were being made.

The software programme I used was *Skymap Lite*, 2005 edition, programmed by Chris Marriott. This enabled me to look at the skies above the Giant, in any direction, on any day, for any hour and minute, going back thousands of years. Sometimes the positions of certain stars changed very little over a thousand years or so, whist at other times alignments only 'clicked in' for a few centuries, especially those involving fast-moving stars close to the Solar System, such as Sirius. Timothy Darvill gives a construction date for the Giant ranging from the 1st millennium BC to 200AD, and I find more alignments within this parameter than any other period. As Bill Putnam stated: *'It is likely that the Cerne Giant was constructed by the Durotriges, whether during the Roman period or before... the Cerne Giant fits well into an Iron Age and Roman context'* (in Darvill et al 1999, p. 51 & 56).

The heavens are constantly moving, so this determines what time of the year any alignment is visible. For instance, the northern point where the Galactic plane and ecliptic meet sits over the Cerne Giant today in winter – almost vertically in fact. But this changes from around midnight (BST) in early September, to 9pm early in November, to around 6pm by the midwinter solstice in December. Finding an alignment in the Cerne Valley is one thing, but its relevance might only become apparent when we ascertain what time of the year it was *observable*.

117

At a recent conference I heard one speaker announce that *intentionality* is the 'big thing' in archaeology at the moment. So we have to consider whether or not an astronomical alignment was deliberate. John North pointed this out with great honesty: *'Deciding between deliberate and accidental alignments is one of the central problems...'* (North 1996, p. 6). I cannot speak for John North, but for my part I am simply putting on record what I have found, and leave it to others to decide concerning matters of coincidence. However, the sheer number of alignments marking 'key events' leaves me in no doubt that something was going on in the Cerne Valley around 2000 years ago that cannot be explained as chance. The ancients were, after all, mirroring in their monuments the principles they saw operating in the cosmos around them, as archaeologist Aubrey Burl observed: *'Death and the heavens were major concerns of the living as they farmed their isolated settlements'* (Burl 2002, p. 85). Life and death, Earth and sky, Man and the gods, were all elements of their cosmology, where all was interlinked and co-existed. Sadly, we no longer see gods in the stars, as our predecessors once did.

Having already put the *Skymap* software to good effect in the Avebury area (Knight 2011), I set out to see what secrets the Giant may have been hiding. What I have found has left me even more in awe of what our Bronze Age and Iron Age ancestors were capable of, and the depths of their relationship with the cosmos. My quest also required me to walk the landscape, to see where the Giant could be viewed from, and where it could not, and to ascertain which alignments were simply lines on a map and which were actually **sight lines**? I had carried out this exercise in my study of West Kennet Long Barrow and I consider it a vital part in the study of any landscape. As well as being essential for viewing suspected alignments, walking the land is invaluable for connecting with it on a deeper level.

I have found that for many astronomical alignments to be realised, it is often a matter of where to stand, and when, and indeed knowing which way to look; only then did the 'open secrets' of the Giant reveal themselves to me. What I present now is, to me, the most exciting aspect of my encounters with the Giant of Cerne. Other than a few isolated opinions, and suggestions for further work from John North, no one had carried out any detailed work on the relationship between the Giant, his landscape and celestial objects. I have come to realise that the Giant belongs not just to the Earth, but also to the heavens – just like the people who first created him.

'We have been living in a world of Astronomical Myth until yesterday'.
(Santillana and von Dechend, 1977.)

118

Chapter 10.
Spring & summer stars -
a swan, a lion, & the Great Rift

'Ride a white swan, like the people of the Beltaine...'
(Mark Bolan)

The summer skies have been dominated for thousands of years by some constellations and configurations that many people may recognise today. These include the Square of Pegasus, the Summer Triangle formed by Deneb, Vega and Altair, the 'W' of Cassiopeia, the lion's head of Leo, and Ursa Major (the Great Bear). On clear summer nights, the Milky Way straddles the sky like a misty ribbon, and in August we may be lucky to see Perseid meteors hurtle across the inky stellar background of seemingly motionless stars.

But nothing is stationery - it is an illusion. For the stars rise a few minutes earlier every day, due to the daily rotation period of the earth, ensuring that over several weeks distinct changes will be noticed, as they surely were millennia ago. The sun appears to move through this stellar background, along a distinct band called the ecliptic, through the twelve (formerly thirteen) zodiacal constellations. The Ancients were watching the sun's slow but steady progress across the heavens, embellishing its journey with myths. In Gaul, the Celts believed that the god Belinos carried the sun across the heavens on a horse-drawn chariot (Biltcliffe and Hoare 2011, p. 128), just as the goddess Diana pulled the moon across the sky.

Two giants, both heroes of myth and legend, seem to compete in an eternal dance around the heavens. Both can be identified with the Cerne Giant, and may well have been thousands of years ago. Hercules is the summer antagonist, striding across the skies and appearing almost overhead at times during the night, a fainter configuration of stars between the brilliant duo of Vega and Arcturus. The stars of Hercules would have appeared brighter in the Iron Age, of course, an easily discernable figure in skies that were truly dark.

As autumn arrives Hercules sinks progressively lower in the evening skies, until two thirds of the figure disappears below the horizon as it approaches north. Hercules' place is now usurped by the brilliant constellation of Orion, with its four magnitude 1 stars and its easily perceived 'belt' of three stars, below which lies the fuzzy patch of the gaseous M42 nebula.

I soon realised that due of their positions in the sky at least one of these mythical heroes is **always** above the horizon, and on occasion they are both visible simultaneously; this happens during the spring and the autumn, which I call 'change-over' times, as the celestial giants 'change shift', so to speak. George Scott comments that in his opinion the god Osiris is identifiable with Hercules (Scott 1966, p. 112); and we already know that the Egyptians regarded Orion as Osiris, so it could be that the *same god* is guarding and orchestrating the heavens and the seasons - continuously and eternally.

We shall speak of this in the next chapter, but for now let me take you on a journey through the spring and summer night skies, and the alignments I have found concerning the Giant and his landscape. Sometimes alignments can be very time-specific, at other times not so. Crucially, regarding the astronomy of the Giant, John North makes the point that *'... no matter what its precise age, it helps to support the argument that chalk figures were astral in meaning'* (North 1996, p. 230).

One other point; we would do well to try and put ourselves in the mindset of the ancient astronomers, and perhaps the people of the Iron Age clans. These folks did not see *stars* clearing Giant Hill; they did not see *stars* rising out of Dogbury Hill. What they saw was Orion the great hero and hunter rising into the sky; they saw the personification of the Kingship Lion rising out of Giant Hill, not the random configuration of stars we now call Leo; and they witnessed the Milky Way as a road to the Otherworld, not simply the plane of our Galaxy. They inhabited a mythic landscape and connected with mythic skies, for through their myths they sought to order their world, just as science seeks to today. The difference between mythology and science today is that the latter has lost the vital component – imagination. When that is restored, the Universe becomes a dynamic, magical place.

Hercules

Hercules is one of the oldest recorded sky figures, which is a curious fact considering it is such a relatively faint constellation. It features in a Chaldean myth (as *Izhdubar*), and a seal dated 3000-3500BC describes how the constellation rests one foot on the Dragon's Head (Draco). Hercules or Orion is shown shaking hands with a king at Arsameia, Mesopotamia (Gilbert 2005, also see p. 161).

I find it interesting that Hercules contains the *Apex of the Sun's Way*, in other words the direction in space towards which our sun and therefore the Earth are heading! (Allen 1899, p. 245).

I could not make sense of some old depictions of Hercules, as he seemed to be portrayed upside down, compared to adjacent figures. Then I realised that he passes more or less overhead when approaching his zenith in the

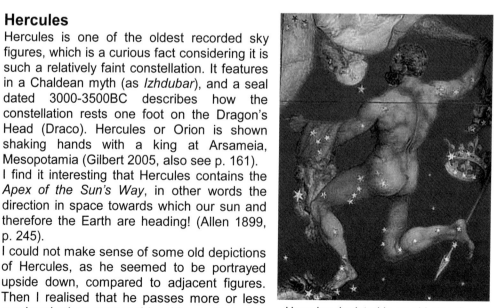

Hercules depicted in an old star chart.

120

south; so when one faces *north* and looks up at him, he is the correct way up as he culminates (reaches the highest point in the sky).

But why was this classical giant of heroic deeds and great strength allotted such a faint set of stars. The answer may be that Hercules used to be an important marker at the celestial pole. Around 10,000BC, Iota Hercules (marking his leading foot) was the pole star, and by 7,500BC Tau Hercules (his following foot) had that distinction. In other words, for around 3,500 years Hercules marked the non-moving part of the night sky - the heavens literally revolved around him. He did, however, do a very diminutive dance through a small circuit, turning, one might say, on a drachma!

These were times when astronomy was in its infancy, when myths were being forged, when our Mesolithic hunter-gatherer ancestors where following the stars as they roamed the landscape, moving around with the seasons, forging mythical links with the star figures. Andrew Collins had previously noted that the celestial pole was in Hercules around 9,500BC, confirming that there was no obvious *'pole star'* (Collins 2006, p. 27). But what he is really saying is that there is no *bright* pole star. Both Tau and Iota Hercules are magnitude +3. Today, even in an urban or near-urban area, I have been able to make out these stars on an average night with little effort. But in the unimaginably darker skies of prehistory they would have appeared much brighter. Hercules is virtually overhead during the night from spring to autumn from southern England, further negating their relative dimness.

In one myth, Hercules cut off the heads of the multi-headed serpent Hydra and cast them into the springs of Lerna. After gradually rising up from the astronomical horizon, the constellations of Hydra and Hercules rise over the Giant when viewed from the valley in front of him. From here, the skyline above the Giant is around 11-

Hercules rising in the Iron Age. Above: Hercules clears Giant Hill (on his side) as seen from the valley below. The club aligns with the phallus as it clears the hill. Right: the whole of Hercules clears the horizon above the Giant, as seen from the vicinity of the Bellingstone.

12° higher than the observer (North 1996, p. 219) so we have to wait a while until it clears the hill. The club of Hercules rises out of Giant Hill in line with the axis of the Giant, or more correctly his phallus, which points slightly to the right (south); you may recall that the phallus is aligned to around 75°. The stars forming club of Hercules pointed directly down to the Giant soon after rising between around 500BC and 300AD, aligning with the Giant's phallus. Hercules then moves south in the sky to stand over Silver Well.

Regarding the valley below the Giant, North commented that, *'The ground runs down to the banks of the river Cerne, which offers what seems to be the most natural place to stand'*. With this in mind, he points to the optimum date for the brightest stars of the constellation of Hercules to rise over the giant to be between 20BC and 200AD: *'... it was very well fitted to mark the rising of the constellation of Hercules over the slope into which it is cut'* (North 1996, p. 219). Hercules clears the horizon earlier if viewed from the Bellingstone, where I discovered that it hangs magnificently over the Giant – the celestial and the earthly giants echoing each other!

Later in the year, Hercules partially disappears beneath the northern skyline, in the general direction of where the Giant is walking, roughly 340° - 345°. I shall return to this later, as this direction has other implications. Also, when seen from Weam Common Hill, the head of Hercules' mythical serpent adversary, the Hydra, rises over the Giant.

There are three important elements of the summer skies that are closely intertwined, and now need to be looked at in detail. Firstly, the constellation of Cygnus, the Swan, which has a long association with Man, with folklore going back thousands of years. Next, the Milky Way, the misty ring that encircles the sky and marks the plane of our galaxy. And finally, a section of the Milky Way in Cygnus that contains some dark patches, known as the Great Rift, which has long been associated with the Otherworld and the soul's journey after physical death.

Cygnus the Swan

This easily recognisable configuration is also known as the Northern Cross, and it's brightest star, Deneb, passes right overhead during summer months seen from Southern England; it is one of the triad of bright stars that forms the *'Summer Triangle'*. It is amazing how cultures all across the world regarded this constellation as a bird of some description. Prior to 2000BC, Babylonians knew it as one of the birds that attacked their god Marduk (aka Hercules). In Hellenic times it was *Ornis the Bird*, whilst in Celtic lore Cygnus was thought to represent a goose. Mankind's association with swans has been a long one; during the Ice Age, mammoth ivory pendants were carved in the form of stylised swans (Trubshaw 2011, p. 116).

This old drawing demonstrates how Cygnus was perceived as a swan.

A north-south world-cosmic axis was once held together by the Northern Cross, Cygnus, and the Southern Cross, Crux. The latter disappeared from British skies in the Upper Neolithic, due to the long-term wobble of the Earth (Mann 2011). Today

Deneb is circumpolar, it never sets, but this has only been the case since around 350BC. Prior to that it was seen to briefly disappear below the northern horizon during winter months; in his *Hymn to Apollo*, Callimachus tells of how Apollo rode on the back of a swan to the land of the Hyperboreans during the winter.

Andrew Collins suggests that the Egyptian god Sokar, a falcon-headed deity, can be identified with Cygnus, as he had the title *'great god with his two wings opened'* (Collins 2006, p. 134). Collins also advocates a convincing north-south alignment between the Giza pyramids, Ursa Major, the north celestial pole, and Cygnus, aka Sokar (op. cit. fig. 34).

Deneb had a profound impact on our ancestors and it seems that people have been watching the star for millennia; Alexander Thom was the first to discover that the axis of Avebury henge is 339.2°, which turns out to be where Deneb was setting in 2600BC (Collins 2006, Mann 2011); Bob Trubshaw and Andrew Collins both found swan symbolism and supportive folklore in the Avebury area. I found alignments with Cygnus nearby, regarding West Kennet Long Barrow and Silbury Hill (Knight 2011). Nicholas Mann comments that in the Neolithic, the Southern Cross (Crux) was visible from Britain, on the opposite side of the sky from the Northern Cross, Cygnus; Avebury's axis was aligned with both crosses, and Silbury Hill was constructed at the time when Crux ceased to be visible from Southern England. Perhaps as Crux was lost from our skies, Cygnus attained greater importance: *'Cygnus was once seen as the entrance and exit to the sky-world, the original location of heaven... and accessed via the pole star and north-south meridian line'* (Collins 2006). An ancient cave painting at Lascaux shows a bird on a stick that represents Cygnus as the 'world axis', the sky-pole, the connection between the earth and other worlds.

Swans were sacred to Apollo, as well as to Venus and Aphrodite, the latter two being

Google Earth image, showing the direction to which the Giant is walking, which has been approximated from the positions of his feet.

the Goddess of Love to the Romans and Greeks respectively. So we have a link between swans and procreation. It is relevant, perhaps, that in some Egyptian paintings Cygnus has a mace, not unlike the Giant's club.

Wayland, the Norse god of blacksmiths, attained astral flight by adorning himself with swan feathers (Biltcliffe and Hoare 2012, p. 131). The axis of Wayland's Smithy long barrow is orientated with the setting of Deneb in the Neolithic (North 1996). Biltcliffe and Hoare state that this was the direction of magnetic north in Iron Age times, and the direction of the axis of the Belinus Line: '... *the Belinus Line, orientated at 346°, targets the setting of Deneb during the reign of the historical King Belinus around 500BC*' (Biltcliffe and Hoare 2012, p. 19). They further speculate that people used Vega (the 3rd brightest star visible from Britain) and Deneb as markers for setting out the Belinus Line, following the apparent position of these stars as they progressed north, lighting beacon fires as they went.

William Shakespeare was once called the *'Sweet Swan of Avon'*, and his Orpheus is sometimes a singing swan. Interestingly, on a proposed 'British Landscape Zodiac', Cygnus sits over Stratford on Avon (Dawkins, in Thorley 2012, p. 73). Peter Dawkins is of the view that, *'There is a great mystery teaching contained in the Swan. By means of the Swan the universe is created'* (op. cit. p. 72).

I find it fascinating that on an astronomical map made by William Schickhard (1592-1635) he depicts Cygnus as a swan but with the crucified Christ superimposed. Christians adopted Cygnus due to its resemblance to a cross; it was their *'Christi Crux'*, a tradition that goes back to at least 592AD. This may have derived from the classical god Orpheus, who was depicted being crucified in the mid-third century AD, and was represented in the sky by the constellation Cygnus. Orpheus is known in popular culture today for his association with the Underworld, and it might be that the

View looking approximately north along the soles of the Giant's feet. Left: showing High Cank and High Stoy on skyline. Right: composite view of Capella, Vega and Deneb above High Stoy in the Iron Age, just before disappearing behind Giant Hill.

Christians merely took over the *'cross in the sky'*, and even the story of the crucifixion, from the myths of this Greek god (Collins 2006, p. 35).

We shall look into deeper aspects of Cygnus soon, concerning ancient concepts that the Great Rift is a portal to other dimensions. For now, let us look at whether Cygnus was regarded as important to Iron Age priest-astronomers of the Cerne Valley. I was amazed to see that it was, and that the very orientation of the Giant may have been determined by Deneb, the brightest star of the constellation.

The Giant is clearly in motion as he walks roughly north along Giant Hill. But to where is he walking? Ascertaining the azimuth of where his feet are pointing is not straightforward, due to the fact that the front foot is slightly raised compared to the other. I have settled for an azimuth range of 346°-348° and, having arrived at this, took a visit to see where this direction pointed to on the ground. I found that the slopes of Giant Hill ensured that the true setting of Deneb or Vega could never be seen from the feet of the Giant. But what I could see were the summits of High Cank and High Stoy, appearing next to each other due to a line of sight effect. During the Iron Age, it was over these hills that the bright stars Deneb, Vega, and Capella would hang before disappearing from view from the Giant – in line with his feet! This is also the direction where the torso and head of Hercules set into the horizon!

It may be remembered that John North regarded the valley in front of the Giant as being ideal for astronomical observations. I went and stood alongside the river, in line with the phallus of the Giant, and calculations soon procured more celestial phenomena that our Iron Age ancestors would have been interested in. For instance, looking north along the valley from this point, I could see Dogbury Hill, an ancient sacred place, on the skyline at around 354-355°, that is 5-6° west of due north. The surprisingly low horizon is due to the fact that we are looking directly north up the

From the river valley below the Giant, Deneb drops in the sky as it approaches Dogbury Hill. Although it then skims the horizon (never setting) but was probably too low to be visible with the naked eye. Here Vega has just risen after briefly going below the skyline. Optimum time: 300BC to 200AD.

Cerne Valley. In the Iron Age, Cygnus came down to Dogbury Hill, and although it then skimmed the horizon through north and beyond, due to the atmosphere was too faint to be visible; it never set but was just below its extinction angle of 2.35°. Later on, it started to rise and went behind Giant Hill. I have noted a similar phenomenon involving Deneb and Windmill Hill when viewed from West Kennet Long Barrow (Knight 2011, p. 203).

In the meantime, the brilliant star Vega, which had preceded Deneb across the sky, had set into the horizon in the vicinity of Dogbury. Later, it reappeared just before it too went, temporarily, behind Giant Hill. The brilliance of Vega meant it would have been visible despite the low altitude, especially in dark Iron Age skies. The best dates for these events would appear to be 300BC – 200AD. An alignment with Vega has been proposed at the Uffington White Horse (Biltcliffe and Hoare 2012, p. 128).

It is worth noting that prior to around 300-200BC, Deneb would have set directly into Dogbury Hill when viewed from our observation point by the river. Perhaps people had been standing in this valley location long before the scouring of the Giant, and that the area was already a sacred place, due to the proximity of the spring. We shall return to this valley setting soon, as it holds more wonders regarding the Milky Way and Leo.

The azimuth from Seldon Hill to High Stoy is around 35-45° (depending where you stand, and allowing for the azimuth spread of the latter). When standing on Seldon Hill in the Iron Age, we would have seen Arcturus (the brightest star of the northern celestial hemisphere) rise out of the right side of High Stoy, as well as the head and torso of Hercules! Local legend says King Arthur was born at High Stoy, and Arcturus is associated with him. This is also the direction that the cross of Cygnus clears the horizon, as well as the full configuration of Lyra, of which only Vega had been prominent until this point. In Greek mythology, Lyra was associated with the myth of Orpheus, the musician who was killed by the Bacchantes. After his death, his lyre was thrown into the river; Zeus sent an eagle to retrieve the object and ordered both of them to be placed in the sky. In Wales, Lyra is known as King Arthur's Harp (*Talyn Arthur*) and King David's harp. I find it interesting that Lyra had sunk into the River Cerne when viewed from our valley view point, as we looked north to High Stoy and Dogbury, an area associated with King Arthur (p. 46).

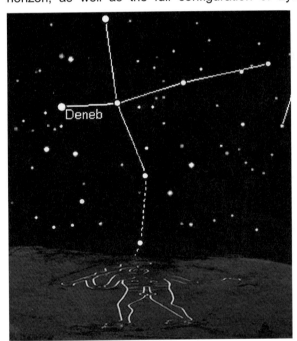

Cygnus rising above the Giant, as seen from the valley below during the Bronze Age through to the Iron Age.

The swan or cross configuration of Cygnus then moved south, continuing to rise, and eventually reached a height where it could be fully seen from the valley below. I believe it is not coincidence that this occurred directly in line with the Giant. The one wing of the swan pointed down to the Giant – the cosmos and the landscape in harmony (image above). Thereafter, Cygnus dominated the south and west part of the sky throughout the summer. This scene had been played out since around 2000BC, and continued through the Iron Age; however, as time went on the constellation was destined to clear the hill further to the north. Today the constellation clears Giant Hill north of the Giant, and hangs in the sky over the Giant somewhat later; this can be seen in pre-dawn skies in February, after midnight in March and April, and just after sunset in May. Unfortunately, as Cygnus is now higher in the sky, we cannot get the effect that once was, during that special time when Cygnus appeared to rise above the Giant's head.

It is now time to look at Cygnus in the context of its position within the Milky Way, and as the location of the so-called Great Rift.

The Milky Way and the Great Rift

The Milky Way is, of course, the densest part of our own galaxy, and is a striking sight to behold as a misty ribbon of light circling the sky on a clear night. In Greek myth, Hercules was being suckled by his Mother Hera, but she spilt some of her milk and this flowed across the heavens creating the Milky Way; the Greek name for it, *Galaxias,* is derived from their word for milk *(gala)*. The Akkadians wrote: *'... connected with the hill of the Sun-God and the passage of ghosts, is the Milky Way.'* They also knew it as the *Crooked Serpent* (Allen 1889, p. 475), whilst the Hebrews called it the *River of Light.* To the Vikings, it was the path that lead to Valhalla, and the Celts knew it as *Arianrod,* or *Silver Street.* Anglo-Saxons knew the Milky Way as *Waetlinga Straet,* the *Path of the Waetlings,* the *giant* sons of King Waetla, and a

memory of this survives as Watling Street, the Roman road. The ancient British called it *Caer Gwydion,* the road down which the god Gwydion travelled.

In England it was known for centuries as the *Way of St James*, making the connection with a pilgrimage or journey (of the departed soul perhaps). Similarly, early Muslim Turks called it *Hagjiler Yûli,* the *Pilgrims Road*, which represented their annual journey to Mecca.

The Milky Way was known as the *'milky pillars'* of the *River of Death,* personified by the goddess Styx, who was said to prop up the heavens and connect it to earthly realms. In Estonian folklore it is believed that migrating birds are led by a white bird with the head of a maiden, who chases away birds of prey. Only later did scientists confirm the observation that migratory birds use the Milky Way as a guide when flying to warmer, southern lands during the winter. In Japanese mythology, 80,000 gods

The Milky Way has inspired the imaginations of people for thousands of years. (Photo: Steve Jurvetson. Wikipedia Common Licence.)

assembled in the Milky Way to coax the sun out of a cave, in an effort to end the winter.

Plato, in his *Republic,* decribes the Milky Way in the context of souls bound for another life, where they encounter: *'... a straight shaft of light – and there, at the middle of the light, they saw stretching from heaven the extremities of its chains; for this light binds the heavens, holding together all the revolving firmament...'*

In Oriental and Native American myths the Milky Way is the road to the Otherworlds, the route of the ancestors. In India, the goddess Sarawati rides on the back of a swan, for she is a swan-maiden who travels down a *'starry river'.* In some Northern and Eastern European myths, the Milky Way is called *Way of the Birds.*

In Egyptian mythology the Milky Way was the goddess Nut. I have shown a papyrus of the Egyptian god Geb with Nut arched over him (p. 80). By superimposing the images of Nut over the Milky Way around winter solstice, Ronald A Wells of the University of California places Cygnus between the her thighs, with Deneb at her vagina. In fact the interstellar clouds that comprise the Great Rift in Cygnus appeared to the Egyptians like the parting of her legs; Nut is birthing the year. Cygnus was the *'womb of the stars',* and may explain why many nude prehistoric figurines have crosses in the region of their genitalia (Collins 2006, p. 171-2).

Nicolas Mann has demonstrated that the Milky Way formed a complete circle around the sky during midwinter around the time Avebury was constructed, and that the white banks of chalk that enclose the stones represented this unique phenomenon (Mann 2011). I have also noted how the Milky Way sat over West Kennet Long Barrow during winter nights in the early Neolithic, just as Orion was setting into the mound (Knight 2011, p. 202).

The Great Rift, a dark area that cuts through Cygnus, formed by interstellar dust clouds.

Cutting through Cygnus the Swan are darker areas where you will see fewer stars, and at one point these dark regions cut a long shadow dividing the Milky Way in two. This is the Great Rift, formed by huge clouds of cosmic dust. It incises right through the Summer Triangle, as if someone has hoovered up the stars! We have already seen how Cygnus, and its representation as a swan, has long been associated with the Otherworld, and in particular a gateway to it. Native Americans, such as the Pawnee and Cherokee, believe that the Milky Way is the road the dead follow to join the ancestors, and that it begins where it bifurcates, i.e. at the Great Rift of Cygnus. Confirmation would seem to come from Scandinavian Saami shaman, who reportedly rode on swans to the Otherworld, and in Neolithic Turkey, Cygnus was known as a vulture (Collins 2006, p. 36). Here we have associations of birds with death and a soul journey into the hereafter. The term 'swan song' is still a term used today for someone about to perform his or her final act. Bob Trubshaw

128

suggests, '... *the annual migration north of swans as taking souls is not merely 'north beyond the north wind' but into the doorway to the Otherworld'* (Trubshaw 2011, p. 126); as we have seen, Cygnus skirts the northern horizon from these latitudes. In countries where storks are not found, birth is sometimes associated with swans bringing the newborn. In Central and North Asia, Africa and Indonesia, the souls of those about to be born perch like birds on the branches of trees.

I find it fascinating that astronomers have is located a massive cosmic ray generator in Cygnus, known as Cygnus X-3. Scientist Carl Sagan proposed that energy bursts of cosmic particles from this source might have caused great leaps in human evolution. This is echoed by Andrew Collins who regards bursts from Cygnus X-3 as being instrumental in, *'accelerating human evolution during the last Ice Age'* (Collins 2006). This object, which is either a neutron star or a black hole, is the only one in our galaxy targeting us, due to the orientation of it's 'one-sided' jet, and recently some scientists have concurred that high bursts of cosmic rays may have altered our DNA (Biltcliffe and Hoare 2012, p. 21). It is somewhat amazing that the Dogons of Mali regard one particular point in the sky as marking their point of origin, their axis of the Universe – and that point is where Cygnus X-3 is located! (Collins 2006, p. 286).

During summer months in the Bronze and Iron Age the Milky Way rose out of Giant Hill at a very oblique angle, at times straddling almost the whole hill when viewed from the west. Midst the Milky Way, Cygnus rose over the Giant, holding the Great Rift within. So perhaps the appearance of Cygnus in line with the phallus of the Giant signalled the return of souls to this earthly plane, which for mere mortals is achieved through sexual union.

It is interesting that another dust-ridden part of the Milky Way in Sagittarius, known as the Dark Rift, similarly has associations with death and the Afterlife. The Maya, for example, called it *Xibalba Be,* meaning *'the Underworld road'* (Mann and Glasson 2007, p. 104).

Going back to Cygnus rising over the Giant during the Iron Age, we can now look at Cygnus and the Great Rift rising over Giant Hill, seen from the river below (image left). This scene is about half an hour prior to that on p. 126, just before the Swan clears the hill.

Cygnus, Vega, the Milky Way and the Great Rift, all rising out of Giant Hill during the Iron Age. This particular scene is on an April evening in 01AD.

With this in mind, we also have added relevance to Deneb setting into the region of High Stoy as seen from below the Giant (image p. 124); for as this happens, the Milky Way and the Great Rift both accompany Deneb down to the horizon, sinking or 'flowing' into High Stoy and Dogbury. This is that magical north direction spoken of by so many cultures – the direction of the ancestors, of the Otherworld.

Let us now turn our attention to what we can see of Cygnus and the Milky Way during summer nights when actually standing at the Giant, or at the Trendle for that matter. At this time, Cygnus follows closely behind Hercules to occupy a spot directly over our heads, a scene that has hardly changed perceptively in thousands of years. At these times, the Milky Way straddles the heavens overhead, with the enigmatic void of the Great Rift clearly seen.

Later in the evening, we could have stood and looked in the general direction of the Giant's gaze, c. 245°-260°, perhaps even lying down on his figure, looking skywards. Either way, we would have seen a wondrous sight. The head of Draco, the Dragon, was now almost overhead. The swan/cross of Cygnus was still high in the sky, the beak of the swan now pointed downward. It now hung vertically like a crucifix, a phenomenon that can only happen in the direction the Giant is facing, the ancient god and the symbol of the new god seemingly in a face-off. But eclipsing this was the sight of the Milky Way, as it plunged from the heights of the zenith down to the horizon, flowing like a misty river into Rowden Hill and Weam Common Hill, seemingly engulfing the Bellingstone. We can perceive this today, on any clear summer night, but light pollution from the streetlights of Dorchester to the south now robs us of the spectacle Druid astronomers would have enjoyed.

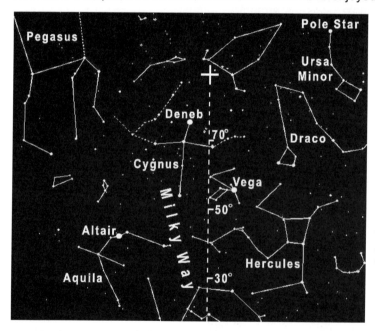

Looking west from the Giant on a summer evening during the Iron Age. Although this example is on August 29, 50AD, the scene would have been very similar for many centuries. The white cross is the zenith, directly overhead.

Pegasus

The *Square of Pegasus* is that familiar figure of summer skies, which in reality is a rectangle formed by four magnitude 2 stars, Scheat, Markab and Algenib in Pegasus, and Alpheratz, now designated to the constellation Andromeda. It can reach an altitude of over 60° from Southern England today, and attained only slightly less than this in the Iron Age. It is involved in some alignments in the Cerne area.

Mythologically, Pegasus was a snowy white, winged horse, the son of Neptune and Medussa, and was said to be Jove's *'Thundering Horse'* that carried divine lightning. Winged horses are clearly shown on Etruscan, Hittite, and Greek art, and Jewish legend speaks of *Nimrod's Horse*. The heliacal rise of this figure marked the winter solstice, and was described as, *'the habitation of the deity Ea... the Way of Anu'*. The

130

The winged horse Pegasus on a Greek plate.

Egyptians showed it as a jackal on the Dendera zodiac (p. 113), linking him to Anubis, whose role it was to welcome Kings and Pharaohs into the afterlife. This is a recurring theme, as horses were symbolic of journeys to the Otherworld, as we saw at Uffington.

To the Romans and the Celts, horses were associated with the goddess Epona or Rhiannon; the Grey Mare and Her Colts long barrow in Dorset (Knight 1996) may have been named after this deity. Under Silbury Hill, King Sil is said to be buried sitting on his horse, and sun gods were often depicted riding their steeds. In Gaul, the Celtic god Belinus carried the sun across the heavens on a horse-drawn chariot (Biltcliffe and Hoare 2011, p. 128). Several Romano-British 'horse and rider' motifs have been found, some of which were votive offerings (Bédoyère 2002). During the Iron Age the horse attained cult status, perhaps now outranking previous bull worship. It was now almost obligatory for a King to ride a white horse.

I was very intrigued to find that ancient Babylonian and Sumerian texts speak of the 'square' of Pegasus as a portal, a gateway to the Otherworld. This is shown on a stellar map reproduced below. The Babylonians described the square as 'L-LKU', an entrance into 'Paradise' (Santillana & von Dechend 1977). The way they depicted it reminded me of simulations of a black hole; it has wavy lines and a feeling of depth to it, of falling into some void. This Babylonian Stargate may be the origin of horses carrying the deceased to pastures new. The Greek name for Pegasus meant 'divine', and one description they had for it meant 'cut in two', meaning it was half hidden by heavenly clouds (Allen 1899, p. 322).

Pegasus was later seen as the Archangel Gabriel; Christians saw it as the ass that carried Jesus into Jerusalem; here too we have a human who is shortly to ascend to heavenly realms with the aid of an equine beast. The word Pegasus itself may come from the Phoenician Pag and Sūs, meaning the Bridled Horse, implying that it carried a rider (Allen 1899, p. 323).

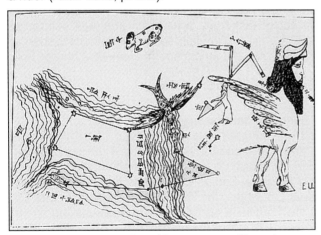
Babylonian depiction of Pegasus as a Stargate.
(After Santillana & von Dechend 1977.)

Running my astronomical programme for various sites around the Cerne Valley, I came upon some Iron Age alignments involving Pegasus. And this was, I might add, *before* I found out about the star-lore.

When viewed from Weam Common Hill, opposite the Giant, Pegasus rose out of the distant skyline directly in line with the Giant. The optimum time for this is between 1500BC and 200AD, after which the square had worked its way too far north along the skyline.

I found another intriguing alignment involving Dogbury Hill; Pegasus galloped up into the sky over Dogbury when viewed from High Stoy (on a bearing of about 100°). This is the locality of the eye of Gary Biltcliffe's proposed landscape horse! I also find it amazing that the star of Epsilon Pegasi was visible over Dogbury an hour before the square cleared the skyline. Arab astronomers called it either Enif or Al Naf, both meaning *'the nose'*, or else Fum al Faras, meaning *'the horse's mouth'*. One 17th century German astronomer called it Grumium, meaning *'jaw'*. So this star was clearly regarded as the head of the celestial winged horse, and the terrestrial landscape horse looked straight at it as it rose! This alignment works best between 500BC to 100AD, but Pegasus is visible over the hill outside of these dates. The appearance of the horse in the pre-dawn skies in April would have heralded Beltaine, and with it the hopes of the summer ahead. It is interesting that Pegasus culminated (in other words, was south at midnight) around the autumn equinox, just as Orion was rising out of the southern end of Giant Hill - both signalling that winter was not far away.

Pegasus, the winged horse, over Dogbury Hill in the Iron Age, as seen from High Stoy, the eye of a landscape horse.

Pisces also rose, below Pegasus, out of Dogbury. This was complemented by the rising of Hydra, the mythical serpent; the head and much of the body of the constellation was visible over Dogbury when viewed from High Stoy: this mirrors the folklore adage that a dragon haunts Dogbury Hill. A small Iron Age enclosure on the hill may have been an important holy place during those times, as it stands virtually equidistant from three main Iron Age centres at South Cadbury, Hod Hill and Maiden Castle. Tradition says that Arthur's Copse at Dogbury was the birthplace of the King. Are the landscape and celestial horses both his noble steeds?

Leo

The sickle-shaped form of Leo's head is a familiar object in our spring and summer skies. The lion is often associated with Kingship – as in the *'King of the Jungle'*. In one of his trials, Hercules had to slay a lion, and the Romans knew this constellation as *Herculeum Leo,* the *Lion of Hercules*. Distinct Egyptian references to Leo are on the walls at Thebes, whilst on the Dendera Zodiac Leo stands on an outstretched serpent; the Egyptian King Necepsos taught that the world was created when the sun rose in Leo. Pliny concluded that the Egyptians worshipped Leo because the rise of the Nile waters occurred when the sun was in that constellation; the Atum, the father-god, was especially worshipped as a lion. Even some Egyptian war goddesses were depicted with the body of Min (including the phallus), and with the head of a lion. To the Akkadians, Leo was *Gis-Mes*, the *'Curved Weapon'*.

132

The Persians, Babylonians, Turks, Syrians and Hebrews all saw Leo as a lion. Throughout history both the lion and the constellation Leo have been identified with the sun, although Chinese astrologers regarded these stars as either a horse or a yellow dragon. Lions abound on heraldry and royal coats of arms.

Regulus, the bright star of Leo, was so called by Copernicus as a derivative of Rex, meaning *King*, from a belief that it ruled the affairs of the heavens. One Phoenician

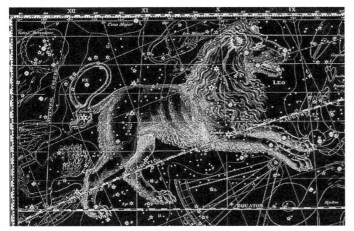

This image, dating from 1280, shows how people viewed Leo as the celestial lion.

god, Byblos, was depicted with a human body and a lion's head. To the Babylonians it was Sharru, *the King*, and he is shown as a lion on a zodiac depiction c. 2000BC. To the Persians it was Miyan, *the Mighty,* and the Sumerian goddess Inanna/Ishtar is sometimes depicted standing on the back of a Lion. Leo was known as the *'house of the sun'*, and the sun was in this constellation when Persephone was carried off to the Underworld with the changing season (Arthur Cook, *Zeus,* Vol 1, p. 230). The 4th initiation level of Mithraism is associated with Leo, and one of their characteristic symbols is the naked lion-headed (*leontocephaline*) figure found in Mithraic temples. He is entwined by a serpent, whose head often rests on that of the lion's. Although the exact identity of this lion-headed figure is debatable, it is largely agreed that the

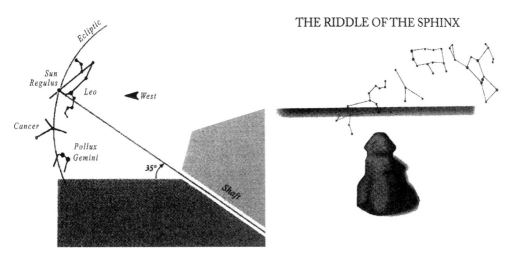

Left: Regulus and the sun aligned with a shaft at the temple of Arsameia.
Right: the rising of Regulus aligning with the Sphinx c.10,500BC.
(© Adrian Gilbert (2005), used with permission.)

god is associated with seasonal change.

Adrian Gilbert has demonstrated how a shaft at the temple of Arsameia in Mesopotamia was aligned to let the sun shine down its length on July 28, the day that the sun, in ancient times, was in conjunction with Regulus, the brightest star in Leo (image previous page). Stone Lions adorned with stars also show how important Leo was to the people who built the temple complex (Gilbert 2005, p. 85 and plate 10). Gilbert suggests connections between this great event and the lion-like sphinx at Giza, whose eyes were looking to where Leo rose c.10,500BC, the controversial date for its construction. Gilbert also found alignments with Regulus and Leo at the Temple of the Phoenix at Heliopolis, dated 3,100BC (op. cit. Plate 14). Like at Arsameia, the Egyptians also seemed to have noted that c. 2,280BC the sun's conjunction with Regulus also marked the summer solstice (op. cit. p. 295).

As if to complement Gilbert's findings at the Sphinx, Chris Street has advocated an east-facing landscape lion 'guarding' London, the head of which is in the Chigwell area of Essex (in Thorley 2012, p. 48-9). The River Lea (Lugh's River) runs down the back and shanks of the feature; in the Welsh language lion is *lleu*, so here we have the fusion of a solar god and a lion. Chris Street also describes how a *Coronation Line* is aligned with the midsummer sunrise and runs through his landscape lion. This links the Kingston Stone, Westminster Abbey and St Paul's Cathedral (site of another *King Stone*); all these sites represent '... *the notion of kingship; features entirely in keeping with the attributes of the regal leonine figure*' (op. cit. p. 52-3). Leo is of course represented in Kathryn Maltwood's controversial Glastonbury Zodiac, whilst John North found alignments with Leo at Wayland's Smithy, and at the South Street long barrow in Wiltshire.

During my calculations concerning the Cerne Giant, I sought to find any possible stellar alignments with Leo during the Iron Age. It will be remembered that when standing in the valley below the Giant, and in line with his phallus, the skyline rises between 10-12°, depending on where you stand and how close you are to the hill. John North commented that this area would be conducive to astronomical

Leo rising over Giant Hill in the Iron Age, as viewed from the river valley. Regulus, its brightest star, aligns with the phallus as it clears the hill.

observation. When standing by the river during the Iron Age, in the vicinity of the *'earthworks'* marked on OS maps, we would have seen Leo rise out of the hill above the Giant, and Regulus, its brightest star, rising directly in line with the axis of the phallus! The best dates for this are c. 50BC to 250AD. Standing on the phallus itself (skyline height +14-15°) Regulus rose a few minutes afterwards with the phallus pointing to the star.

I find it amazing that of all the places Leo could have arisen in the Iron Age it was above the Giant. Leo is associated with solar gods and kingship, the latter of which is connected with the fertility of the land; the Giant is a fitting epitaph to both. Later in the year, as the sun rose out of the Giant at Beltaine and Lughnasad, it was right next to Regulus in the sky.

Today, as seen from the riverside, Regulus clears the skyline further south (to the right) of the Giant (azimuth 85-86°). This can be seen about 1am mid-November, around 11pm mid- December, 9pm mid-January, 7pm mid-Feb, and so on. To see the view the ancients had, one has to walk north for a short while, so Leo also moves to the left and appears to align with the Giant (although Regulus is not in line with his phallus as it once was). If you do this, please try and visualise that it was a *lion* rising above the Giant, not just a configuration of stars. Only then may you get into the mindset of those who were watching this scene some two thousand years ago.

The bright star Regulus rising in line with the phallus. The optimum time for this view was c.50BC – 250AD.

Regarding the Iron Age *setting* of Leo and Regulus, this was between azimuths 300-330°, which was into High Cank (site of a henge) and Seldon Hill; the latter seems to have been pivotal to so many alignments.

Staying down in the valley, between 1500BC – 500AD to be exact, the head of Hydra, the sinuous celestial serpent, rose just to the right of the axis of the Giant, over his extended left hand in fact! Serpents have long been associated with phallicism and fertility rites. From the same vantage point, Pegasus cleared the hill to the right of the Giant. Andromeda and Perseus, the lovers in classical mythology, rose over the summit of Giant Hill and both stood resplendent above the Giant as if they had come to seek his fertilising powers; Perseus was an heroic warrior, who rescued Andromeda from a sea leviathan. The sky figure of Andromeda lay horizontally over the phallus of the Giant, reminding me of the Egyptian scenes of the goddess Nut arching over the amorous Geb. Later on during summer evenings, the brilliant Arcturus rose out of the summit of Giant Hill, whilst at the same time the long arm of Ursa Major, *King Arthur's Wain*, pointed directly down to the Giant, as if showing us the way.

It must also be remembered that the brighter planets, Venus, Mars, Jupiter and Saturn, inevitably and periodically rise over the Giant. Occasions such as these may have been seen as important omens. One planet outshines all the others – Venus. I document the following here, as the events I describe can only occur during the late-summer month of September.

Venus

In mythology, Venus is of course the Roman goddess of love. She was certainly worshipped in Britain in the Iron Age, as Roman-British carvings of her have been found at several sites. The goddess was connected with the phallus, proven by the carrying of phalli by naked women to the Temple of Venus in Rome at her festivals, held in April and in October (Scott 1966, p. 130-1).

Venus is often brilliant in the sky, and is in fact the brightest of all the 'stars'. There were several alignments of Venus with the phallus of Giant in the Iron Age; the star of love rising in line with the male member must have stirred the imagination, the emotions, and perhaps the loins! These occurred every eight years in September, when the planet was a morning star, when near its maximum elongation from the sun. From down in the valley in front of the Giant, we would have seen Venus rising over him in pre-dawn skies in September 5BC, 4AD and 12AD. During some of these elongations Venus and Regulus would have been very close to each other in sky, as the latter is very close to the plane of the ecliptic; this occurred on September 12th, 12AD, which was a particularly close conjunction. Venus was again over the Giant in September 20AD, and was close to Regulus around September 11th. The next two occasions were in 28AD and 36AD.

I have shown previously that at eight-year intervals Venus would have shone directly down the passage of West Kennet Long Barrow (Knight 2011, p. 208-9). During its orbital cycle the rising of Venus sometimes coincided with the midwinter sunrise point. I was privileged to witness Venus in the dawn sky prior to the great alignment of 2012 – the planet twinkled in the southwest, as if heralding in a new age, the goddess of love leading the way.

Chapter 11.
All change for the heroes

Eventually summer turns to autumn, just as winter turns to spring. These turning points of the year are marked by ancient festivals that mirror the astronomical cycles. In the spring we have Imbolc (Feb. 1) and the spring equinox (Mar. 21/22), and later, after the summer has passed, we come to the autumnal equinox (Sept. 21/22) and Samhain (Oct. 31 - Nov. 1). These events are dictated by the movements of the sun, of course, but almost imperceptible changes also occur in the stellar background of the night sky.

I have suggested that the super-heroes of myth, Hercules and Orion, are pivotal to understanding the Giant, and not simply in terms of *symbolic* parallels between the Giant and these ancient strongmen. By looking to the heavens, I sought to ascertain the times of appearance of the *constellations* of Hercules and Orion, and how these fitted into the Giant's landscape. John North speaks of a close association between myths and changes in the seasons: *'What is surprising of the myths known to history is how very many have to do with periodic natural change and the seasons'* (North 1996, p. 532). An example would be how the Goddess (the personification of life-force and fertility of the land) comes and goes with the seasons *to another realm,* born out by this Sumerian text, spoken by Inanna, in her role as Queen of Heaven and goddess of the rain:

'I step onto the heavens, and the rain rains down;
I step onto the earth, and grass and herbs sprout up'.

Way back in the February skies of 4000BC, Taurus set just as Leo was overhead: *'This would signal the start of springtime sowing of barley in Babylonia and the agricultural year'* (Bailey 1998, p. 202). In a Baltic myth, recorded in the 15th century, the sun is trapped inside a tower, causing all the earth to be in darkness. The constellations told a smithy that the only way of releasing the sun was by forging a *'great hammer'*. Having made this, the smith god broke the walls of the tower, releasing the sun to shine upon the world once more. This tale reflects the loss of the sun in winter and its return in the spring. I remind you of the myth of Dionysus, who sent satyrs to put Orion into a deep sleep so he could be blinded; this refers to

Orion's absence during summer months. He had to travel to the east to be healed by the sun. The Greek Corina sang of Orion, '... *conquering all the land of the dawn*', surely referring to its reappearance in pre-dawn skies in the autumn.

British folklore connects giants with the changing seasons, such as the tale of Wandil. He was a giant who stole spring, so winters grew longer and more severe. Later, he was captured by the gods, who made him relinquish spring. Wandil was immortal, so the gods threw him up into the heavens, where he is the constellation Gemini. His eyes are the two brightest stars, Pollux and Castor; it is said that there will be a heavy frost when they stare brightly down on the earth.

It has been suggested that it was not just Orion, but also Taurus that heralded the rainy season, because bellowing bulls were associated with storms; crashes of thunder were taken as the sounds of the celestial bull. An ancient Rig-Veda poem announces, '*Let the heaven, the tawny bull thunder*'. In one myth, Hercules strikes the bull Achelous, causing spring waters to issue from his mouth, explaining how the rainy season coincides with the appearance of Taurus.

For six months the skies are dominated by Cygnus the Swan and Leo the Lion. But Hercules, I believe, was the guardian of this summer cortège of stars, the superhero around which, you may remember, all the heavens once revolved when his stars were close to the celestial north pole. He is relatively faint compared to Orion, his winter counterpart - it is the Swan and the Lion who hold centre stage.

Looking at the star charts for the Iron Age, I found that in the autumn, as Orion gains prominence in the southwest, Hercules sinks into the northwest horizon, as if sneaking out by the back door. He never disappears completely, however, as a few

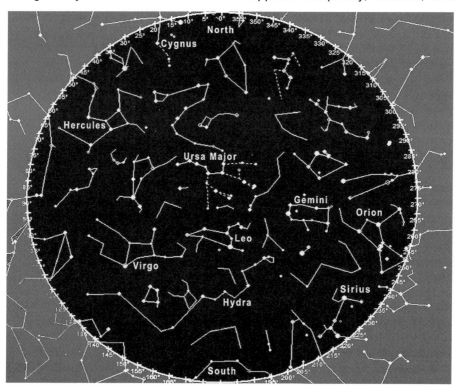

Star chart for Iron Age skies above the Giant: midnight Feb 1, 10pm early-April, 7pm mid-May. Orion sets earlier in the west each evening as Hercules rises in the east. Leo and Ursa Major are prominent in the south.

stars stay above the horizon as he swings by due north; these are so faint, however, that to all intents and purposes he has gone into the Underworld. Hercules has handed over the reins to his winter rival, Orion, who now rides high in the south. This arrangement also holds good for today.

The appearnace of Orion (as Sahu-Osiris) marked the changing of the seasons as this Egyptians text demonstrates:

'Osiris! You went away, but you have returned,
you fell asleep, but you have awakened,
you died, but you live again'.

Ursa Major (the Great Bear) and Ursa Minor (the Little Bear) are lowest in the skies during winter nights. This ties in with the winter hibernation of bears in caves; as they emerge in the spring, so the sun also comes back to life.

Six months later, as spring approaches, Orion sinks into the west earlier each night, so Hercules raises his whole body above the northeast skyline. Soon after, most of Orion has set into Weam Common Hill just as Hercules clears Giant Hill, as seen from the valley below; he announces, if less dramatically than Orion, the approach of warmer times. It is now Hercules' time to be high in the south, almost overhead, whilst Orion disappears from our night skies for most of the summer.

I also noticed that because these two constellations are 180° apart in the sky, at least one of them is **always** above the horizon from the latitude of the Giant. It would not have been seen as pure coincidence that these two superheroes were at opposite

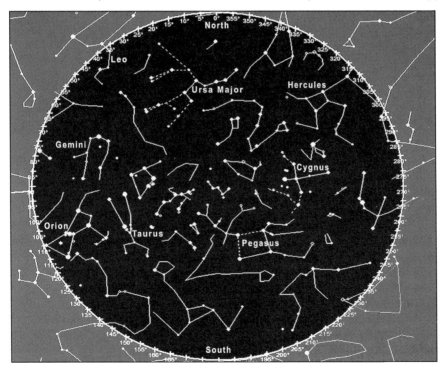

Star chart for Iron Age skies above the Giant; 1am mid-Sept, 10pm early-Nov, 6pm early-Jan. Hercules is about to set as Orion rises. Cygnus and Hercules set progressively earlier each night, as Taurus, Gemini and Orion rise to prominence, to dominate the winter skies.

139

sides of the heavens. Orion is prominent and bright, a fitting constellation to portray Osiris, Gwyn and other deities. But why was Hercules relatively faint compared to his winter counterpart? The answer is because mythology demanded it; they had to be 180° apart so that at least one of these guardians was always above the horizon. So regarding the allocation of Hercules to this particular configuration of stars, the ancient astronomers **had no choice!** Though I am sure they would not have looked at it in quite that way; they were looking for an arrangement of stars that fitted the bill in a precise location in the sky - and that is exactly what they were gifted by the gods.

Lion-headed Mithras, whose slaying of the bull brings forth spring.

At times, Hercules and Orion are *both* above the horizon, such as during the evenings in early spring, or during autumn/early winter evenings. These 'all change' positions herald the seasonal changes. It is as if the two giants are jostling for position, in an eternal celestial tug-of-war, just as the Oak King and the Holly King take turns over dominion of the land. In mythology, Hercules and Orion share many characteristics: they are both giants, both human and very strong, their weapons are a club, bow and arrow, they are both hunters, they slew lions, and may carry a lion's head in their hand or over their arm; *and* they were both transported up into the heavens. But they share more than that, for between them they were the heroic celestial gatekeepers that orchestrated the changing of the seasons.

It is interesting that as Taurus begins to fade from the skies in the spring, this is when Leo is south at midnight – the Lion rules! In some classical myths a lion slays a bull, reflecting this change of the seasons. A Roman hymn to Cebele from the second century AD contains the line, '*... mother of the immortal gods, seated in a chariot drawn by bull-killing lions ... who occupies the central throne of the cosmos, and thus of the earth*'. Mithras, the ancient sun god of the Persians who was popular with the Romans, is sometimes depicted with a lion's head (image above); he kills the bull and brings in the spring. He is sometimes carved as a youth emerging from a rock, which is indicative of the appearance of the new shoots of spring (image at beginning of chapter). Some see Mithras as the sun moving around the heavens, others see him as Time itself.

You may recall that Yuri Leitch linked Gwyn to Orion: '*... he is the constellation Orion... This great constellation is also the 'Winter King' because it appears in the sky from October... '* (Leitch 2007, p. 32). So Hercules begrudgingly makes way to the relentless march of Orion, accompanied by Sirius and Procyon, his two hunting dogs. Time now to see what wonders the Iron Age winter skies held.

Chapter 12.
Winter stars –
Orion & the bull

'I see the motion of the holy constellation Orion'.
(Egyptian *Book of the Dead*)

Few amateur astronomers would disagree with the statement that the winter stars are more spectacular to the naked eye than their summer counterparts. The brightest of the constellations is Orion, its belt pointing down to Sirius, the brightest star in the sky. The Milky Way passes overhead, with the brilliant Capella embedded within. Five other magnitude 1 stars are in attendance and the whole assembly is dazzling in dark winter skies. This section of the sky had special relevance to the Egyptians, for it contains the celestial personifications of Osiris, Isis, and a Stargate to other realms. Gods, goddesses, heroes and bulls, with their interlinked myths, all parade above our heads in a magnificent pageant.

Orion

This constellation is one of the easiest to spot in the night sky, and one of the best known. A configuration of magnitude 1 and 2 stars define Orion the Hunter, with his belt slung around his midriff. A few fainter stars and a nebula are his sword scabbard, hanging from the belt. The belt itself aligns with Sirius in one direction, and Aldebaran in the other. His one hand is raised to hold a weapon, like the Giant, and the other is extended, variously holding a bow, a shield, or a lion's head. All this sounds very familiar from our earlier studies of the Giant. A small cluster of stars above the belt are known as the 'eye' of Orion, defining his head.

The oldest image of a star pattern is that of Orion on an ivory tablet some 32,500 years old; the tiny sliver of mammoth tusk contains a carving of a man-like figure with arms and legs outstretched in the same pose as Orion's stars. It is now generally agreed by scholars that the myths of Orion existed prior to the constellation being assigned to him, making him one of the most enduring global heroes.

Middle Eastern myths speak of Orion as Baal, the *'storm god'*. His festivals took place in autumn, to mark the end of the agricultural season – just as Orion appears in the evening skies. The Babylonian star catalogues of the Late Bronze Age name Orion as *SIPA.ZI.AN.NA*, *'The Heavenly Shepherd'* or *'True Shepherd of Anu'* - Anu being the chief god of the heavens. This Babylonian constellation was sacred to Papshukal and Ninshubur, both minor gods fulfilling the roles of *'messengers to the gods'*. The Akkadians called Orion Uru-Anna, *'The Light of Heaven'*.

To the early Irish, Orion is Caomai, the *'Armed King'*, but was later known as An Selgaire Mhór, *The Great Hunter*. Kerbstone 52 at Newgrange has inscribed holes in groups of three, and this may be depicting the belt of Orion. The Norse held the constellation to be Orwandil, and to the Saxons he was Aegil the Archer, or the giant of winter, Waendel. In Arabic the constellation is Al Najid, the *Conqueror*. Orion's brightest star, Betelgeuse, has several Arab names, variously meaning, *'Armpit of the Central One'*, *'Right Hand'*, *'Shoulder'*, and *'The Arm'*.

I wonder if Orion was originally seen as Inanna/Ishtar by the Sumerians. In some images, she is shown with a bow and arrow, and as a huntress she is associated with Sirius the Dog Star, Orion's companion. She is also the goddess of the rains and storms, whose appearance, as with Orion, coincides with the end of summer and the onset of the stormy half of the year. It is interesting that Inanna is also the Goddess of War, like Mars, who I listed as one contender for the Giant's identity.

The belt of Orion attracted many myths in itself. It was also called *The Golden Nuts* by the Arab astronomers. Interestingly, Arabs knew the belt as Al Mizan al Hakk, the *Accurate Scale Beam*, whilst the ancient Chinese knew them as the *Weighing Beam*. This reminds us of St Michael who weighs up the souls of people, and harks back to the Egyptians, for it may be remembered that the shafts of Khufu's pyramid at Giza were aligned with Orion's belt (Bauval and Gilbert 1994). David Furlong suggests that the three main pyramids on the Giza Plateau represented Osiris, Isis and Horus, the Egyptian 'holy trinity' (Furlong 1997, p. 75). Mark Vidler has found correspondences between many terrestrial sacred sites and celestial objects (Vidler 1998).

In the UK, Thornborough Henge (Yorkshire) and the Priddy Rings (Somerset) are two prehistoric monuments that seem to represent the three stars of Orion's belt (Leitch 2007, p. 51). There are also the Three Fates, three Plagues of Britain, three ribs of Corineus, the three Cyclops, three Wyrd Sisters, three festivals of Sirius, three Celtic gods of art, three witches in *Macbeth,* Faith Hope and Charity; the Greeks also held that Mount Olympus, home of the gods, had three peaks. In Norse myth, the shaman figure Vainamoinen searches the body of a dead giant for *three* lost runes. Christians knew the belt of Orion as the Three Magi or Three Wise Men. A remnant of the mystery cults of Orion is the belt worn by the dancing Dervishes, which has three knots, said to represent the Orion' belt (Gilbert 2005, p. 187).

In some depictions of Mithras, there are seven stars on his cloak, making a possible connection with the seven bright stars defining Orion's configuration. The main Mithras myth, and the chief ceremony of his adherents, involved the sacrificing of a bull. Orion of course faces Taurus the bull in the sky. Further interest comes from scholar James Moulton, who suggests that Mithras may have derived from *metru,* the Assyrian word for *rain*. It will be remembered that Orion was associated with the rainy season (Moulton 1911, p. 36). The Syrian storm god Jupiter Dolichenus is shown standing on a bull with a weapon in his raised hand (Bailey 1998, p. 221).

In Aesop's Fable 123 (Greek 6th century BC) we read: *'Orion with his golden bow is on watch during the night.'* The Greek myth in which Orion is blinded clearly parallels the story of Samson, the Biblical strong man, who was blinded by the Philistines; Samson pulls down the halls of his captors, letting in the light of the sun.

Orion is the only figure in constellation mythology that was blinded. One account of Orion's death states that he boasted he would conquer all animals, clearing the earth of all wild beasts, and that the Earth Goddess sent forth a scorpion, whose sting killed him. This myth plays out Orion's winter dominance, the time when many animals are hibernating - he has indeed temporarily 'conquered' them.

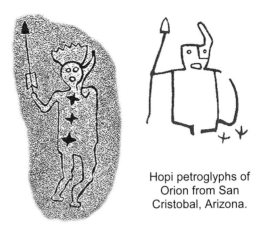

Hopi petroglyphs of Orion from San Cristobal, Arizona.

In Cambodia, Orion was seen as a trapper of tigers, whilst in China the constellation is *War Lord Tsan,* the hunt master of autumn skies. Orion is also referred to by Hebrews and Christians in the Bible: *'The Bear, Orion, and the Pleiades, and the chambers of the south'* (Job 9:9); *'See him that maketh Pleiades and Orion'* (Amos 5:8). Recently, Gary A David (on *The Orion Zone* website) has suggested that Orion myths were familiar to the Hopi Indian of Arizona. They certainly made images of the constellation, as petroglyphs from San Cristobal verify (images above).

According to a 6th century poet called Jacob of Serug, a deity worshipped at Harren in the Middle East was *'Mari [lord] of his dogs'.* Adrian Gilbert suggests that, *'It seems likely that this 'lord' was the constellation Orion the Hunter'* (Gilbert 2005, p. 80). Gilbert believes that when Hercules was originally designated a constellation in the sky, it was not the faint one now assigned to him, but the stars we know as Orion: *'I believed now that Hercules, like those other heroes, Samson and Osiris, were represented in the sky by the Orion constellation'* (op. cit. p. 85).

It is perhaps in ancient Egypt, above all else, that the movements of Orion were most keenly followed, because it was regarded as the celestial representation of one of their main gods, Osiris, known as Sahu-Orion: *'Thy sacred image, Orion in heaven, rises and sets every day';* the soul of Osiris was laid to rest in Orion. The Book of the Dead tells us, *'The Osiris N is the constellation Orion...'* and *'Osiris... In your name of Dweller in Orion'.* Egyptian Pharaohs and kings hoped to join Osiris in the skies, becoming one of the stars of Orion. This is why several major sites are aligned with Orion. This image (right) is from a wall at Teotuhuacan, and Orion is painted carrying a staff or mace in the same hand as the Giant.

The Sphinx at Giza aligns to where the head of Orion was rising in the east around 1800BC (Gilbert 2005, p. 273). The belt of Orion is famously featured in *The Orion Mystery* by Robert Bauval and Adrian Gilbert, in which they propose that the plan of the pyramids at Giza reflects the positions of the belt stars (Bauval and Gilbert 1994). They also confirmed earlier work that shafts running through the Great Pyramid

Sahu (Orion) painted on the western wall at Teotuhuacan, Egypt. (© A Gilbert (2005) used with permission.)

aligned to both Sirius and the belt of Orion around 2600BC, as well as to former pole stars (op. cit. p. 100). It has also been implied that several Egyptian sacred sites are located to form the shape of Orion on the earth.

Gardiner and Osborn have traced the similarity between Egyptian myths and some Arthurian tales, plus those of Odin and Bran the Blessed. They conclude that, *'It seems that everything leads back to Osiris, as if he is the archetypal Shining One...'*

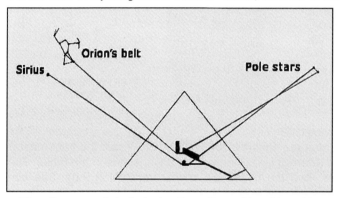

The alignment of shafts in the Great Pyramid at Giza with Orion, Sirius and two pole stars. (After Bauval and Gilbert.)

(Gardiner and Osborn 1997, p. 71); and Osiris, as we have seen, is Orion. Odin and Orion are further connected in that they both heralded impending storms, or could indeed cause them. In one Teutonic myth, giants called upon Odin for help, where upon he caused a storm to rise and removed a great mill to the Milky Way, after which it was known as *Mill Way*.

We shall return to Orion as Osiris in the next chapter, when we look into the Egyptian belief that a Stargate existed in the region of Orion, and that Osiris lead them through it.

Throughout later history, Orion was still seen as the hunter-warrior figure on most star charts and globes, as seen by these two examples below. Sometimes he carries a sword, or else a club, and bears either a shield or a lion's head before him. Poets have been moved to write about Orion, such as Shelley: *'Far o'er southern waves immovably, belted Orion hangs'.*

I am about to propose some alignments concerning Orion and the Giant. But are there any precedents for the constellation of Orion aligning with any other sacred sites in Britain? It turns out that there are plenty!

John North (1996) has shown that during the Neolithic, Orion hovered over the skyline above the Long Man of Wilmington, with Rigel just skimming the horizon as it reached its culmination (see image next page). This alignment not only

Time-lapse photograph of Orion against the starry background.
(By 'Mouser', Wikipedia Common Licence.)

worked in the Neolithic, but at later times also, for one had only to walk closer to the Long Man to see Orion 'stand' on the hill above him. Even today, Orion continues to, *'walk along the Downs'* (North 1996, p. 204). As said before, the Long Man may have inspired the Giant at Cerne, as it is almost certainly much older. One of the adjacent

144

barrows to the Long Man is *Hunter's Burgh,* suggesting a link with *Orion the Hunter.* North noted a similar phenomenon at West Kennet Long Barrow, as Orion 'walked' along the barrow mound if viewed from the valley to the north (Knight 2011, p. 201). John North also found alignments with Orion at the White Horse of Uffington, (North 1996, p. 195).

Neolithic star-gazers at West Kennet Long Barrow produced an alignment with neighbouring East Kennet Long Barrow that resulted in Orion rising over the latter (Knight 2011, p. 200). The orientation of the axis of West Kennet Long Barrow also means that Orion sank into the mound when viewed from outside the entrance (op. cit. p. 202).

Nicholas Mann and Philippa Glasson have convincingly described Orion alignments in the Glastonbury area (Mann and Glasson 2007) and Yuri Leitch suggests that Orion was the god Gwyn at Glastonbury (Leitch 2007). Orion is said to be represented in the Glastonbury Zodiac as a giant, whose head is Dundon Hill Fort. He raises his arm to fight, it seems, an adjacent figure of a bull (op. cit. p. 42). Mann also found intentional alignments between Orion and sacred sites around the Avebury landscape (Mann 2011).

Adrian Gilbert has proposed that Orion may later have been identified with Jesus, as some Christian Middle Eastern sites align with the constellation, and suggests that, as in previous ages, the constellation can again guide us into a new age (Gilbert 2005).

The Giant and Orion

If we run with the premise that the Cerne Giant may possibly have been regarded as Orion, Gwyn or Osiris, or at the very least by certain people during part of its long history, we would expect to find some alignments involving the figure and the constellation. My research did not disappoint me. Again, it was all a matter of where you stood, when you stood there, and at what time of the year. For when one stands in front of the Giant, as we did to observe Leo rise, we see the main body of Orion rising to the south of Giant Hill. I shall return to this in the next chapter, because what is important here is that the Giant aligns with something significant that lies at the end of Orion's outstretched club – the Stargate!

Two astronomical star charts, showing how depictions of Orion can vary. The club, however, is present in both examples.

Orion rises out of Dogbury Hill during the Iron Age. The three stars of the belt have just risen out of the hill, and now point back down to it.

But for now, we shall now go back, Tardis-like, to the Iron Age and return to three important hills in terms of the Giant's story. Firstly, we shall stand on High Stoy, at the eye of the landscape horse (image p. 46), and look over to nearby Dogbury Hill, the sacred Iron Age sanctuary. You may recall that Pegasus cleared the horizon over Dogbury. Under winter skies we find a more spectacular and a very precise alignment. Viewed from High Stoy, Orion's belt rose straight out of the summit of Dogbury Hill, and the whole of the figure cleared the horizon directly over the hill. More than that, the three stars of the belt pointed straight down to the hill! This must have been a profound sight to the Druid astronomers standing on High Stoy. They would have first witnessed this in pre-dawn skies in early August; after that Orion would have risen earlier each day until, by the autumn, it rose around midnight - signalling that winter was not far away. This alignment worked best between about 500BC to c. 500AD, after which Orion moved too far north. Even now, however, Orion floats over Dogbury soon after rising – so the effect can still be appreciated.

From Seldon Hill, Orion rises out of the distant skyline directly over Giant Hill in the Iron Age. The last star rises right over the Giant. This example is on Oct 20, 50AD. The arrow marks Giant.

Orion 'walking' across the hill above the Long Man of Wilmington in the Neolithic. (After J North 1996.)

Let us now stand on Seldon Hill in the Iron Age, and look towards the Giant (a bearing of 112º), as we have already during the daytime (see image p. 44). This was the site of prehistoric activity, and later Iron Age settlements. From here we would have seen Orion (aka Lugh or Gwyn) rising directly out the distant skyline (which is almost the same height) directly above Giant Hill (image above) and that the very last star of the Orion's figure (Saiph) cleared the hill directly in line with the Giant!

From Weam Common Hill, directly west of the Giant, the distant skyline is only a few metres higher than the observer, a long, unbroken skyline that stretches out in front of us. From here, we have another variation on a theme regarding Orion. We first would have seen Orion's shield or bow, as well as his outstretched arm holding his weapon, rise out of Giant Hill. Then came the bright star Bellatrix, marking the giant hero's shoulder. Next to rise was the brilliant Betelgeuse, the Arab *Armpit of the Central One,* and Orion's head, formed by a triangle of fainter stars. Gradually the configuration moved upward and south, until we would have seen the stellar giant standing directly over the spring (Silver Well) with the belt pointing down to its sacred waters. Because of the width of the constellation, the date range for this is around 500BC – 500AD, but Orion rose over Giant Hill centuries either side of this.

As Orion rose out of the southern end of Giant Hill, it gradually became visible from the valley below, at the foot of the hill figure; Orion's belt pointed down to the Giant and Trendle as it rose, seemingly out of the spring and the nearby mounds. We shall return to this location shortly, as we witness the Milky Way rise vertically out of the hill directly above the Giant, including the intersection of the ecliptic and the galactic plane - the Stargate point.

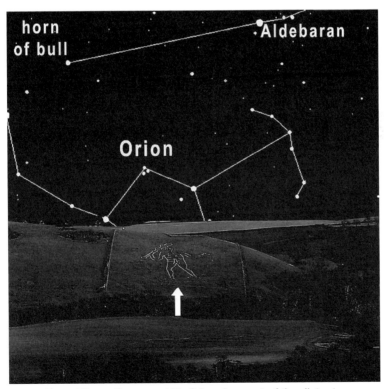

From Weam Common Hill, Orion rises out of the distant
skyline above the Giant. Arrow marks Giant. This view is
around 50AD.

147

Orion as it began to set into Rowden and Weam Common Hill. Standing on the Giant, this was the view, as the earth giant witnessed the sky giant descend into the Underworld. This scene is from a late-winter evening, c.100AD.

The Giant's 36.5m (120ft) long club is also relevant, in terms of the direction it is pointing. Its axis would appear to be 108-110°, so standing at the bottom of it in the Iron Age, Orion's belt would have risen directly over the Trendle, its three stars aligning back down to it. The club points the way!

But what of Orion's *setting* from the Giant? The hill opposite is only about 2° higher than the Giant's head, so appears virtually level to an observer. You may remember that the Giant looks in the general direction of 245-260°. Just prior to setting in the Iron Age, Orion's bow and arrow pointed directly down to the Bellingstone! Soon after, the main stars of Orion started to set at azimuth 245°, as Rigel disappeared in the vicinity of the Bellingstone; Rigel set exactly at the Bellingstone c. 300BC! The belt of Orion then set into the hill just south of due west, with Bellatrix setting into the summit of Weam Common Hill, followed by Betelgeuse further north, at around 272°. From the Giant and the Trendle to the summit of Seldon Hill is 294°, marking where the extended club of Orion set. Again, it depended on where you stood; if you were positioned on the top of Giant Hill, at the Trendle, you would have seen the stars set slightly later and further north than from down in the valley below the Giant.

Philip J Grant, Yuri Leitch, and Adrian Bailey had suggested that the Cerne Giant may be Orion, as I have acknowledged. I hope I have now given convincing evidence to link these two superheroes as never before.

Harking back to William Holloway's poem, 'The Giant of Trendle Hill' (see page 29) he tells us that,

'Thrice he essays to rear his head,
… And thrice to raise his arm…
… The night was cool, the turf was soft…
… From here, when cheerful summer comes… '.

I think the number three is important as it links to the two pairs of three ribs of the Giant. Or is this referring to the three giants, Hercules, Orion and the Cerne Giant himself? More than this, the tale clearly took place in winter - when Orion ruled the

148

skies. The role of Orion in British myth was played out by Herne the Hunter, and by Mabon of the Celts. This winter deity was the only god who could handle the hunting dog Drudwyn. Let us now meet the hound.

Sirius

Sirius, the Dog Star, derives its name from the Ancient Greek *glowing* or *scorcher*, although the star has over 50 other designations and names attached to it. It is the brightest in the sky at magnitude −1.46, and follows Orion across our winter skies, the belt of Orion pointing more-or-less to it. It is in the constellation of Canis Major, the Great Dog, and nearby is Canis Minor, the Little Dog, marked by the star Procyon; Betelgeuse, Procyon and Sirius form a celestial equilateral triangle. The Sirius system is one of Earth's near neighbours at 8½ light years, and is currently heading towards us at around 10 miles a second. It has moved position equivalent to the diameter of the moon since Rome was built, and will increase in brightness over the next 60,000 years.

Images of dogs on sacred objects go back at least to the Neolithic, and a record of Sirius by name dates to the 7th century BC, in Hesiod's poetic *Works and Days*. Sirius is the only definitively named individual star of the Egyptians (Allen p. 123). Its hieroglyph is a dog, and the star was regarded as the resting place of Isis. The Temple of Sakkra may have been erected in the star's honour (Allen 1889, p. 123), as well as the Temple of Satis at Elephantine and the Temple of Horus at Djebel Thoth. The latter two had to be dismantled and realigned to take account of Sirius' rapid motion across the sky (Mann and Glasson 2007, p. 77). In Egyptian mythology, Sirius was known as Sothis and Isis Hathor, as well as Sopdet, Sihor, Sed, and the *Nile Star*. Egyptians based their calendars on Sirius' heliacal rising, namely the day it became visible just before sunrise, when far enough away from the glare of the sun after a 70-day absence. This occurred just before the annual flooding of the Nile and the summer solstice; Isis had returned after her journey through the Underworld.

The goddess was revered in Britain too, following Scotia's arrival on these shores. Part of the River Thames and Isis Parlis Cave (Cumbria) are named after her (Biltcliffe and Hoare 2012, p. 335).

In Egyptian sacred manuscripts called the Pyramid Texts, we read:

'... you are this Great Star, the Companion of Orion, who traverses the sky with Orion... In your name of Dweller in Orion, with a season in the sky and a season on the earth, O Osiris, turn your face and look upon this King, for your seed which issued from you is effective'. In another text, a later Ptolemaic manuscript, Isis speaks to Osiris: *'Thy sacred image, Orion in heaven, rises and sets every day; I am Sothis following after him, and I will not forsake him.'* As shown above in this chapter, one of the shafts in the Great Pyramid was aligned with Sirius (Bauval and Gilbert 1994, p. 174).

To the Greeks, the period following the star's appearance were known as the *Dog Days* of summer. The universality of Sirius myths may be due to the fact that the star can be seen from almost every inhabited region of the Earth's surface, with only those living north of latitude 73° being unable to see it. The

To the Egyptians, Sothis-Isis was the personification of the star Sirius.

culmination of Sirius was celebrated on February 11th at the temple of Ceres in Eleusis. Homer, in the *Iliad*, describes Sirius and Orion: *'That star [Seirios the dog-star] which comes on in the autumn and whose conspicuous brightness far outshines the stars that are numbered in the night's darkening, the star they give the name of Orion's Dog, which is brightest among the stars'.* From around 238BC onwards, the Romans sacrificed dogs to Sirius at May festivals, as the sun approached the star in the sky (Allan 1899, p. 121).

In Chinese astronomy the star is the *'celestial wolf'*. Further afield, many of the indigenous peoples in North America also associated Sirius with canines; the Seri and Tohono O'odham of the southwest held the star to be a dog that followed mountain sheep, while the Blackfoot called it *'Dog-face'*. The Cherokee paired Sirius with the star Antares as dog-star guardians at either end of the *'Path of Souls'*. A Cherokee folktale tells of a dog who stole some cornmeal and was chased off. He ran away to the north, spilling the cornmeal along the way; the Milky Way is thus called *Gili Ulisvsdanvyi* – *'The Way the Dog Ran Away'*. The Wolf (Skidi) tribe knew it as the *Wolf Star*, whilst others knew it as the *Coyote Star*.

In Scandinavia, Sirius has been known as Lokabrenna, *'burning done by Loki'*, or *'Loki's torch'*. Sirius was a British Wolf Goddess, the form taken by the Irish goddess Morrigan. Irish myths speak of the god Lugh being accompanied by his magical hound:

'That hound of mightiest deeds,
Which was irresistible in hardness in combat,
Was better than wealth ever known,
A ball of fire every night'.

This suggests another connection between Lugh and Orion, and for Lugh's hound being Sirius. Perhaps the link between Lugh and a dog was because in the Iron Age Sirius first appeared in dawn skies around the end of July, thus marking Lugh's festival in Northern Europe! Lugh, as Orion, had already appeared in dawn skies a couple of weeks before, but the festival was held when his dog made it's appearance! Sirius became visible when the sun was in conjunction with Regulus.

Sirius is mentioned in *the Koran*: *'... That He is the Lord of Sirius (the Mighty Star)'*, and the Arab astronomers knew Canis Major as Al Kalb al Jabbār, *'The Dog of the Giant'*. In India, sanskrit texts say the star represents the god Shiva.

Dogs often guarded the threshold between the realms of living mortals and the Otherworld of the dead and the gods. The Egyptians had Anubis, and the Greeks Cerberus, who both guarded portals to other realms.

And it wasn't just the Egyptians who had been awaiting the return of Sirius, for here in Britain the early farmers, *'... would have come to value the dawn risings and dusk settings of Orion and Sirius, as vital signs of the best time to plant and harvest the grain crops'* (Mann and Glasson 2007, p. 78). Farmers would have seen that Sirius was no longer visible from early April, and made it a marker for planting; the star's heliacal reappearance in August signalled harvest time.

Research by Mann and Glasson at Glastonbury and Avebury, and my own findings at West Kennet, have proven that British farmers had been accurately watching the motions of Sirius and Orion since the Neolithic; star-gazers at West Kennet Long Barrow, for instance, had produced an alignment between neighbouring East Kennet Long Barrow and the rising of Sirius (Knight 2011, p. 200). In the lower Neolithic, Sirius briefly rose in the same position as the winter solstice sunrise, which may explain why so many sites are aligned with this direction (Knight 2001 & 2011, and Mann 2011).

Modern writers, such as Aleister Crowley, Murry Hope, Robert Temple and M Temple Richmond, have advocated that Sirius has affected the development of human evolution. Philip Coppens believes that, '*Sirius and Canopus* [the second brightest star] are associated with evolution*ary affairs of Earth and Humanity, and herald potent global experiences… Sirius holds specific responsibility for Earth*' (Coppens 2004). Robert Temple, in *The Sirius Mystery,* cited how the Dogons of Mali had identified Sirius' dwarf star companion, Sirius B, long before science discovered it, and that they had been contacted by a civilisation from the Sirius star system (Temple 1975). He also argued that the sudden rise of the Egyptian civilisation was due to this '*alien intervention*'.

The Druids, as I have mentioned, had to pick Vervain at the moment Sirius rose (Whitlock 1979, p. 87), and the rising & setting of Sirius was recorded by the Iron Age Chaldeans, c. 300BC.

Seen from Seldon Hill, Sirius rises over the spring, an alignment specific to a narrow time band in the Iron Age.

As Sirius rose much further south than Orion, around 115° between 100BC and 100AD, I was not expecting many alignments between the star and the Giant. From the Giant, it rose to the south of the Trendle, as it did from the valley below the Giant, where it cleared the distant skyline at around 135°. This is the direction, however, of the sacred spring, the Silver Well. Sirius (aka Isis and Morrigan) was therefore seen to rise over it (out of it?) reminding me that most springs were associated with goddesses: Sirius was known to the Egyptians as, '*the bringer of water*'.

The spring has, of course, associations with St Catherine, who replaced the feminine Pagan deity of the spring. The spot where the star *visibly* rose, around Piddle Wood near St Catherine's Farm on Black Hill, is close to the site of a lost Christian chapel.

Shortly after clearing Giant Hill (viewed from the valley below), when Sirius was around 12° high, the Giant's empty left hand pointed to Sirius. Was this Osiris pointing to Isis, his divine wife - the '*Hand of God'* no less?

From Seldon Hill, Sirius again rose over Black Hill, but further to the east, on an azimuth of c.120°-122°. This is because Seldon Hill is only slightly lower than the height of the hill over which Sirius rises - so the star rises earlier and further east than down in the valley. Despite this, Sirius still rises over the spring (image above); soon after this happens, Orion's belt also points down to the Giant.

Regarding the setting of Sirius in the Iron Age, when viewed from the Giant or the Trendle, the star set into Rowden Hill, just south of the Bellingstone. You may recall that the Giant is facing this general direction. The belt of Orion had also set just minutes before Sirius.

In 1976 a dog figure was reported near the Giant (p. 58). I felt the location of it to be amazing, for the dog lay in the same positon in relation to the Giant that Sirius is to Orion in the night sky! Orion's raised arm, and the Giant's club, both extend back to their respective canine companions! Philip J Grant, from Bournemouth, had already made this connection in a letter to *Dorset Magazine* (1978, 54, p. 32), *'A dog figure to the left of Cerne [Giant] would relate directly to Sirius in astronomical terms'*. No one had picked this up and investigated it further, until now!

Eridanus – the river

I do not think it would have gone unnoticed by ancient astronomers that the constellation Eridanus, the river, rose out of the skyline directly above the spring when viewed from the valley immediately below the Giant. This long and sinuous configuration of fainter stars begins next to Orion's right foot, and takes its name from the Babylonian constellation known as MUL.NUN.KI, the *Stars of Eridu*. Eridu was an ancient city situated in marshy regions in the south of Babylonia; it was sacred to the god Enki-Ea who ruled the cosmic domain of the Abyss, the mythical fresh-water reservoir below the Earth's surface. It was linked to the River Nile in Egyptian myth, and identified with the Po in Italy. The stars that correspond to Eridanus are also depicted as a river in Indian astronomy; Eridanus is called *Srotaswini* in Sanskrit, *srótas* meaning the course of a river or stream. It is depicted as the Ganges on the head of Dakshinamoorthy, an incarnation of Shiva. Dakshinamoorthy himself is represented by the constellation Orion.

Before Orion reached due south, it was Eridanus that stretched across the lower half of the southern sky, at one point 'flowing' into the horizon. It is as if the River Cerne, which flows south, connects with its celestial counterpart. This would have been the view from the Trendle or, better still, from further up the river valley, such as on High Cank or Dogbury, where the view to the south was less impeded, as the river stretched away southwards.

Taurus the bull

Taurus is another prominent constellation of the winter skies. Its brightest star is Aldebaran, of magnitude 1, whilst Taurus is also the home of the Pleiades and Hyades star clusters, both visible to the naked eye. Taurus and Orion are inextricably bound together, not just by their close proximity in the sky, but also by their myths. Further to this, the hero and the bull are central elements of the cult of Mithras, which we shall look at. The *'Horns of Taurus'*, as we shall see, are also connected with the proposed Orion *Stargate* of various mythologies. A 19th century poet spoke of this connection:

'I mark, stern Taurus, through the twilight grey,
The glinting of thy horn,
And sullen front, uprising large and dim,
Bent to the starry Hunter's sword at bay'.
(from *Hymn to Taurus*, Bayard Taylor)

Bull worship is very ancient; a cave painting at Lascaux, dated c.15,000BC, depicts a phallic bird-headed man with a bull to his right (p. 62). Taurus is one of the oldest recorded constellations, due to the fact that between 4000BC and 1700BC, a period when astronomy was birthing as a science, it marked the spring equinox. More than most constellations, the naming of this configuration is remarkably similar in different cultures, such as El Taur (Arabia), Taura (Syria) and Tora (Persia), proving that they

saw the same beast. Around 3000BC the Sumerians regarded the spring equinox as the start of their year, and the reappearance of Taurus in dawn skies also heralded the reappearance of Sirius. Its loss was sung about in hymns:
'The wild bull lives no more, the shepherd, the wild bull lives no more.
Dumuzi, the wild bull, lives no more' (Baring and Cashford 1991, p. 222).
Aldebaran is the brightest star of Taurus and 5000 yrs ago the Persians held it as one of their four Royal Stars. Baal, the son of *'the Bull El',* was a fertility god, said to bring the rains from the heavens. Orion and Taurus appeared in the sky when the rainy season was nigh; sometimes shown as a bull, Baal gave his creative power to the Earth.
Taurus is the bull tamed by Jason the Argonaut, and is also the Cretan Bull. At Catal Hüyük in Turkey, several bull images and relics were found; the bull, *'... was the principle animal epiphany of the god... all these compositions are images of the dynamic fertilising power that calls out or awakens new forms dormant in the old'* (Baring and Cashford 1991, p. 75). The people of Catal Hüyük even named their local mountain range the Taurus Mountains, after the bull god. The Chaldeans had noted that in spring the sun rose in the Bull, and to the Akkadians Taurus was the *'Bull of Light'.* In Greece the god Bacchus was at times depicted with the head of a bull, linking the fertility god with Taurus, the celestial bull; because of his high sex drive and virility, the bull has a long association with fertility, one that is universal, seen as a fitting symbol for masculine creative vitality.

Mithras slaying the sacrificial bull, whilst looking back at the sun. (Koln Museum. Wikipedia Common Licence.)

Like Orion, Taurus also represented the bull-god Osiris, and in fact Egyptian creation myths say the human race was created when the sun was in Taurus. Text on an obelisk at Thebes declares, *'Horus, the Mighty Bull'* and alignments with Taurus and the spring equinox were made around that time (Gilbert 2005, p. 100 and p. 106). Taurus also represented Isis, who is often shown with horns on her head, or as a milk-giving cow. She leads Orion/Osiris into the sky and again follows later as Sirius. The sky goddess Nut is sometimes depicted as the *'heavenly cow'* and in one tale carries Ra (the sun) across the sky.
In Iron Age Britain bull worship was prolific. Inscriptions to Serapis, the local equivalent of Apis the Bull, were found at Romano-British sites at York and Kirkby Thore (Bédoyère 2002). Mithras is often depicted slaying a bull (image above). The Druids held their festival of Tauric when the sun entered Taurus and it has been suggested that the tors of Britain might be old sites of their Taurine cult (Allen 1899, p. 382). Scotland has its Candlemas Bull, an old Imbolc purification icon.

Taurus and the Giant

Bull worship was present in Dorset in the Iron Age; effigies of them were found at such places as Maiden Castle, Stoke Abbot and Lychett Minster, all of which can be seen in the County Museum in Dorchester (Knight 1998, p. 82). In fact, the frontispiece of the 10th century *Book of Cerne* is embellished with a bull representing St Luke, through whom Christianity sought to take over the bull as a spiritual icon. In Dorset, it was a custom to place a bull's heart up the chimney to ward off evil spirits (Knight 1998, p. 94). The sun passes through Taurus between April 20 to May 21 each year – at Beltaine. Beltaine was the festival of Bel/Baal, and was a time when cattle were purified, giving us a link with Taurus the constellation. Medieval documents record bull-baiting, which was followed by the slaughter of the bull, and the carrying of the carcass up a hill to be roasted.

Considering the astronomical alignments of hill figures, John North suggests that back in the Neolithic the Uffington Horse may have been a bull. Over the centuries it became a dragon (thus Dragon Hill) and is now a horse. The head does have two horn-like extensions that could easily have started out as horns. It is prehistoric in origin, and in Iron Age times, when a large settlement was established nearby on top of the hill, a new mythos developed, indicative of the beliefs and totem animals of the new clans. Nicholas Mann has also proven that the rising of Orion and Taurus were marked out as far back as the Neolithic in the Avebury area (Mann 2011, fig. 16).

You may recall the account of 1865 folklore that the Cerne Giant used to, *'stride over to the opposite hill, where Belchalwell nestles under Bulbarrow'*. The *Bel* and *Bul* elements link this tale to bull worship and the constellation Taurus.

In the Iron Age, an observer standing on the higher slopes of Weam Common Hill would have seen Taurus gradually rise over the distant skyline, which mirrors that of Giant Hill below. The full extent of Taurus did not become

Taurus the Bull rampages across the heavens directly above the Giant, as seen from Weam Common Hill. This example is on Dec. 25, 01AD. Arrow marks Giant.

visible until it was directly above the Giant. Aldebaran was bright, with the two horns of the bull reaching out horizontally northwards, running almost parallel with the skyline. The image I show here is about half an hour after it became visible, just as the shield or bow of Orion appears, and this view held good from around 800BC to 200AD. Taurus also appeared to rise directly over the Giant when viewed from the Bellingstone, but from here it was the tips of the two horns that aligned with the Giant,

154

just after they rose. This works between 500BC to 100AD. Outside these dates the angle of the tips of the horns still align to Giant, but they rose further north. I also found it amazing that, as seen from down in the valley in front of the Giant, Taurus finally clears the hill just as the tips of the horns align with the phallus!

So, up in the heavens, above the fertility earth giant, the celestial bull, symbol of fertility, charged across the heavens. What a spectacle this would have been to an Iron Age shaman-astronomer, and, as Orion rose, the eternal battle between the hunter and the bull commenced.

When viewed from the Giant, Taurus set into both Weam Common Hill and Seldon Hill, the Pleiades being the last to disappear into the latter. This happened in the pre-dawn skies at Samhain, just as Leo was due south; Taurus and Leo were Samhain *'time keepers'*.

The Pleiades

The Pleiades, commonly known as the *Seven Sisters,* is the well-known cluster of magnitude +2 and +3 stars in Taurus. The cluster is easily visible on most clear winter nights, and keen-eyed people can make out more than seven stars. The Pleiades are mentioned in Chinese texts in 2,357BC, making them some of the first stars to be mentioned in astronomical literature. The Greeks regarded the heliacal rising of the Pleiades in May to mark the beginning of the seafaring season. To the Egyptians, they represented Nit or Neith, one of the principle deities of Lower Egypt (Allen 1899, p. 399). Ancient knowledge had been given to Native Americans by *Star Women* who came down from the Pleiades. The heliacal rising of the Pleiades in May was marked at Cuzco, Peru, where the cluster was known as the *Storehouse*, because of its connection with agriculture. In fact, Indian texts (c. 1,730BC) speak of *The Great Year of the Pleiades,* their term for the 25,900 year precessional cycle.

John North found an alignment with the Pleiades at West Kennet Long Barrow (Knight 2011, p. 205-6). It has been suggested that the seven chambers of the Great Pyramid commemorate these stars. Greek temples, such as the Great Parthenon, were orientated to them; the Temple of Bacchus in Athens, dated 1030BC, was aligned with their setting,

The Pleiades have attracted much interest from New Age circles in modern times. In Theosophy, it is believed the *Seven Stars of the Pleiades* transmit the spiritual energy of Seven Rays from the *Galactic Logos* to the *Seven Stars of the Great Bear;* from Sirius these energies are sent via the sun to the Earth, and finally through the seven Masters of the Seven Rays to the human race.

The Pleiades preceed Aldebaran and the horns of Taurus out of the horizon. From the valley below the Giant in the Iron Age, the little star cluster clears the hill directly over Giant's left hand and the Trendle. The stars would have been visible from the moment they rose out of Giant Hill as they were already 12° above the astronomical horizon. From across the valley, anyone standing at the Bellingstone would have seen the Pleiades rise directly above the Giant.

Mithras

The solar hero and the sacrifical bull merge in the worship of Mithras. This deity originated in ancient Persia, but continued to flouirsh in later times, reaching Rome by the 1st century BC, thereafter becoming a widespread cult across the Roman Empire. Mithras is closely associated with the sun and is a god of war. Mithraism was a complex cult, where adherants went through seven grades of initiation, involving a symbolic death and rebirth, some rituals including the infliction of pain and being showered with blood from a sacrificial bull. The nobility of Rome, including Emperors, aspired to this cult and it came to Britain via the Roman elite.

Mithras is often depicted rising out of a rock, emerging as a nude youth, with a dagger in one hand and a torch in the other, and wearing a Phrygian cap. He represents the 'rebirth' of the sun following winter. However, there are variations on this and sometimes he is shown as coming out of the rock as a child holding a thunderbolt. This thunderbolt links him to Orion, who is the god associated with the stormy season of the year.

Mithras is closely associated with bulls, which were ritually sacrificed in his name in the *Tauroctony,* depictions of which have been found across Britain. The Mithras cult was alive and well in London in Roman times, and a marble carving of a Tauroctony in was unearthed in Walbrook in 1889. In this scene Mithras is sacrificing a bull, surrounded by a zodiac (image p. 163). We shall return to this important relic in the next chapter. Mithras was very popular with Roman soldiers and most of Britain's Mithraea turn up in military contexts (Bédoyère 2002, p. 177). At Roman Chester, the

This star chart from 1601 epitomises how cultures have envisaged Orion and Taurus for thousands of years.

bull is named as Actae, which must be killed in the autumn enabling the springs to be filled.

Other Mithraea were found at Lanchester, Carrowburgh, and Housesteads on Hadrian's Wall, and at High Rochester and Caerleon. One major centre seems to have been at Brading on the Isle of Wight, which became a focus for this mysterious cult. It has been suggested that St Paul landed on the Isle of Wight to preach the new faith because of this local Mithras veneration (Biltcliffe and Hoare 2012, p. 44-5).

Mithras temples or shrines could be built anywhere that water was available (Bédoyère 2002, p. 175). In one story, Mithras strikes a rock and a spring opens up in the ground – just like the miracle of St Augustine. Was this myth surviving at Cerne when St Augustine arrived and was replaced by his *'miracle'*?

Mithras is probably one of the least plausible suspects to be the Cerne Giant

per se, although Michael Speidel does associate Mithras with Orion (Speidel 1997). But that does not mean that there is no connection, or that the god was not influencial locally after the Romans arrived. The deity had his birthday on December 25th, giving him links with the midwinter sun and the new solar god, Jesus. Mithras was the Sol Invictus, the *'Unconquered Sun'*, who returned after midwinter, and it has been suggested that his cult was part of an increased interest in the concept of monotheism (Bédoyère 2002, p. 179). This is reminiscent of the 'One God' of some ancient cultures, such as the Atum in Akhenaten's reign in Egypt, and Baal in Syria. Mithras is often depicted with a billowing cloak and a dog, two of the 'lost' elements of the Giant.

It has recently been proposed that the symbols of Mithras - the bull, snake, dog, raven and twin torchbearers - are all star constellations, representing the sun's passage through the heavens by the solar god, Mithras himself (Bailey 1998, p. 217). D Jason Cooper regards the images of Mithras slaying the bull as astronomical illustrations, with Mithras portraying the constellation Orion (Cooper 1996, p. 66). Mithras was later assimilated into St Michael and St George, the patron saints of soldiers. In William Holloway's poem *'The Giant of Trendle Hill'* (see page 29) he describes:

'The sturdiest bull that graz'd at large,
With single stroke he slew',

I wonder if this is a distant subconsious memory of Mithras and Taurus? We shall return to meet Mithras again soon, concerning a mythic sky portal. All the above myths give us an idea of how the bull was associated with fertility and human virility, and how the celestial bull was Taurus. Although Orion and Taurus are in a celestial stand-off, eternally in opposition, the bull must be slain if winter is to end; like Mithras, Orion has to be victorious for the sun to return. The horns of the bull tower menacingly over Orion, our hero, but they are also pointing to something else. They guard a secret – but one that was once well-known by astronomer-priests for thousands of years.
The horns of the bull, and Orion the Hunter, both guard the Stargate.

157

Chapter 13.
The Giant and the Stargate

'I open the door in heaven'.
(Egyptian text.)

In this chapter I shall bring together elements we have looked at previously – Orion, Osiris, Mithras, Gwyn ap Nudd, and the bull, and I will detail the concept that a celestial *'Stargate'*, a door to the afterlife, was existent in myths across the ancient world. I shall present the case that the Iron Age designers of the Cerne Giant knew of the Stargate and aligned him with it, and did so with great accuracy.

The heavenly gates

Ancient cultures often spoke of portals in the sky where there was interaction between our earthly domain and the Otherworld, places to where the dead journeyed, and where many of the gods resided. This is because they believed that the Otherworld was not somewhere below us, but rather above our heads.

In the *Book of the Dead,* the Egyptians often refer to the soul's **celestial** journey. The *Book of Gates* is an ancient Egyptian funerary text dating from the New Kingdom, c. 1133BC), and narrates the passage of a newly deceased soul into the next world; it is analogous to the sun's journey through the Underworld during the hours of nightime. The soul was required to pass through a series of 'gates' at different stages on its journey; each gate was associated with a goddess or god, and the deceased was required to recognise that deity. As well as being *exits* from our world, these gates could also be *entrances* to it. John North is of the view that prehistoric people saw the stars as carriers of the dead: *'It is conceivable that the stars were seen, if not as the souls of the dead themselves, then as genial visitors to the dead, possibly famous ancestors. Perhaps they were thought to carry the soul of the dead upwards'* (North 1996, p. 526).

I have already described two regions, in Pegasus and Cygnus, which were regarded as portals to the Otherworld. Two other areas in the sky, however, greatly eclipse these as locations for so-called *'Stargates'*, in terms of the sheer weight of star-lore. These two sacred places are where the ecliptic (the sun's annual path around the heavens) converges with the galactic equator, the plane marking the axis of our galaxy. These crossing places were known as Saltire Crosses; Saltire literally means *'leap into heaven'*. Anthony Thorley comments, *'… they were considered to be portals, or star-gates, to the celestial Elysian Fields of Heaven… the souls of men were considered to incarnate to Earth through the star-gate between Gemini and Taurus'* (Thorley 2012, p. 99). Nicholas Mann comments on these convergences: *'As far as esoteric significance of the crossing-points is concerned they are central in several astronomical traditions'* (Mann 2011, p. 334). Mann found alignments with these points at Neolithic sites around Avebury. Much later, St Peter's keys to Heaven, his crossed *Saltire Keys,* were enshrined in Vatican heraldry.

The southern convergance of the ecliptic and the galactic plane is in Sagittarius, near its border with Ophiuchus, close to our galactic centre; the northern convergance is on the borders of Orion, Taurus and Gemini, above Orion's upwardly pointing club. Both of these crossings are embedded in the Milky Way, which, as we have seen, was integral to one's journey to the afterlife: *'Universally, indigenous peoples and ancient civilisations have seen the Milky Way as the 'road' or 'river' to the sky-world…'* (Collins 2006, p. xv).

Its name comes from its appearance as a dim "milky" glowing band that arches across the night sky, because the naked eye cannot distinguish the myriad of individual stars. Our Solar System is located within this disk, around two thirds of the way out from the galactic center, on the edge of a spiral-shaped concentration of stars, gas and dust called the *Orion–Cygnus Arm*.

The Greek Aratos wrote of the Milky Way: *'That shining wheel, men call it milk… all through historic time it has been thought of as the River of Heaven'* (Allen 1899, p. 474). To the Akkadians of Mesopotamia (c. 2300-2150BC) it was, *'connected with the hill of the Sun-God and the passage of ghosts, is the Milky Way'* (op. cit. p. 475). In Hungarian mythology, Csaba, the mythical son of Attila the Hun and ancestor of his race, rides down the Milky Way whenever Hungarians living in Transylvania are threatened; they called it, *'The Road of the Warriors'*. Siberian Altaic people call the Milky Way the *'tracks of God'*. In the Bible, Jacob sees a ladder ascending to Heaven. Jacob says, *'Surely the Lord is in this place, and I did not know it'* (Gen. 28:16); the three stars of Orion's belt are called Jacob's Staff. As two scholars conclude: *'The way of the dead to the other world had been thought to be the Milky Way, since the oldest days of high civilisation'* (Santillana & von Dechend 1977, p. 211).

The Roman writer Ambrosius Macrobius (4th century AD) states quite clearly that the *'gate' through* which souls arrive and leave the earth is, *'… where the Zodiac and the Milky Way intersect'* (op. cit. p. 242). Some southern hemisphere cultures, such as the Polynesians, speak of an entrance to the Otherworld being at the galactic-ecliptic convergence in Sagittarius, which is more prominent in southern skies. The sun occupies Sagittarius at the midwinter solstice, when the sun symbolically dies. A tympanum at Kencot (Oxfordshire) depicts Sagittarius the archer slaying a dragon: *'This carving may represent the symbolic slaying of the Earth dragon at the winter solstice'* (Biltcliffe & Hoare 2012, p. 140).

The Northern Stargate

It is the northern portal, above the figure of Orion, that we shall concern ourselves with regarding the Cerne Giant. Several things amaze me about this northern convergence point. Firstly, it is not marked by any prominent stars. One would not expect an area lacking bright stars to attract the attention of ancient people - but it did! Secondly, the upheld club or mace of Orion is immediately below the point and, more than this, ***points directly to it***.

Thirdly, on running my astronomical programme, I was amazed to discover that the configuration of Orion's club pointing to the convergence point has held good since c. 3500BC, and will continue to do so until around 3500AD. Orion (aka Lugh or Gwyn ap Nudd) eternally directs 'traffic' in the direction of the Stargate. This crossing-point has always been in the same location in the sky; stars inevitably move, if but slowly, across the stellar background, the Stargate does not - it is a stellar constant. The Ancients would have noticed this. Such important points in the sky would have been seen as crisis-resistant portals, where the dead could 'change platforms' on their journey, so to speak: *'The constellations that serve as "gates" to the Milky Way must "stand" upon the earth… and once precession had been discovered, the Milky Way took on a whole new and decisive significance'* (Santillana & von Dechend 1977, p. 244-5). Finally, the horns of Taurus the bull direct us to this portal.

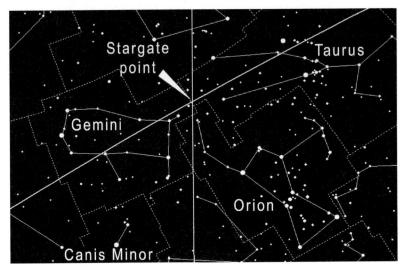

The Stargate point, marked by the intersection of the galactic plane and the ecliptic (the sun's path), as it was relative to the stars in 50AD.

Many cultures tell us that this point is important for humankind, where we either enter or leave our world, and there are many substantiating myths. The two 'gates' are 180° apart, so as one point rises, the other sets – another celestial constant. The only thing that changes is what time of the year the sun passes through these points, due to precession. There is no physical reason why the northern Stargate should be above the outstretched arm of Orion, for it could have been anywhere in the sky. It is fate, one might say, a mere coincidence (if there is such a thing), but one that had huge implications for the religious, political and social history of Mankind. I find it interesting that the two main 'protagonists' or 'guardians' at each cross-over point are both hunter/ archers, Sagittarius and Orion. Sagittarius is shown as an archer with the

In this Egyptian painting, Orion (Osiris) leads the divine cow Sothis (Isis - Sirius) across the heavens.

face of a lion on the Dendera zodiac, and rules the heavens during the summer, at the opposite time of the year to Orion.

Key to my understanding of this special place came by way of best-selling author Adrian Gilbert. He was a speaker at the 2012 *Convention of Alternative Archaeology and Earth Mysteries,* an event I host annually in Wiltshire. After his enlightening presentation, he inadvertently left behind two copies of his book *Signs in the Sky* (Gilbert 2000 and 2005); they had been meant for someone else. It was one of those magical, synchronistic moments, for I soon saw why the book had been drawn into my consciousness. Gilbert proposes that several ancient sites in the Middle East, including Egypt, were aligned to this particular place in the sky, described as a gateway to other worlds. He established that it was the god Osiris who helped people cross over to the Afterlife, and Egyptians saw his stellar representation as the constellation of Orion. Macrobius, in his *Commentaries on the Dream of Scipio,* also expressed the concept that between lives men's souls dwelt in the Milky Way.

Years earlier, Gilbert (with Robert Bauval) had concluded, '*... the constellation of Orion was one of the dwelling places of the souls of the departed kings, who became stars*' (Bauval and Gilbert 1994, p. 77). Adrian Gilbert believes the Egyptians regarded this place as something of a '*Stargate*'. In some images, Osiris/Orion is shown holding an ankh, which Gilbert concludes is the key to the Stargate. He points out that although the hieroglyph for a five-pointed star, *s'ba,* means *star,* it has a secondary meaning, which is '*door*' (Gilbert 2005, p. 198). Another Egyptian text says, '*I open the door in heaven*', and Gilbert proposes that the ankh may also represent the Stargate itself. It is interesting that Persian astronomers saw Orion's upward-reaching line of stars as Al Taj, *Crown of Kings;* this is the road to the Otherworld, along which the departed Kings and Pharaohs journeyed.

If we take Orion as Osiris, and that the 'doorway' to otherworlds is in Orion, then the following Coffin Text is interesting, which appears to tell of Osiris' **phallus** being a door bolt or latch to heavenly realms:

'*The phallus... is drawn back, and the doors of the sky are opened, the King has*

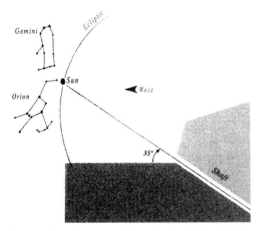

Above: the alignment of the shaft at the temple at Arsameia with the Stargate and the sun. (© A Gilbert, used with permission.) Right: a King shaking hands with Orion or Hercules at Arsameia. (Image: Klaus Peter Simon, Wikipedia Common Licence.)

opened the doors of the sky because of the furnace-heat which is beneath what the gods pour out' (Coffin Text 313). I shall return to this phallus-Stargate connection soon. The idea of being accompanied to the heavens by a deity was widespread; on his deathbed, Socrates talked about this journey to the 'other side': *'When a man dies his guardian deity, to whose lot it fell to watch over the man while he was alive, undertakes to conduct him to the other world'.*

In another Pyramid Text (PT 1717) we read, *'… The Duat [Osiris's realms] has grasped the king's hand at the place where Orion is… betake yourself to the Waterway [Milky Way]'.* An Egyptian magic spell states, *'I am the guardian, I am his [Osiris'] heir on earth. Prepare a path for me, O you who are at peace; see, I enter into the Netherworld, I open up the beautiful West, I make firm the staff of Orion...'* In some temple paintings it is Osiris as Sahu (Orion) who leads the dead to the afterlife, sometimes standing on a boat.

It may be recalled that a shaft at the Mesopotamian Mithras temple at Arsameia was once aligned with Leo. Gilbert also discovered that the same shaft aligns with the Stargate of Orion, which is also where the sun stood on the ecliptic around May 27th. Orion reaches up to the sun as it is in, what Gilbert calls, *'the shake-hands position'.* On this date, the sun shone down the shaft, allowing the soul of its departed King to journey to the afterlife. This is mirrored by St Christopher carrying Jesus (solar god) across the river on his shoulders: Orion 'carries the sun' when it is over the constellation in May. At this time of year the sun is midstream in the Milky Way, the *'river of the heavens'.*

The Arsameia temple complex has statues seen previously as a King shaking hands with 'Hercules', but Adrian Gilbert now believes this club-wielding figure is Orion (image above). It is interesting that Hercules carried out his 'labours' with the help of Orthus, his two-headed dog. This links with the two dogs of Orion, Canis Major and Canis Minor, which accompany the hunter across the skies.

You may recall that the Akkadians of Mesopotamia, c. 2350-2150BC, called Orion *'the Light of Heaven'* (Allen 1899, p. 304). The idea of a celestial road and doorway to the afterlife was not restricted to the Middle East. Euripides spoke of the Milky Way as the place of the Creator: *'Thee I invoke, thou self-created being, who gave birth to Nature'* (Allen 1889, p. 476). Macrobius also called this the *'portal of man'*, said to be where souls incarnate. The Greek scholar Porphyry comments thus: *'A cavern pleasant… a lofty gate unfolds on the either side; that to the north is pervious to mankind'* (in Mann 2011, p. 334).

The re-birthing aspect of the Milky Way is born out by the Arabian name for it: *'Mother of the Sky'*, whilst to Ethiopians it is *'Mother of the Bend'.* The Vikings knew it as the *'Path of Ghosts'*, the route to Valhalla; did they see Orion as Odin?

The Bella Cool Indians of Canada tell of how the gates of sunset and sunrise are guarded by a giant warrior named the Bear of Heaven, who only lets the sun pass through, but not humans. Cherokee Indians believe that after death souls pass on through an entrance at the *'Northern End of the Milky Way'*, in the Taurus/Gemini area of the sky, from where they are then transported to a *'Spirit Star'* at the other end of the galaxy in the constellation of Scorpio (Santillana and von Dechend 1977, p. 407).

The Celtic god Gwyn returns to earth at Beltaine in a boat-shaped coffin; the Egyptians often depicted Osiris, Horus and Sirius journeying in boats. Like Osiris, Gwyn, *'… escorts the dead to the gates of the Underworld'* (Mann 2002, p. 17). Gwyn-ap-Nudd himself said, *'I have been where the soldiers of Britain were slain… I am the escort of the grave'.* **Orion's stars were quite literally seen as Gwyn leading the departed through the Stargate!**

Vedic texts from India speak of the Gemini/Taurus 'gate' as the home of Brahma, the creative male principle, source of the vitality of the gods. The closest bright star to it, Alnath, represented the fire god Agni.

The concept of celestial rivers interacting with the earth is confirmed by Indian texts called the *Vishnu Purana,* which tell us that the Ganges was born of the Milky Way, as it literally falls down from heaven. The Aborigines of Australia speak of seven sisters, probably meaning the Pleiades, who came through a great hole in the sky *in Orion* (Knight and Lomas, 1999, p. 127). Readers of classical mythology may recall how Hercules had to draw his bow in order to settle the seas that Oceanus had whipped up; if Hercules were indeed the constellation Orion, as Gilbert suggests, then it would seem that Orion is leading us out of the troubled waters of mortality - to Paradise. Orion is the Gate Keeper; an Egyptian text advises us that, *'Orion leads the way so follow in his footsteps'.*

Expanding his theory about Orion being the home of the northern Stargate, Gilbert notes that Orion's belt points directly down to the Mount of Olives in Jerusalem when viewed from the Citadel (Gilbert 2005) and at Jesus' Ascension (on May 27, 29AD) the sun was very close to the *'shake-hands'* position in the sky. The same point to where the Arsameian King ascended via the shafts was now the cosmic focus for the ascension of Jesus. *'… just as the Orion constellation symbolised Osiris, the 'Father' of the Egyptian Pharaohs, so in the new Hermeticism of Christianity it stands for Jesus' 'Father in Heaven' '*(op. cit. p. 235). Gilbert concludes that, *'This makes sense of Jesus' statement that he was going to the right hand of his father in heaven. The right hand of Orion symbolized in the starry world his spiritual transition back through the 'Stargate''* (op. cit. p. 297).

On one sculptured relief of the god Mithras, he is **shaking hands** with the sun god Sol. In some temples, Mithras held a thunderbolt, again linking him to Orion, who is associated with the stormy season. It may be remembered that Mithras was associated with the sacrificial bull; this portal lies midway between the main stars of Gemini and Taurus, right in front of the tips of the

Mithras depicted from the Roman Mithraeum at Walbrook in London. Is he inside the Stargate?

bull's horns (beta and zeta Tauri). The horns always set just before the portal, and Nicholas Mann finds the relationship between the horns and this point was recognised by Neolithic astronomers at Avebury: *'The horns appear to draw the crossing-point down to the horizon, embracing Silbury Hill [as seen from the Sanctuary]'* (Mann 2011, p. 207). The bull symbolises fertility, new life, re-birth and, like Orion, Taurus was often depicted as Osiris, as a bull god. The Phoenicians and Hittites had a weather-god that held lightning bolts in his hand and is carried along on a chariot pulled by bulls, such as on a Hittite frieze at Malatya, which dates back to the 10th century BC. This links with Orion and other European

163

weather/thunder gods. Mithras was one of the dominant early cults of the Middle East and the bull was inextricably linked with him. The god's birthday on December 25th was adopted by Christianity for the birth of their own 'sun-god'. Was the bull so prominent in these cultures because the Stargate was right in front of the horns of Taurus?

When we look to the sky, the bull seems to be rushing towards the Stargate, as if its horns are about to gore it. The brightest star in Taurus is Aldebaran, which in Hebrew is called Āleph, meaning *God's Eye;* the bull is looking straight at the Stargate point. Sumerian texts tell us that Mithras *'... passed through the Horned Gate that marked the entrance to the Nether World'* (Baring and Cashford 1991, p. 223). This *'Horned Gate'* is the Stargate point. So Mithras, the sacrificial god, slays the bull and goes through the portal to be reborn. In several Tauroctony depictions, Mithras is looking behind him, over his right shoulder, as he stabs the bull. Is he looking at the Stargate - is he in fact Orion? A Tauroctony found at the Roman Mithraeum at Walbrook, London, shows Mithras slaying the bull whilst looking back over his shoulder, accompanyed by a figure holding a torch (image previous page). Around him is a circle containing the zodiac symbols, representing the sun god's annual passage through the heavens. But is the god also standing at the door of the Stargate? It is quite interesting that this Romano-British work is very similar to the *Stargate* machine in the movie of the same name; on that device some of the heiroglyphs resembled the configuration of Orion!

As we have seen, the horns of Taurus are visible over the Giant, preceding the Stargate (image p. 154). These horns have both been visible over the Giant since around 100BC, although the upper star (beta tauri) has cleared the hill (seen from the valley) since around 1400BC. Above the Stargate is Capella, the brilliant star of the constellation Auriga. To the Egyptians, the star was known as the male god Ptah, meaning *'The Opener'*, and at least half a dozen Egyptian temples, and at least two Greek temples, were aligned to it (Allen 1899, p. 87-8). His main centre was at Memphis, where his worship involved creation myths. We have a direct link with Orion at Memphis, where he was worshipped as *Ptah Seker Osiris.* Interestingly, Ptah's consort is the lion-headed goddess Sekhmet – Mithras was sometimes shown with a lion's head.

Sirius the arrow

My research has revealed that some ancient cultures, such as the Chinese, the Egyptians and some Mesopotamian cultures, depicted Canis Major (the Great Dog) as a bow and arrow, with Sirius as either the target or the tip of the arrow. As if to confirm this, on the Egyptian Dendera Zodiac the divine goddess of archery, Satit, aims her arrow at Hathor, who is Sirius. The Babylonian name for the star is KAK.SI.DI, meaning *arrow.* The Persians knew Sirius as Tir, and portrayed it as an arrow. The Babylonians and Sumerians configured a bow and arrow from the constellations Canis Major and Argo, whilst the Chinese also associated Sirius with an arrow (images right and below). It got me wondering as to where this arrow was being aimed, as no one seemed to have looked

Ancient Chinese illustration of the Stargate point, midst a watery whirlpool, above an archer. The bow and the dog represent Sirius.

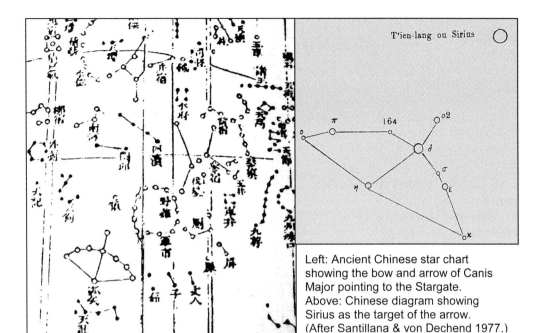

Left: Ancient Chinese star chart showing the bow and arrow of Canis Major pointing to the Stargate.
Above: Chinese diagram showing Sirius as the target of the arrow.
(After Santillana & von Dechend 1977.)

at this before. On running my *SkyMap* programme I was astonished to see that it pointed to the raised arm of Orion, towards the Stargate! Incredibly, this has been the case for at least 6000 years, and continues to this day – it is an additional celestial constant. True, the arrow, if released from the bow, would have passed no closer than 5° to the Stargate in ancient times, but in the general direction of the Stargate it certainly would fly. This alignment is just as accurate as some other so-called 'markers' in the sky; for instance, the Belt of Orion does NOT point to Sirius, as is often quoted on *The Sky at Night* and elsewhere, but misses it by about 4°; a line drawn from the two *pointers* of Ursa Major actually misses the Pole Star by around 5°. Even though these examples do not *exactly* line up, to the naked eye they work as effective guides. I find it interesting that although the Sirius arrow does not point *exactly* at the Stargate, on one chart (above left) the Chinese astronomers depicted it **as if it did**. This is not an error – they were making a point (quite literally!). I am not aware anyone else has made this connection.

From a 1825 star chart called the *Urania*. This shows the Little Dog (Canis Minor) and Monoceras, the unicorn, pointing to the Stargate.

Just as Orion had his great hunting dog Sirius, so too Gwyn had his dog, Dormarth. His name literally means *Death's Door*. Is this because Dormarth is Sirius, and therefore relates to the Stargate? Gwyn is extended to *'Gwynfa'* meaning *'Paradise"* (Leitch 2007); Gwyn, as the celestial Orion, is pointing to and guarding the *Gate of Paradise*. Like Osiris, Gwyn ap Nudd, *'... escorts the dead to the gates of the Underworld'* (Mann 2002, p. 17). The Celtic god Lugh was known as *'Lugh of the Long*

165

Arm'. Was Orion seen as the celestial Lugh, stretching his *'long arm'* up to the Stargate?

Something else I believe has not been commented on previously is that the two brightest stars of Canis Minor, the Little Dog, also point to the Stargate! This dog is also one of Orion's hunting companions, whom the Egyptians saw as Anubis (the Jackal-god), a deity with obvious connections to the Otherworld; incredibly, the ancient Chinese also saw Sirius as a celestial jackal, T'ien-lang! The more I look at all these myths, the more I see common threads running through them, many of which lead to Orion - and the Stargate.

The Stargate and the Giant

I am sorry if some may feel I have laboured some points above, but I felt it imperative to detail how cultures had seen this particular spot in the sky (one that contains *no* bright stars) as a portal to other realms – a Stargate no less. But what of the Cerne Giant? When I ran the sky programme for the Iron Age I was, not for the first time, astonished to discover that of all the places the Stargate might have risen - **it rose above the Giant!**

Even during previous millennia, the Stargate point had risen over Giant Hill if viewed from Weam Common Hill, the Bellingstone, or indeed from the valley below the Giant. But it had been rising to the south of where the Giant would later be (a full 12° further south back in 2000BC, for instance). Bronze Age astronomers had watched Orion undertake a slow precession northwards along Giant Hill, and I believe that their Iron Age brothers noticed that something was about to 'click'. By creating the Giant when and where they did, they joined the heavens and the land, through an alignment and imagery that had not been possible before.

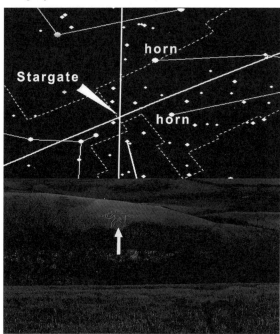

From the Bellingstone, the Stargate point hovers above the Giant not long after rising in the Iron Age. It aligns with the phallus just as the club of Orion clears the skyline.

During these inspiring times, an observer standing in the vicinity of the Bellingstone would have seen the Stargate point right over the Giant, just as Orion's 'club' became fully visible (image left). The galactic plane was **almost vertical** as it rose out of the distant skyline, the Milky Way appearing as a misty road that joined the heavens with the landscape. Again, this phenomenon had not, and could not, have occurred until the Iron Age. The example shown here is from 50AD.

And what about the view from next to the river, in line with the Giant, a spot we have visited previously? Around 30 minutes after viewing it from the Bellingstone (image left), the Stargate point cleared Giant Hill from our valley viewpoint – and it did so directly in line with the phallus! This event occurred from about 700BC to around 200AD. As I have said, the galactic plane rose *vertically* out of Giant, and on autumn-winter nights there are times we can still observe this; at other times of the year, the Milky Way rises at a much shallower angle (image p. 129). In the diagram below I have added in the misty course of the Milky Way for extra effect. Donning their mythic hats, I wonder if our ancestors would have seen the contact between the Giant and the Milky Way (rising from out of Giant Hill) as the ejaculation of the Giant! I have already described how the Milky Way is connected with gods and fertility; and, after all, this whole scene is being overseen by Taurus, the virile bull.

The Stargate was south at midnight at the midwinter solstice, as is still the case today – a celestial constant. Later on during winter nights, we would have seen the Stargate point set into Seldon Hill, a hill that has been involved with some of our other astronomical studies, and will be again regarding the sun; we saw, for instance, that this was the place from which to see Orion rise over the Giant.

During the Iron Age, the sun passed through the Stargate, immediately above the outstretched club of Orion, around the end of May; the date varies depending on the era. For instance, c. 600BC the sun was in this position in the third week of May, but

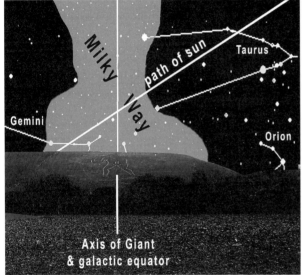

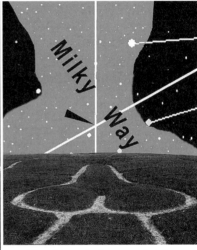

The Stargate (arrowed) rising over the skyline in the Iron Age, as viewed from the phallus.

When viewed from the valley below the Giant, the galactic plane and the Stargate point cleared Giant Hill above the Giant's phallus. The Milky Way was vertical as the tip of Orion's club rose. This example is c. 50AD.

by 01BC – 100AD it was the around the end of May. At this time of the year, Taurus the bull was too close to the sun to be visible - it had been 'killed' by the sun, in the guise of the mythological solar hero Mithras/Orion/Osiris.

You may recall that Rodney Castleden suggested that the Long Man of Wilmington might be holding open the doors of some sort of *'portal'*. Orion soared over the Long Man, carrying the Stargate point (image p. 146 – bottom right); the Long Man, like the Giant, stood at the doorway to the Otherworld!

I have previously demonstrated how at West Kennet Long Barrow during the lower Neolithic, Orion set into the mound when viewed from the entrance (Knight 2011, p. 202). Looking at this again, I can now see how the Stargate point also set into the barrow, in line with its axis. Looking in the opposite direction, viewing Orion rising around that time, the Stargate point is right in front of the entrance, a few degrees above the skyline! This is the direction of the passage and the entrance of the barrow. Were the shamans directing their consciousness along the passage to the Stargate, and was this the destination of the souls of the dead whose bodies had been interred within the chambers?

It should come as no surprise that our shaman-astronomer ancestors were watching the skies in later-Iron Age Dorset, recording what they observed with great skill. Do not forget that this was over three thousand years since the astronomers at Avebury and West Kennet had laid out those sites with the stars in mind; it was one or two thousand years since the latter stages of Stonehenge, with all the astronomical forethought that went into that monument's design. Countless other Bronze Age stone circles across Britain were astronomically designed. Astronomy was already an ancient science; its skills had been well practiced for many generations prior to the time that people carved a Giant into a Dorset hillside. These people left few clues as to the depth of their awareness, as their knowledge was passed down by oral tradition. We are well aware of the level of respect the Romans had for the skills and profound knowledge of the Druids, our **British** Druids, so we should be left in no doubt whatsoever that these learned people had the knowledge to find a sacred and topographically-unique landscape, where they could articulate their myths, speak to their gods, and focus on the skies above.

Every now and again during the Iron Age the ancients would have observed that the brighter planets would rise in line with the Giant during the night, sometimes very close to the Stargate point. Venus, Saturn and Mars all pass close, but it seems to be Jupiter that makes a 'direct hit' most often; as Jupiter stood at the Stargate point, it was a brilliant magnitude –2 star rising above the Giant. Jupiter was one of the main Roman gods, the equivalent of Zeus to the Greeks; he was a strong 'protector' deity, and his worship was widespread in Roman Britain.

Jupiter takes about 12 years to circle the sky, yet at the midsummer solstice of 2013 it will be on the Gemini-Taurus border - standing at the door of the Stargate! Astrologically, Jupiter represents growth, expansion, prosperity, humanity, freedom, and protection. Let us hope this alignment brings positivity to Mankind.

The Stargate point still rises out of Giant Hill today, as a nightly event played out during the autumn and winter, visible after sunset until around mid-January. Although it only rose in line with the Giant from around 500BC to 500AD (it now rises further north) it nevertheless still hangs above the Giant, the point marked out by Orion's outstretched arm and the tip of his mighty club. By another wonderful piece of synchronicity, since the 1930's the summer solstice has occurred when the sun is at the Stargate point. It is signalling in a new age.

Chapter 14.
A man for all seasons –
the Giant and the sun

'Unite, unite, let us all unite,
For summer is a-come unto day,
And whither we are going we will unite,
On the merry morning of May'.
(Anon, Padstow May Day Song.)

More than any other celestial object, it was the sun that determined the lives of prehistoric people, just as it does today. Our nearest star was at the heart of many ancient cultures around the world, most famously the Egyptians, the Incas, the Mayans, and the Aztecs. Solar myths and folklore tell of the triumph of light over dark, and how we too can be reborn; we are conceived and born, we live our lives, and then must die, and it is the sun that can guide us from the darkness back into the light. Every morning the Egyptians saw the sun-god Ra's epic return as a metaphor for the journeyings of the human soul; but the time spent in the Underworld the during the night was not a period of rest and recuperation after its daytime journey, but a period to wrestle with the serpent god Apophis. They saw the orange red glow in the dawn sky as the blood that flowed in childbirth, as Nut gave new life to the sun. The giants were perhaps the earliest representatons of gods, and their defeat was often at the hands of solar heroes. In Greek mythology, the chief solar god Zeus had to defeat the Titans, a race of giants. Lucien Richer comments that, *'In all popular tales the giant Gargantua is essentially linked with the movements of the Sun… and the forces of the Earth'* (in Miller and Broadhurst 2000, p. 14). French writer Henri Dontenville, referring to French mythology, made a direct link between the original Earth-god Gargantua and the Christian dragon-slayer St Michael. The latter is associated with the sun and hill tops, epitomised by the St Michael Line, which aligns with Beltaine and Lughnasad sunrises.

To the Norse, the sun rose everyday through *Deling's Dore ('Dawn's Door')*. In the 6th century British poem, *'The Spoiling of Annwn',* we learn of how King Arthur and his men go on a treasure hunting foray into the Underworld; what they seek is the magical cauldron of inspiration and plenty. His return with the golden booty symbolises the return of the sun following winter or, indeed, the night? This has parallels, of course, with the Grail Quest. It was said that the energy of Arthurian hero Gawain waxed and waned with the sun.

In Gaul, the Celtic god Belinos carried the sun across the heavens on a horse-drawn chariot (Biltcliffe and Hoare 2011, p. 128). Place names such as Solsbury Hill (near Bath), Silbury Hill (Wiltshire), and Silchester are all memories of solar worship. I have already suggested links between the Giant, Orion, and Mithras. The close association between the god Mithras and the sun is attested at Housesteads on Hadrian's Wall, where an altar in the Mithraeum was dedicated to Sol. Emperor Aurelian ruled from 275-270BC, and he was a devotee of Mithras, making the god central to Roman state religion. It will be remembered that Mithras was the solar lion who annually killed the bull.

Baltic myths recorded in the 15th century tell of the sun trapped inside a tower, causing the Earth to be plunged into darkness. The stars told the smith god that the only way to release the sun was by forging a *'great hammer'*. Having made the hammer, the god broke the walls of the tower and released the sun to once more shine upon the world. This story is typical of countless tales reflecting the loss of the sun in winter and its return in the spring.

The Kings of Judah dedicated horses to the sun (Kings 2, 23:11) and King Solomon built a high place, known as Chemosh, for solar worship (Kings 1, 11:7): *'There is evidence that Samson was a solar god, the equivalent of Hercules... he met with a lion, which, like Hercules, he destroyed'* (Scott 1996, p. 17).

But it was the Egyptians who took sun worship to a whole new level. The Pharaohs were called *'Sons of Ra'*, and they regarded themselves as the personification of the sun god; every temple is adorned with solar orbs, which are depicted over the heads of many deities (the origin of the Christian halo). Their creation myths involve the personification of the sun as Atum-Ra or Re, the Creator sun god, whose semen brought into being the other deities at Heliopolis, *City of the Sun.* The largest obelisk at Heliopolis was worshipped as a petrified ray of the sun; Atum-Ra was born each morning as a child, who grew until midday and afterwards fell into decline, dying at dusk as an elderly man.

On my visit to Egypt in 1995, I marvelled how the massive columns and corridors of the Temple of Karnak were aligned to the midwinter sunrise. At Abu Simbel, I was equally amazed at the gigantic carvings of the sun god Ra Horakhete, and the huge sun disks above his head. This is complemented by Adrian Gilbert's discoveries at the Mesopotamian Mithras temple of Arsameia (image p. 161), where the sun shone down carefully orientated shafts.

The ithyphallic Roman deity Bacchus was a sun god, a 'saviour' born of a virgin mother on December 25th. Parallels with his story can be found with Osiris, Krishna, Adonis, Apollo, Hermes, Quetzalcoatl and, of course, Jesus. All were either crucified or crushed to death, symbolic of the sun's loss of creative power during the winter, and his eventual rebirth.

John Allegro comments on the sun's phallicism: *'The ancients saw the glowing orb as the tip of the divine penis, rising to white heat as it approached its zenith, then turning to a deep red, characteristic of the fully distended glans penis, as it plunged into the earthly vagina'* (Allegro 1970, p. 24). The Greek word Gaia means *'earth'* and comes from the Sumerian GALLA, meaning *'womb'*. Referring back to the 'saviour gods', the word saviour actually comes from the Sumerian SUTUN, meaning, *'giver of life to the womb'*.

The azimuth that the sun rises and sets on the skyline varies depending on the time of year. These directions are also greatly determined by one's latitude, longitude, elevation of the observer, and the height of the horizon. From the Giant's latitude, the sun rises approximately SE at midwinter, gradually moving northwards along the horizon until it rises due east at the spring equinox. It then continues northwards until the summer solstice, when it rises approximately NE. The whole process then reverses, until midwinter solstice is reached around December 21st. So too with the sunsets, which move from roughly SW in midwinter to NW at midsummer. The solstices and equinoxes, however, do not divide the year equally, due to the Earth's elliptical orbit, meaning that the so-called Celtic fire festivals are not equally spaced in the calendar. Over thousands of years, these sunrise and sunset points have also moved slightly, and one has to consult software programmes when one looks back over millennia. This applies equally to the moon, whose movements are in fact even more complicated due to an 18.61-year cycle.

The 2007 winter solstice sunset at Stonehenge. Countless ancient sites are aligned with solar events.

Ask most people to name one ancient site connected with a sunrise and there is a good chance they will answer Stonehenge. This is of course the famous midsummer sunrise, loved by the Druids and Pagans who arrive en mass to witness the sun rising over the Heelstone. I have seen several sunsets at Stonehenge and I never tire of the experience of seeing the sun-god sink into the Underworld. But Stonehenge is not the exception, rather it is the rule. I have previously shown how 47 long barrows in Dorset show a bias in the direction of the midwinter sunrise and the equinoxes, with 18 orientated towards the southeast and 14 to the east (Knight 1996, p. 7). I have shown how the sun would shine down the passage of West Kennet Long Barrow around the

Left: May Day 'Obby 'Oss at Padstow, Cornwall. Right: children dancing around the maypole at Barwick-in-Elmet, West Yorkshire. (Both images, Wikipedia Common Licence.)

time of the equinoxes, lighting up the west chamber, a phenomena which can, surprisingly, still be witnessed today (Knight 2011, p. 183-5).

In Dorset, I have demonstrated how the Nine Stones, the Grey Mare and Her Colts, Hampton Hill stone circle, and the Great Barrow at Knowlton, were aligned with solar events back in prehistory (Knight 1996 and 1998).

John North asks a good question: '... *might it perhaps be a mistake to focus on the Sun as an individual? Might it not have been the light of the Sun that mattered?*' It is the *light* of the sun, seen as a long phallic beam, that enters the passages of both Newgrange and West Kennet Long Barrow, penetrating these womb tombs with the life-giving and fertilising *'shaft of light'* (Knight 2011, p. 186).

The Giant and the sun

As with the stars, when looking for solar alignments for the Giant it is all about where one stands and when one stands there. Regarding the Giant, Prof Barbara Bender commented, *'Of course there's also the possibility that he's relating to features in the landscape: that he talks to the combe or the rounded hill, or to something on the other side of the valley'* (in Darvill et al 1999, p. 132). It has been said that the Giant's phallus points due east, and may be associated with equinoxes. It does not in fact point in that direction, but around 15° north of that. The Giant's unashamed, salacious display naturally connects him with Beltaine, the May festival associated with the fertility of the land, which signals the return of the sun's vitality. Folklore from the Brecon Beacons says that at every May Day a secret door to the Underworld was opened by the fairies. This practice was ended when someone stole some of the fairies' flowers (Whitlock 1979, p. 35). This links us with the Giant's azimuth and the Stargate of the previous chapter.

Let us recall the extract from the Gentleman's Magazine of 1764: *'This monstrous figure viewed from the* **opposite** *hill appears almost erect... just going to strike a blow which seems sufficient, as it were, to overturn a mountain'* (my emphasis). Hilary Jones comments that, *'There is strong evidence for the Giant to be linked to May Day observations... on May Day a sight-line taken vertically up the middle of the phallus would have pointed directly at the rising sun as it came over the downs'* (in Darvill et al 1999, p. 148). At Cerne we certainly have records of maypoles, the quintessential image of spring revelry, a tradition re-established in recent years. Folklore at Silver Well speaks of local girls visiting the well at May Day, placing their hands on the 'wishing stone' whilst reciting a rhyme (p. 38). On this stone is a wheel with eight spokes, the divisions of the solar year. Newborn babies were dipped into the water at the exact moment sunlight hit it, great care being taken to ensure that infants faced the *rising sun*; and anyone wishing to see a vision of who would die in the coming year should look into the waters at *sunrise* on Easter Day.

At Symondsbury, near Bridport, the waters of a local well had to be taken as sunlight struck the water. Well-dressing traditionally takes place at Beltaine and Lughnasad, and not far from Cerne, at the Ebenezer Chapel at Cripplestyle, a Whit-Tuesday festival used to attract over 1000 people. In recent years a May Festival has been established at nearby Maumbury Henge, Dorchester. Festivals such as this occur sporadically around the country, and include the popular 'Obby 'Oss parade at Padstow, Cornwall. The church of St Andrew Undershaft in the City of London is named after the maypole that was kept under its eaves and set up each spring until 1517, when *mayhem* caused by students put an end to the custom; the maypole itself survived until 1547 when a Puritan mob destroyed the *'pagan idol'*.

A link between the Giant, Hercules and the harvest comes from ancient Rome, where on August 12th Hercules *'the invincible'* manifested as a generous god, and at the entrance to the Circus Maximus food and wine were given out to the poor in his name. Michael Dames advocates that this and other festivals might have been transferred to Britain via the Roman army (Dames 2010, p. 87).

It is a well-known modern belief that the phallus of the Giant aligns with the sunrise at Beltaine. This May Day sunrise point is also close to that of sunrise on Lughnasad, the old harvest festival. But if one stands at the feet of the Giant during the first week in May, the sun does not clear the hill until it is well to the south, when it rises over the Trendle. We must return, once again, to the valley below the Giant. When standing by river, where earthworks were recorded by the RCHM, we now look up and can in fact see sunrises over Giant Hill for several weeks during the summer months. So the Giant is the keeper of the agricultural season – orchestrating the complete farming cycle.

The fact that alignments with the Giant seen from the valley occur well after sunrise does not invalidate them. When I studied the temples on Malta a few years ago, many of the solar alignments were realised sometime *after* sunrise, sometimes several hours after, as the higher sun was then able to shine into the interior of the temples, sometimes through high windows. At West Kennet Long Barrow, the sun at Samhain only begins to penetrate the NE chamber half an hour after sunrise (Knight 2011, p. 185-189).

Standing next to the river in front of the Giant, we see the sun's daily march north along the hill from mid-April, until in early-middle May, when it rises over the phallus.

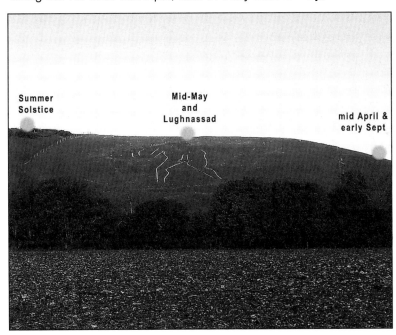

Iron Age sunrises from the valley in front of the Giant. The sun has to clear skyline heights of 9-12° before it is visible.

It then continues, at a slower pace, until the soltice standstill point is reached in June. It then returns south, rising over the Giant at Lughnasad. From this vantage point, the sun rises over the hill about 1hr 20mins to 1hr 30mins after the true time of sunrise, due to the 9-12° elevation of the hill, but again this depends on where you stand; the nearer the Giant, the higher the hill appears, the later the sunrise. The fact that the sun rises over the Giant at Lugh's festival bolsters the case for the Giant being Lugh/Nudd/Gwyn, as it does Bel or Helis. Maybe the valley was where the Lughnasad ceremonies were held – as the sunrise-phallus alignment was realised.

Either way, seen from east, the Giant is the *Summer King*; the Giant does not have a beard, so is this a sign that he is associated with spring and summer? There is the story of John Barleycorn, the British harvest god, who only grows a beard at harvest time, seen as the wheat and barley sheaths. He is cut down, eaten as bread or made into beer, yet he has a triumphant return in the spring. Lugh's time is also marked by the spectacular Abbots Bromley Horn Dance, held in early September, whose ceremonial deer antlers, *'... have been carbon dated to prehistoric times'* (Matthews 2002, p. 139). As already noted, the association between Lugh and hounds may be because Sirius appeared in the pre-dawn skies around the end of July-early August (after 70 days of invisibility). If we see Lugh as Orion, then that constellation had already appeared in dawn skies a couple of weeks before; but the festival was only held when his hunting dog, Sirius, finally made an appearance! During winter months, Orion is the *Winter King*, magnificent in the night sky when the sun has retreated.

We have already established the ancient association between the bull and fertility; it is interesting, therefore, that the sun passes through Taurus between April 20 to May 21 each year – around the time of Beltaine.

Beltaine and Lughnasad are the festivals either side of the midsummer solstice.

The view of the Giant from just down slope from the Bellingstone, (enlarged image using some zoom).

However, the position the sun rises over the Giant around these two dates is not the same because of the difference in the sun's angle of ascent following the sunrise, and the fact that the theoretical sunrise point at Lughnasad is north of that at Beltaine, if that is taken as May 1st. Regarding the Iron Age, I find mid-May to be a more accurate alignment with the phallus from the valley below the Giant, although it varies with one's distance from the hill.

But what about the Beltaine sunrise as observed from around the greater landscape? Well, the naming of the Bellingstone perhaps gives us a clue. This stone stands alone on the hill across the valley (image p. 40). A hedge now impedes the view across to the Giant, but a footpath and a gate takes us into the field beyond. As we walk away from the stone, towards the reservoir in the field, the Giant slowly appears in the valley below. The view is very good, and the Giant lacks the foreshortening we see from down in the valley. The Bellingstone to Giant azimuth is around 65° (25° north of due east), very close to the Beltaine sunrise in early May. From here, there is an almost level horizon - there is no hill for the sun to clear before it becomes visible. Of these hills opposite the Giant, Rodney Castleden stated, '... it is as if the Giant was made with the intention that it should be viewed from them... ' (Castleden 1996, p. 13). Castleden also concluded that the 1.8m (5.5ft) stone, '... *would originally have been plainly visible up on the western skyline from the Cerne Giant'* (op. cit. p. 90). As I have said, more to the point is that the Giant was visible from the stone! If the Giant was once regarded as Bel, Belis, Helith or Helis, then this stone was named after the solar god. V L Oliver, writing in 1921, confirmed the tradition that the stone was once called Hell- or Hel- Stone. The stone might even be the sole remnant of a stone circle, an important meeting place within sight of the Giant.

The stone stands on Rowden Hill, the *row* element perhaps deriving from the local dialect for roe deer, which are associated with Cernunnos. The Abbey's deer park was on this hill, and one of the 'Park Vale' boundaries aligns with the Giant.

To check all this out I went to observe the May Day sunrise in 2007. It was a glorious morning, not a cloud in the sky, and I arrived as the first blue glow appeared in the east. When the time came, the sun rose as a magnificent orange ball directly over the Giant. The Giant was barely visible in the gloom, but I could see that the sun was not in line with the Giant's axis, which I estimate it would be a few days later. In fact, it rose over the outstretched left hand, as if he was about the juggle with it! Remember that every year in May the sun passes through the sky immediately above this outstretched hand – the *'Hand of God'* perhaps.

The magic was complete when two deer ran across the field in front of me – as if Herne himself had come to witness this wonderment. I stood there watching the sun climb higher, taking a whole sequence of colour photos (which can be seen at my presentations), as I was unwilling to leave the spectacle. Eventually I dragged myself away, bidding the Bellingstone a fond farewell as I passed by. I wondered to myself

Minutes after the Beltaine sunrise of 2007, seen from near the Bellingstone.

175

how long it had been since a Beltaine sunrise had been witnessed from where it was originally intended. I had looked towards the east, like the blinded Orion, and had witnessed the sunrise. I prayed that I too might be granted the gift of sight – in the form of insight.

From the Bellingstone, the sun also rises over Giant Hill at Lughnasad. It may also be recalled that from the vicinity of the Bellingstone, the midsummer sunset occurs over Ellston Hill, also named after the sun god.

Rodney Castleden had discussed the case for a May Day sunrise association with the Giant: *'It may be, as some have pointed out, that the sun rises over the Giant Hill in line with the phallus on May morning... but from which vantage point this solar event should be observed is not clear'* (Castleden 1996, p. 16). I believe that this is now perfectly clear.

Conversely, when viewed from the Giant or the Trendle, the sun goes down in the vicinity of Bellingstone in early February and November, marking the festivals of Imbolc and Samhain! The Giant's head is at a height of 182m (587ft) above sea level; this western skyline is slightly higher at around 230m (754ft), so the sun sets slightly earlier than if it were a level horizon. I was privileged to witness the 2013 Imbolc sunset with some dear friends of mine – it was a perfect evening; the orange ball of the sun sank into the horizon close to where the Bellingstone stood - I felt as if I had been transported back in time. I followed the sun's disappearance as it crept up the Giant; it vanished around 16.45pm when viewed from his feet, 16.52pm from the tip of the phallus, and finally at 16.57pm from the Trendle.

Imbolc sunset on Feb 2nd 2013. It was a perfect sunset, with the sun (arrowed) about to set where the Bellingstone stands. Compare to image p. 41, which is the same view.

Seldon - *Hill of the Sun* revisited

We have already seen how Weam Common Hill, Seldon Hill, Dogbury Hill, and High Stoy were involved in stellar alignments. The geographical relationship between these hills also enabled observation of sunrises and sunsets on key dates. I cannot believe the Iron Age shamans of the Cerne Valley did not acknowledge these.

From Seldon Hill to High Cank is 35-50° depending where you stand (they are not precise points on the landscape because they are relatively close together). This is the direction of the midsummer sunrise around June 21/22. A henge and a tumulus on High Cank mark sites of prehistoric sanctity.

Seldon Hill is involved in another solar alignment. Because the hill is higher than the Giant, when viewed from the latter the sun sets into the sides of Seldon Hill around both May Day and Lughnasad!

Even more than this, you may recall that we could see the Giant from Seldon Hill (image p. 43). Well, when viewed from the latter, the sun rose out of the distant skyline over Giant Hill at Imbolc, and again around Samhain; the latter alignment was directly above the Giant in the Iron Age. And there is more! For when one stood on High Cank, the midwinter sun sank into Seldon Hill.

Seldon Hill probably derived from Sol, the sun. It is interesting that Michael Dames traces the mythic origin of the naming of Silbury Hill not back to *King Sil*, but to a 17th century record of *'King Sel'* (Dames 2010, p. 77). Dames suggests that King Sel was the *'harvest monarch'*, who was annually, *'... delivered anew from beneath the hill'*. Is this why Seldon Hill was marked out for a settlement? Was the site being used centuries before for more spiritual purposes? I have spoken elsewhere that solar alignments can be associated with occupation and seasonal ceremonial sites, such as in the Avebury area (Knight 2011, p. 178), and how **all** monuments should be taken in the context of their landscape setting. For it has been my experience that very few sacred sites are truly secular and separate from those with which they share the landscape. Everything is connected on some level, and this would have been part of the mindset of our Iron Age ancestors.

Around the valley, more solar alignments took place. Viewing the midsummer sunrise from the sacred spring, Silver Well, would also have been spectacular at this time, as the sun rose at the top of Yelcombe Bottom, the long valley that aligns with the sun only at this time of the year. The midwinter sun rose out of Black Hill directly in line with the spring when viewed from our well-established viewing point in the valley below the Giant; it would have reflected its light.

When viewed from High Stoy, the eye of the landscape horse (p. 46) the sun rises out of Dogbury at the end of October, Samhain.

From the Giant and the Trendle, the equinox sun sets into Weam Common Hill and, conversely, the equinox sun rises out of Giant Hill when standing on the northern side of Weam Common Hill.

The Trendle would have been an excellent place to observe sunrises and sunsets, as it is today. However, the level distant skylines offered few astronomical markers. I believe that people moved around the valley for the different festivals, explaining why we have settlements at some of the key observation points.

The Abbey mounds

Immediately to the east of the site of the old Abbey, in Beevor Field, there are a series of earthworks, which have never been dated or excavated. Sited next to the

This bank aligns to the midwinter sunrise point over Black Hill.

177

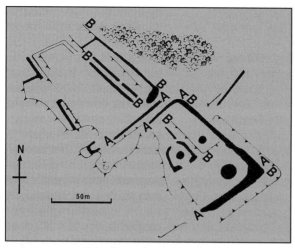

Astronomy of the features east of the Abbey and spring. **A-A** = midsummer sunrise and midwinter sunset. **B-B** = midwinter sunrise and midsummer sunset. The alignments take account of the local topography (After RCHM).

spring, the linear banks and round mounds are thought to be part of a monastic garden, but there may be more here than meets the eye, as Rodney Castleden suggests: *'No one has supplied a convincing explanation of either the mounds or the enclosures'* (Castleden 1996, p. 65). Some round mounds, resembling tumuli, can be made out, as well as depressions and long banks. To me, the site always seemed to be far older and more enigmatic than a monastic precinct. Finds of pottery and coins are sometimes thrown up out of rabbit burrows on the banks, some of which suggest dates much older than the Abbey. I did a site visit in 2012 and measured the azimuths of the two main linear banks, to see if there were any astronomical alignments; there were! The diagram above shows my results. Running my *SkyMap* programme, two alignments were clear: The first aligns with where the sun sets at midwinter, at around 231°. This is not where it sets into a flat horizon, but where the sun falls below the skyline of Dickley Hill, which is slightly higher than the site from which we are observing. Although the hill is about 88m (289ft) higher at the sunset point, it is over half a mile away, so the sun sets just 2° south of a level horizon event. In the opposite direction, the same bank points to the midsummer sunrise, which is well observed due to Yelcombe Bottom being uncannily orientated in that direction.

The long NW-SE embankment points to the west end of Piddle Wood on Black Hill. If it were a horizontal horizon, the midwinter sun would rise about 128°, and yet the

The Wessex Morris with the Dorset Ooser on Giant Hill, May Day, 2009.
(© Dark Dorset, used with permission.)

banks align to 130°; this is because they point to where the sun actually appears over the hill. This is the vicinity of the former chapel dedicated to St Catherine; the hill was once known as Cat-and-Chapel Hill. In the opposite direction, a line extended from the bank skims the bottom of Giant Hill, and heads off to our old friend Seldon Hill. The midsummer sun sets into the hill in alignment with the bank. Some of the other linear features here run parallel with those already mentioned.

I believe that these mounds and banks, although possibly used for more mundane purposes in

178

medieval times, are much older, at least Iron Age, and possibly Bronze Age. There are plenty of precedents of prehistoric linear features being astronomically aligned, and I believe that there might have been a sanctuary here, right next to the sacred spring. Gary Biltcliffe and psychic Marie Moon think a Druidic bardic college once stood here, where astronomy was taught (pers. comm.).

A henge-like feature at the Giant Hill settlement (map p. 34) has entrances that are aligned to the midsummer sunrise and the midwinter sunset. This may be an ancient prehistoric feature, the banks of which can still be seen today.

Solar eclipses at the Stargate

Going back to the Stargate briefly, it is worth noting that the sun occupied the Stargate position during the last week in May in the Iron Age, and had done so for a long time: this was around May 27 in 129AD, on May 26 in 01AD, and May 25 c.100BC. Today, by a magical piece of synchronicity, the sun passes precisely across the Stargate point at the midsummer solstice!

The 1999 total eclipse of the sun, which was visible from Britain. (Luc Viatour. Wikipedia Common Licence.)

The chances of any total eclipses being visible from Cerne Abbas in the Iron Age were slim. However, I found that four did occur – all in June! June 1st 409BC and June 21st 400BC were two. The next was not until June 19th 9BC, but was barely visible as the sun rose. On June 21st 19AD, not long before midday, a total eclipse of the sun was visible from India, Northern Europe, through southern England and across the Atlantic as far as the Bahamas. The Cerne Valley fell well within the 100% zone, and around 3 minutes of totality was witnessed. We do not witness many total solar eclipses from southern England, and I think it amazing that such a prominent one as the event of 19AD should occur *on the day of the summer solstice.* What would the Iron Age farmers of the Cerne Valley have made of this as they gathered for their midsummer festivities? Did their astronomer-priests know it was coming? We may never know, but who is to say that this monumental event did not inspire the building of the Giant – to be their *'protector god'* against such future events.

Knowing how Iron Age people related to the changing positions of the sun, moon and the stars brings the history of the valley to life. People were standing on Giant Hill and Seldon Hill, and at the Bellingstone, waiting for the sun to rise or set at key times of the year. The movements of the heavenly bodies had been worked out thousands of years before by their ancestors. They were continuing this ancient tradition, one that connected the skies with the land they farmed.

179

Chapter 15.
Staying power –
the Giant as an icon today

"It is the survival of the Giant that is remarkable,
not its creation' (Rodney Castleden).

History is constantly being rewritten, and this is how it should be, for a history that does not evolve is doomed. We inhabit a world where tomorrow's history is all around us. So too is the case with the Giant; there should always be periodic reappraisals in the light of new technology and new perspectives.

Even now people debate the origins of the Giant, as I have done: *'It is this difficult question of origin and purpose that makes the hill-figure of the Cerne Giant so enigmatic, problematic, and challenging'* (Darvill et al 1999, p. 7).

Some people, such as my fellow-Pagans and Druids, suggest that the Giant and other sacred places may help us reach out to find tangible ways to connect more with Planet Earth. Perhaps the Giant could again be an icon for Britain, as he once was when our land was the magical Isle of Albion. If the Giant had had no meaning in the past, he would not still be on that Dorset hillside today. Perhaps part of the answer to the Giant's mysteries, and his ultimate value, is what he means to us today, and what he will mean to us in the decades ahead. Future histories are indeed being written now, by all of us, every day; likewise, the Giant has generated his own history, and will create his own future.

The Giant can perhaps give all of us what we seek from him, whatever that may be. That does not invalidate anyone else's beliefs, which I feel may have been the case many generations ago; whatever message the Giant bestowed on any individual was valid. Being able to bequeath what any pilgrim seeks is the nature and quality of all major sacred sites. Katherine Barker's comment that the Giant, *'... is an image which is capable of demonstrating a continuum of meaning',* was meant to bolster her case that the Giant was a post-Iron age construct. Yet it also confirms how the Giant may have been all things to all-comers during the Iron Age. Whether Celt, Saxon, Phoenician or Roman, people could relate to a Giant as a hero-figure they recognised from their own mythologies. Myths were a universal vehicle by which cultures passed on knowledge from one generation to the next and although we have concentrated on the Iron Age in this study, we have to acknowledge that the belief systems of the Durotriges had their origins millennia before, many hundreds of miles away.

Our older hill figures were once more than the quaint curiosities many regard them as today. They were the focus for whole communities to gather together, as they gazed up to them from below, honouring and reaching for the gods. The Giant represented virility, fecundity, potent forces of the land and the heavens, and the divine powers that linked the two. He was an intermediary of colossal proportions, for he represented forces that were beyond human control.

I am not suggesting, as others have done, that the Giant represents some 'Golden Age', when Man and the landscape were interwoven in some Utopian shamanic wonderland - far from it. The Iron Age was a violent time, when old values were fading away, and human life was less sacrosanct than before. Perhaps the Giant, rather than a symbol of spiritual and cultural greatness, was a last-ditch attempt to stem the rot, so to speak. It was hoped that the symbol they created would protect the local clans from outside interventions, from forces and evils known and unknown. Although the gods were to be feared, they could also be called upon to help when help was needed – perhaps the Giant is a symbol of people's fears as much as their reverence. Things had been going 'downhill' for some time, and Gary Biltcliffe believes the Giant represents this time of transition: *'People in ancient times knew that a 'time of separation' had come, that*

The scouring of the Giant by the National Trust in 2008.
(Image: Nigel Mykura. Wikipedia Common Licence.)

Man was becoming disconnected from the land. With the Giant they left us a reminder of times when we had not been' (pers. comm.).

The Cerne colossus is not some lofty King or mighty god per se, but was equipped simply with 'primitive' objects that any clan member could associate with. In this respect he can be identified with Jesus, Buddha or Ghandi, as he inspired the common man, the average tribal member, rather than a chieftain. He appealed to the ordinary man, proof of that being how he survived through the Middle Ages, when intolerance of Pagan practices resulted in women being burnt at the stake. If he is the local equivalent of a Hercules-like persona, then it is interesting that archaeologist Stuart Piggott regarded Hercules as, *'a domestic god with very human qualities'* (Piggott 1938, p. 325). At the end of the day, regardless of what label we stick on the Giant, his role was local guardian and protector, a sort of Elder figure to the local clans. He was *their* giant, *their* god. Although we may seek out comparisons to other myths and cultures in an effort to pigeonhole him, and this may be a worthwhile enterprise, **the Cerne Giant is unique**. If there hadn't been some specific factors at play here, then there would be ithyphallic chalk figures all over Southern Britain.

Perhaps the miracle of the Giant is not how old he is, but that he is still around. If the giant was created in the Iron Age, then we are talking about 60-65 generations having come and gone. He is certainly a survivor who now dwells in the 21st century - with us, here and now. Prof Barbara Bender makes the point that, *'He is not an object, he is a figure in a working landscape... he lives on because he goes on being meaningful'* (in Darvill et al 1999, p. 128). Amen to that.

Hilary Jones makes the good point that although monuments such as the Giant are fragile, it is all too easy to become carried away with preserving them, to the extent that they become mere ornaments, with no human interaction (op. cit. p. 150). I have made suggestions elsewhere that we can use sacred sites today and do it responsibly and mindfully (Knight 2011). The Giant was intended to be part of a community, to be incorporated in a community's spiritual and social activities. In these times of ecological and environmental uncertainty, what better place to honour Nature than at places such as the Giant; I have hopefully demonstrated how he marks the changing seasons and the movements of the heavens – he can help 'connect' us once more to the cycles of Nature and the cosmos.

Myths can be brought to life today, every time we stand at the viewing point and stare across the valley to the Giant, or look up at the stars above his head; this brings the Giant to life. Our focus today should perhaps change from, *'How old and who is he?'* to *'What does he represent to us today?'* What messages does he have for us? In what direction might he lead us? What truths does he hide? This was, after all, the thought process behind the people who first scoured him on the hillside around 2000 years ago.

As the sun rose on December 21st, 2012, on the occasion of the great 'galactic alignment', the Stargate was about to set! 2000 years ago, it had already set over an hour before sunrise. The balance point is **now** – inviting us to perhaps examine concepts we have not looked at before. The Stargate is open for business once more.

Cerne Abbas, and its surrounding sacred landscape, is a place where the past and the present seem to merge together, a place where time does not stand still for anyone, and never has; yet it can also be a place where even the future may be glimpsed.

Finally, as our journey comes to an end, I would argue that although we repair him and tend for his needs, the Giant does not belong to Mankind, for he is more than this, and he is certainly more than a mere tourist attraction that requires our upkeep. He belongs to the landscape across which he strides. We fence him in, yet he refuses to be restrained. He calls to us across the valley, enticing us and inviting us to walk alongside into his mysteries. It is an invitation we would do well to accept.

'What space is depends on who is experiencing it.'
(Christopher Tilley.)

About the Author

Peter Knight is well known for his inspirational PowerPoint presentations, workshops, and field trips on topics relating to sacred sites, ancient wisdom and dowsing. He has been leading tours to sacred sites since 1995 and has spoken at several international conventions in the USA, Malta, and across the UK. He is co-founder of the Dorset Earth Mysteries Group and has been awarded honorary member status of both the Dorset Dowsers and the Antiquarian Society. He is also a member of the Wyvern Dowsers, the Society of Leyhunters, and the British Society of Dowsers.

Peter has previously had seven books published, and has contributed to several magazines and journals. He has appeared on BBC local radio, and on TV, such as on Channel 4's *Don Roamin'* with Monty Don. Peter is the founder and organiser of the *Convention of Alternative Archaeology and Earth Mysteries*, held annually in Wiltshire, which gives a platform to both new and leading researchers. In 2004 he established Stone Seeker Publishing, and in 2006 founded Stone Seeker Tours, which promotes holistic tours of sacred sites across the UK and Europe. He also conceived and hosts the *Ancient Ambient Chill-Out*, combining funky world music with large-screen images of sacred sites, planet Earth, and tribal cultures.

His PowerPoint presentations are informative and inspiring. The subjects include the Cerne Giant, West Kennet, Avebury, Stonehenge, Ireland, Malta, Dorset, Glastonbury, Brittany, dowsing, stone circles, the symbolism of Church architecture, sacred geometry, and several other subjects (see website).

Peter lives near Avebury and his interests include walking, drumming, world music, dowsing, prehistoric art, astronomy, shamanism, and nature photography. He is a father, a vegetarian and follows a goddess-orientated spirituality, whilst honouring all spiritualities and religions. He is co-founder of the Calne Environmental Network, which seeks to help make his town more sustainable and wildlife friendly.

His 'mission' is to help people connect with sacred sites and sacred landscapes, as a means of enhancing the lives of individuals, and to actively help, and promote, planetary healing.

Peter is available to do an inspiring full-colour presentation about this book to local groups and societies, as well as to lead field trips to Cerne Abbas.

Contact Peter by e-mail: stoneseeker@waitrose.com
Web site: www.stoneseeker.net
Peter also has a Facebook page

Also by Peter Knight

Ancient Stones of Dorset
Published in 1996 by Power Publications. 208 pp. The most comprehensive work on Dorset's megalithic sites. 180 illustrations. Maps of alignments, site plans, and grid references, earth energies, astronomy, newly discovered stones. Recently reprinted.

Sacred Dorset ~ On the Path of the Dragon
Published in 1998 by Capall Bann. 292 pp, 200 illustrations. A thorough work on Dorset's ancient spiritual heritage, including hillforts, wells and springs, hills, sun and moon, the green man, fairy and giant folklore, dragons, trees, and much more.

Dorset Pilgrimages ~ A Millennium Handbook
(with Mike Power)
Published in 2000 by Power Publications. 144 pp (gloss finish), over 100 photographs and line drawings. Day-long pilgrimages across Dorset, visiting churches, stone circles, megaliths, wells, etc, en route. Includes Cerne Abbas!

Earth Mysteries ~ An Illustrated Encyclopaedia of Britain (CD-ROM)
Published in 2003 by Stone Seeker Publishing. Over 350MB of information – the biggest overview of British earth mysteries ever published. Compatible with Windows Word (Windows 98, XP, etc). Over 250 illustrations. A-Z format, plus resources and fully cross-referenced - like a giant website, with over 1000 hyperlinks.

Thirteen Moons ~ Conversations with the Goddess
Published in 2007 (new ed. 2010) by Stone Seeker Publishing. Peter's novel has received rave reviews. The book's hero is contacted by the Earth Spirit on 13 full moons at sacred sites across Europe (such as Roslyn, Stonehenge, Avebury, Glastonbury, Ireland and Brittany). The Goddess guides him on how to connect with the Earth Spirit, and divulges what the human experience is all about and how we can live fulfilling lives in harmony with the planet – before it's too late! The culmination is the gift of 13 Insights in Glastonbury.

The Wessex Astrum – Sacred Geometry in a Mystical Landscape
(with Toni Perrott).
Published by Stone Seeker Publishing in 2008. Fully illustrated. The story and details of the groundbreaking discovery of the huge landscape hexagram, involving Stonehenge, Avebury, Glastonbury, and the St Michael Line. New megaliths, forgotten wells, Knights Templar sites, a secret cave, and much more are revealed.

West Kennet Long Barrow – Landscape, Shamans and the Cosmos
Published by Stone Seeker Publishing in 2011, and full of illustrations. This is the most thorough and all-embracing guide to this 3,500 year-old Neolithic tomb near Avebury. Includes everything you need to know about the monument and surrounding landscape, including many of Peter's new discoveries. Deals with the landscape, alignments, astronomy, excavations, archaeology, acoustics, earth energies, shamanism, psychic phenomena and how we can use such places for ceremony.

Signed and dedicated copies are available from the author.

Bibliography

Allegro, John (1970). *The Sacred Mushroom and the Cross.* Hodder and Stoughton.

Allen, R Hinckley (1899). *Star Names and Their Meanings.* The Lost Library ed.

Ashe, Geoffrey (1990). *Mythology of the British Isles.* Guild Publishing.

Bailey, Adrian (1998). *The Caves of the Sun.* Pimlico.

Baring, Anne, and Cashford, Jules (1991). *The Myth of the Goddess.* Viking Arkana.

Bauval, Robert, and Gilbert, Adrian (1994). *The Orion Mystery.* Heinemann.

Bédoyère, Guy de la (2002). *Gods and Thunderbolts – Religion in Roman Britain.* Tempus.

Biltcliffe, Gary (2009). *The Spirit of Portland – Revelations of a Sacred Isle.* Roving Press.

Biltcliffe, Gary, and Hoare, Caroline (2012). *The Spine of Albion.* Sacred Lands Publishing.

Bord, Janet and Colin (1982). *Earth Rites.* Granada.

Bremmer, Jan, ed (1987). *Interpretations of Greek Mythology.* Croom Helm.

Brennan, Martin (1994). *The Stones of Time: Calendars, Sundials and Stone Chambers of Ancient Ireland.* Inner Traditions International.

Bryce, Derek (1994). *Symbolism of the Celtic Cross.* Llanerch Publishers.

Carr-Gomm, P (1983). *The Wilmington Giant.* Element.

Castleden, Rodney (1996). *The Cerne Giant.* Dorset Publishing Co.

Castleden, Rodney (1998). *The Long Man: the Wilmington Giant Reconsidered.* In *The Ley Hunter Journal*, Vol 131, 27-30.

Castleden, Rodney (2000). *Ancient British Hill Figures.* S B Publications.

Clarkson, J, and Tappenham, S (1998). *Precise Angles of Light.* White Box.

Cooke, Grace and Ivan (1971). *The Light In Britain.* White Eagle Publishing Trust.

Collins, Andrew (2006). *The Cygnus Mystery.* Watkins.

Conder, Claude (1883). *Heth and Moab.* Palestine Exploration Fund.

Cooper, D Jason (1996). *Mithras – Mysteries and Initiation Rediscovered.* Samuel Wiser.

Cope, Julian (1998). *The Modern Antiquarian.* Thorsons.

Coppins, Philip (2004). *The Canopus Revelation.* Frontier Publishing.

Cutler, Richard (1865). *Original Notes on Dorchester and the Duritriges.*

Dames, Michael (2010). *Silbury: Resolving the Enigma.* The History Press.

Darvill, Timothy, et al (1999). *The Cerne Giant – An Antiquity on Trial.* Bournemouth University, Oxbow Books.

Devereux, Paul, and Thomson, Ian (1979). *The Ley Hunter's Companion.* Thames and Hudson.

Edwards, Brian (2005). *The Scouring of the White Horse.* In *Wiltshire Archaeological and Natural History Magazine.*

Furlong, David (1997). *The Keys to the Temple.* Piatkus.

Gardiner, Philip, and Osborn, Gary (2005). *The Serpent Grail.* Watkins.

Gelling, Peter, and Davidson, Hilda (1969). *The Chariot of the Sun.* Dent.

Gibbons, A O (1962). *Cerne Abbas.* Longmans.

Gilbert, Adrian (2005). *The Signs in the Sky.* A R E Press.

Green, Miranda (1989). *Symbol and Image in Celtic Religious Art.* Routledge.

Grinsell, Leslie (1980). *Antiquity,* Vol 54, p. 29-33.

Harte, Jeremy (1986). *Cuckoo Pounds and Singing Barrows.* DNH&AS.

Harwood, Jonathan (2000). *Sacred Geometry on the Dorset Landscape.* Self-published.

Hawkes, Christopher (1965). *The Long Man: A Clue.* In *Antiquity,* Vol 39, p. 27-30.

Hodges, Michael (1998). *Helis, the Cerne Giant and his Links with Christchurch.* Self-published.

Hutchins, John (1774-1814). *The History and Antiquities of Dorset.* (2 editions).

Hutton, Ronald (1996). *The Stations of the Sun.* Oxford University Press.

Jones, Mary (1952). *Cerne Abbas: the Story of a Dorset Village.* Allen and Unwin.

Knight, Christopher, and Lomas, Robert (1999). *Uriel's Machine.* Century.

Knight, Peter (1996). *Ancient Stones of Dorset.* Power Publications.

Knight, Peter (1998). *Sacred Dorset – on the Path of the Dragon.* Capall Bann.

Knight, Peter, and Power, Mike (2000). *Dorset Pilgrimages: A Millennium Handbook.* Power Publications.

Knight, Peter (2001). *The Grey Mare and Her Colts – The Goddess, the Sun God and Sirius.* Journal No. 2, Dorset Earth Mysteries Group.

Knight, Peter (2007 and 2010). *Thirteen Moons – Conversations with the Goddess.* Stone Seeker Publishing.

Knight, Peter (2011). *West Kennet Long Barrow – Landscape, Shamans and the Cosmos.* Stone Seeker Publishing.

Knight, Peter, and Perrott, Toni (2008). *The Wessex Astrum – Sacred Geometry in a Mystical Landscape.* Stone Seeker Publishing.

Leitch, Yuri (2007). *Gwyn – Ancient God of Glastonbury and Key to the Glastonbury Zodiac.* The Temple Publications.

Lethbridge, Tom (1957). *Gogmagog – the Buried Gods.* Routledge.

Lévy-Bruhl, Lucien (1983 ed.). *Primitive Mythology.* University of Queensland Press.

Mann, Nicholas R (2002). *Reclaiming the Gods.* Green Magic.

Mann, Nicholas R (2004). *Energy Secrets of Glastonbury Tor.* Green Magic.

Mann, Nicholas R (2011). *Avebury Cosmos.* O Books.

Mann, Nicholas R, and Glasson, Philippa (2007). *The Star Temple of Avalon.* The Temple Publications.

Massingham, H J (1926). *Fee Fi Fo Fum.* Chapman and Hall.

Matthews, John (2002). *The Summer Solstice.* Godsfield Press.

Michell, John (1969). *The View Over Atlantis.* Sago Press.

Miller, Hamish, and Broadhurst, Paul (2000). *The Dance of the Dragon.* Pendragon Press.

Moulton, James (1911). *The Early Religious Poetry of Persia.* Cambridge University Press.

Mysliwiec, Karol (2004). *Eros on the Nile.* Cornell University.

Newland, Robert, and North, Mark (2007). *Dark Dorset.* CFZ Press.

Newman, Paul (1987). *Gods and Graven Images.* Robert Hale.

Newman, Paul (1997, 2009). *Lost Gods of Albion.* The History Press.

North, John (1996). *Stonehenge – Neolithic Man and the Cosmos.* Harper Collins.

Norvill, Roy (1979). *Giants – The Vanished Race of Mighty Men.* Aquarian Press.

Orchard, Andy (2002). *Norse Myth and Legend.* Cassell.

Piggott, Stuart (1938). *Antiquity,* Vol. 6, p. 214-6.

Piggott, Stuart (1938). *The Hercules Myth: beginnings & ends.* In *Antiquity,* Vol.12, p. 323-31.

Pollard, Joshua, and Reynolds, Andrew (2002). *Avebury – The Biography of a Landscape.* Tempus.

Rose, A (1967). *Pagan Celtic Britain.* Routledge.

Russell, Jesse, and Cohn, Ronald (2012). *Orion (Mythology).* Bookvika Publishing.

Santillana, Giorgio de, and von Dechend, Herth (1977). *Hamlet's Mill.* Godine.

Scott, George Ryley (1966). *Phallic Worship - a History of Sex and Sexual Rites.* Senate.

Screeton, Paul (1977). *Quicksilver Heritage.* Abacus ed.

Speidel, Michael P (1997). *Mithras-Orion: Greek Hero and Roman Army God,* Brill Academic Publishers.

Squire, Charles (2000). *The Mythology of the British Isles.* Wordsworth.

Street, Chris (1990). *Earthstars.* Earthstars Publishing.

Street, Chris (2009). *London's Camelot and the Secrets of The Grail.* Earthstars Publishing.

Stukeley, William (1724). *Itinerarium Curiosum.*

Temple, Robert (1975). *The Sirius Mystery.* St Martin's Press.

Thomas, Chris (1999). *The Fool's First Steps.* Capall Bann.

Thompson, E W (1977). *General Pitt-Rivers: Evolution of Archaeology in the Nineteenth Century.* Moonraker Press.

Thorley, Anthony, ed (2012). *Legendary London and the Spirit of Place.* Archive Publishing.

Trubshaw, Bob (2011). *Singing up the Country.* Heart of Albion.

Underwood, Guy (1969). *The Pattern of the Past.* Museum Press.

Vidler, Mark (1998). *The Star Mirror.* Thorsons

Weir, Anthony, and Jerman, James (1999). *Images of Lust.* Routledge.

Westropp, H, and Wake, C (1875). *Ancient Symbol Worship.* The Book Tree (1999 ed.)

Wightman, Ralph (1977). *Portrait of Dorset.* Robert Hale.

Whitlock, Ralph (1979). *In Search of Lost Gods.* Phaidon Press.

Willis, Roy, et al (1993). *World Mythology – the Illustrated Guide.* Duncan Baird.

Index